NINJA FOODI
DOUBLE OVEN
COOKBOOK FOR BEGINNERS

Master the Art of Fast Cooking with the All-in-One Ninja Double
Oven Recipe Book and Make Your Life Easier

Bertha Zimmer

CONTENTS

Introduction

Welcome to the culinary journey that will redefine your cooking experience - the Ninja Foodi Double Oven Cookbook. With each turn of these pages, you're about to embark on a voyage of flavors, innovation, and sheer cooking mastery. This cookbook is your key to unlocking the full potential of your Ninja Foodi Double Oven, seamlessly blending creativity and professionalism to elevate your home cooking to extraordinary heights. Whether you're a seasoned chef or just beginning your kitchen adventures, prepare to discover a world of delectable possibilities as you harness the power of this remarkable appliance. Get ready to savor the art of culinary excellence like never before.

In the Ninja Foodi Double Oven Cookbook, we've meticulously crafted a collection of recipes that showcase the versatility and efficiency of this kitchen marvel. From succulent roasts to delicate pastries, from quick weeknight dinners to grand feasts, our recipes are thoughtfully designed to suit every occasion and skill level. With clear instructions, elegant presentation ideas, and a dash of inspiration, we invite you to explore the magic of double oven cooking, where simplicity meets sophistication. Unleash your inner chef, redefine your cooking routine, and create meals that resonate with both creativity and professionalism - all with the ingenuity of the Ninja Foodi Double Oven as your culinary accomplice.

The Ninja Foodi Double Oven emerges as an embodiment of culinary innovation, offering a multifaceted solution that transcends traditional kitchen boundaries. Seamlessly blending the reliability and precision of a conventional oven with the inventive capabilities of an air fryer, this appliance redefines cooking dynamics while occupying a modest countertop space. Its significance extends beyond its physical presence, characterized by the symphony of culinary possibilities it orchestrates. Central to its design is the ingenious incorporation of twin autonomous cooking chambers, operating in unison to orchestrate a culinary symphony of parallel cooking experiences, each tailored to distinct temperatures and modes. This remarkable feature empowers aspiring chefs and seasoned cooks alike to effortlessly embark on a culinary odyssey that spans the realms of baking, roasting, air frying, dehydrating, and beyond, harmonized within the confines of a singular and consolidated culinary marvel.

Beyond its dual-chamber symphony, the Ninja Foodi Double Oven acts as a true culinary maestro, enabling creative minds to compose intricate gastronomic harmonies. As one chamber diligently roasts a succulent cut of meat to perfection, the other can craft a delicate confection with the finesse of a dedicated baker's oven. This synchronous dance of flavors and aromas showcases the artistry that can be achieved within a limited space, underscoring the appliance's prowess in accommodating a spectrum of culinary desires. With the Ninja Foodi Double Oven as their stage, chefs can experiment with flavors, techniques, and cuisines without constraint, as this innovative appliance liberates their creativity and amplifies their capabilities. In the heart of every kitchen, it stands as a testament to the union of innovation and tradition, where the past and future of cooking coalesce, and where aspiring chefs compose their culinary symphonies with finesse and flair.

What is Ninja Foodi Double Oven?

The Ninja Foodi Double Oven is a groundbreaking countertop appliance that merges the capabilities of two ovens into one compact unit. Its standout feature, the FlexDoor™ design, splits the oven's interior into distinct cooking chambers, enabling simultaneous preparation of separate meals with individual cooking requirements. This streamlines meal prep without requiring extra space. The Smart Finish™ technology syncs both ovens, guaranteeing synchronized cooking times. The Smart Cook System ensures precise temperature monitoring, while 12 cooking functions cover diverse techniques. Altogether, the Ninja Foodi Double Oven redefines countertop cooking by offering dual oven power and efficiency in a single unit.

Benefits

The Ninja Foodi Double Oven offers a plethora of benefits, from the FlexDoor™ technology with the power of two appliances in one unit. Its versatility, energy efficiency, and capacity make it an exceptional addition to any kitchen, allowing you to cook with precision and creativity while saving time and effort.

FLEXDOOR for Versatile Cooking

The Ninja Foodi Double Oven introduces the innovative FlexDoor feature that revolutionizes countertop cooking. With this unique design, you have the freedom to create two separate ovens within a single unit. This means you can even access the top portion only for quick snacks and sides or even conveniently open the full door to utilize both the top and bottom ovens simultaneously. This flexibility empowers you to cook two different meals with distinct temperature and cooking time requirements, all within the confines of one compact appliance.

Flavor-seal Technology for Distinct Flavors

One of the standout benefits of the Ninja Foodi Double Oven is its FlavorSeal Technology. This ingenious feature ensures that the aromas and flavors of dishes prepared in one oven do not cross over to the other oven. This means you can confidently cook savory and sweet dishes simultaneously without worrying about flavor contamination. Experience the joy of preparing delicate desserts alongside savory roasts without the fear of flavor fusion.

Smart Finish Technology for Time Management

With Smart Finish Technology, the Ninja Foodi Double Oven takes the guesswork out of multitasking in the kitchen. By syncing both independent ovens, you can cook two different meals that finish cooking at the same time. This technology empowers you to create harmoniously timed multi-course meals without the hassle of juggling cooking times and temperatures.

Faster Meal-Making for Busy Lifestyles

The Ninja Foodi Double Oven is a time-saving marvel, boasting a 65% faster meal-making capability compared to traditional ovens. Thanks to its dual oven cavities, you can prepare two different dishes concurrently, eliminating the need for back-to-back cooking. This advancement is a game-changer for busy households and individuals who value efficient cooking without compromising on quality.

Diverse Cooking Functions for Culinary Creativity

Equipped with an impressive repertoire of 12 cooking functions, the Ninja Foodi Double Oven caters to a wide range of culinary desires. From baking and broiling to air frying and dehydrating, this countertop appliance is a versatile tool that lets you explore various cooking techniques, ensuring every meal you create is nothing short of exceptional.

Family-Sized Capacity for Gathering and Entertaining

The Ninja Foodi Double Oven boasts a substantial family-sized capacity that's perfect for gatherings and entertaining. With the ability to fit up to 6 lbs of wings or a 12-inch pizza, you can easily prepare enough food to satisfy a crowd of up to 8 people.

Top Rapid Oven for Quick Culinary Creations

The Ninja Foodi Double Oven features a top Rapid Oven that's perfect for preparing quick meals, snacks, and sides. Whether you're reheating leftovers or toasting bagels, this compartment's efficient heating ensures speedy results without compromising on taste or quality.

Bottom Convection & Air Fry Oven for Culinary Excellence

The Bottom Convection & Air Fry Oven of the Ninja Foodi Double Oven is a culinary powerhouse designed for larger roasts, bakes, and air frying. From succulent roasts to perfectly crisped air-fried dishes, this oven compartment lets you showcase your culinary prowess with exceptional results.

Precision Air Frying for Healthier Delights

Air frying is a standout feature of the Ninja Foodi Double Oven, allowing you to enjoy your favorite fried foods with significantly less oil. This means you can relish crispy, golden delights without the guilt, making your meals healthier and more enjoyable.

Whole Roast Capability for Impressive Feasts

Impress your guests and loved ones with the Ninja Double Oven's "whole roast" function. Whether it's a succulent chicken or a tender pork loin, this oven lets you create show-stopping roasts that are sure to be the centerpiece of any meal.

Dehydrate Function for Homemade Snacks

Health-conscious individuals will appreciate the dehydrate function of the Ninja Foodi Double Oven. Transform simple ingredients into delicious homemade snacks without the need for specialized dehydrating equipment.

Space-Saving Design for Countertop Efficiency

The Ninja Foodi Double Oven's ability to house two separate ovens within a compact countertop footprint is a space-saving marvel. Enjoy

the benefits of dual ovens without sacrificing precious kitchen space, making it an ideal addition to kitchens of all sizes.

Elevated Cooking Experience with Convenience

Elevate your cooking experience with the convenience of the Ninja Foodi Double Oven. Its intuitive controls, versatile cooking functions, and thoughtful design elements make it a must-have for both culinary enthusiasts and those seeking an easier way to create delicious meals.

Energy Efficiency for Reduced Utility Costs

The efficiency of the Ninja Foodi Double Oven translates into energy savings. With its faster cooking times and the ability to prepare multiple dishes at once, you'll not only save time but also reduce your energy consumption and lower your utility costs.

Step by step use

Discover a detailed walkthrough on effectively utilizing the Ninja Foodi Double Oven, a cutting-edge countertop appliance that maximizes kitchen space. With its array of functions, this oven redefines efficiency and convenience in your culinary endeavors. Whether you're aiming for quicker meal-making, family-sized feasts, or simultaneous diverse dishes, the Ninja Foodi Double Oven delivers with its innovative design and comprehensive capabilities.

Step 1: Unboxing and Setup

Carefully unbox your Ninja Foodi Double Oven and ensure that all the included components are present, including the countertop oven itself, sheet pans, wire racks, an air fry basket, and a removable crumb tray. Find a suitable location for your oven on your kitchen countertop, ensuring there is enough space for the FlexDoor™ to fully open without any obstructions. Plug the oven into a power outlet.

Step 2: Familiarize with Cooking Functions

Take a moment to completely understand the 12 cooking functions offered by the Ninja Foodi Double Oven. These functions include bake, broil, reheat, keep warm, bagel, toast (in the Top Rapid Oven), as well as air fry, convection bake, pizza, air roast, whole roast, and dehydrate (in the Bottom Convection & Air Fry Oven). Understanding these functions will help you choose the right cooking method for your dishes.

Step 3: Preheating the Oven

Decide whether you'll be using the Top Rapid Oven or the Bottom Convection & Air Fry Oven. Turn the function dial to the desired cooking mode and set the temperature using the temperature control dial. Allow the oven to preheat to the desired temperature, and the indicator light will signal when it's ready for cooking.

Step 4: Using the FlexDoor

If you're cooking multiple dishes with different requirements, utilize the FlexDoor. To access just the top oven, open the top portion of the door. If you need both ovens simultaneously, open the full door. This is particularly useful when cooking separate meals at different temperatures and cooking times.

Step 5: Cooking with FlavorSeal Technology

The FlavorSeal technology prevents flavors from crossing between the two ovens. This ensures that the distinct tastes of your dishes remain separate even when cooking multiple items concurrently.

Step 6: Employing Smart Finish Technology

For synchronized cooking of two separate meals that finish simultaneously, make use of the Smart Finish™ technology. This feature lets you coordinate the cooking times of both independent ovens, resulting in a well-timed and convenient cooking experience.

Step 7: Monitoring with Smart Cook System

Utilize the leave-in thermometer provided by the Smart Cook System to precisely monitor the temperatures of your dishes. This thermometer eliminates the need for constant checking and ensures your food is cooked to perfection.

Step 8: Enjoy Faster Meal-Making

Experience the efficiency of the Ninja Foodi Double Oven as it reduces cooking time by up to 65% compared to traditional ovens. The ability to cook two dishes at once eliminates the need for back-to-back cooking, allowing you more time to spend with your family.

Step 9: Cooking Family-Sized Meals

Leverage the family-sized capacity of the Double Oven to prepare substantial meals. It can accommodate up to 6 lbs of wings or a 12-inch pizza, making it ideal for feeding larger gatherings of up to 8 people.

Step 10: Separate Meals Simultaneously

Enjoy full advantage of the convenience of two independent ovens. Prepare a meal for your children in one oven while simultaneously cooking a separate dish for the adults in the other. This feature streamlines dinner preparation for families with diverse tastes.

Tips to use accessories

Before your first use of the Ninja Foodi Double Oven, familiarize yourself with the accessories provided. Taking a moment to understand each accessory's purpose will help you make the most of your cooking experience.

Optimal Rack Placement

Experiment with the 2 wire racks to find the best placement for your dishes. For even cooking results, ensure proper airflow by leaving enough space between racks. Adjust the racks based on the cooking function you're using and the size of the dish to achieve ideal outcomes.

Efficient Sheet Pan Usage

The 2 sheet pans are versatile tools for baking, roasting, and more. To prevent overcrowding and ensure proper cooking, avoid placing items too close together on the sheet pans. If cooking multiple items, consider rotating the sheet pans halfway through the cooking time for uniform results.

Air Fry Basket Expertise

The air fry basket is perfect for creating crispy, golden delights. When air frying, evenly distribute your ingredients within the basket, allowing hot air to circulate freely. This will help achieve the desired crispy texture while maintaining consistent cooking throughout.

Crumb Tray Maintenance

The removable crumb tray is a handy accessory for keeping your Ninja Foodi Double Oven clean. Place it at the bottom of the oven to catch any food debris or drippings, making post-cooking cleanup a breeze. Regularly remove and clean the crumb tray to maintain hygiene and extend the lifespan of your appliance.

Accessory Preheating

Depending on the cooking function, consider preheating your accessories along with the oven. This helps ensure that your dishes start cooking immediately upon placement, leading to better results. For instance, preheating the sheet pans can aid in achieving a crispy crust on baked goods.

Mixing and Matching Accessories

Don't hesitate to combine accessories for certain recipes. For example, you can use a wire rack on a sheet pan to elevate food for more even cooking. Experiment with different configurations to suit your cooking needs and achieve optimal results.

Monitoring During Cooking

Keep an eye on your dishes while they're cooking. Accessories like the sheet pans and wire racks can influence cooking times, especially if you're layering items. Adjust cooking times or positions as needed to prevent overcooking or undercooking.

Air Fry Basket Shake

When air frying with the basket, remember to shake it gently or give it a quick toss halfway through the cooking time. This ensures that all sides of the food are exposed to the hot air, promoting even browning and crisping.

Cooling Down Accessories

After cooking, give the accessories a few minutes to cool down before handling them. Use oven mitts or protective gloves to safely remove hot accessories like sheet pans or the air fry basket. This precaution prevents accidental burns and ensures a safe cooking experience.

Straight from the store

Straight from the store to your kitchen, this innovative appliance brings a new dimension to home cooking. Combining the prowess of two ovens in the footprint of one, the Ninja Foodi Double Oven offers a dynamic cooking solution that caters to diverse culinary desires.

Unboxing and Initial Inspection

When you bring your brand-new Ninja Foodi Double Oven straight from the store, start by carefully unboxing the appliance. Make sure to remove any packing materials, stickers, and protective coverings. As you do this, pay close attention to any visible damages or defects. If you notice any issues, contact customer support immediately for assistance.

Read the User Manual

Before diving into using your Ninja Foodi Double Oven, take a moment to read the user manual thoroughly. This manual contains important information about setup, operation, safety precautions, and maintenance. Familiarizing yourself with the manual will help you make the most of your appliance while ensuring safe and effective usage.

Prepare a Suitable Location

Choose a suitable spot in your kitchen for the Ninja Foodi Double Oven. It should be a flat, stable surface with enough clearance around the appliance for proper ventilation. Keep in mind that the oven's FlexDoor™ will require ample space to fully open, so position it accordingly. Avoid placing the oven near flammable materials or under cabinets that might obstruct the door.

Plug In and Power On

Find a safe and nearby electrical outlet to plug in the Ninja Foodi Double Oven. Once plugged in, turn on the appliance using the power button. You should see the control panel light up, indicating that the oven is ready for operation. If the oven doesn't power on, double-check the power connection and consult the user manual troubleshooting section.

Initial Setup on the Control Panel

Navigate through the control panel to set up the oven according to your preferences. This might involve setting the clock, choosing temperature units (Celsius or Fahrenheit), and other initial settings. The control panel is intuitive, but referring to the user manual can help you navigate these steps seamlessly.

Preheating the Oven

Before your first cooking endeavor, it's a good idea to preheat the oven to ensure accurate cooking temperatures. Select the desired oven cavity (Top Rapid Oven or Bottom Convection & Air Fry Oven), set the temperature, and allow the oven to preheat. This step is essential for achieving consistent cooking results.

Test Run with a Simple Dish

For your first cooking experiment, choose a simple dish or recipe that you're familiar with. This could be toasting bread, reheating a snack, or baking a small batch of cookies. This test run will help you become acquainted with the cooking process and ensure that the oven

is functioning as expected.

Explore Cooking Functions

Delve into the Ninja Foodi Double Oven's array of cooking functions. Familiarize yourself with the options available in both the Top Rapid Oven and the Bottom Convection & Air Fry Oven. Try out different functions like baking, toasting, roasting, or air frying to get a sense of the oven's versatility.

Cleaning Before First Use

Before preparing your first official meal, take a few moments to clean the oven's interior and accessories. With the help of a soft cloth remove dust or residue that may have accumulated during shipping and handling. Wash the included sheet pans, wire racks, and air fry basket with warm, soapy water before using them.

Experiment and Learn

With your initial cooking success under your belt, embark on a culinary journey of experimentation and learning. Try out various recipes, explore different cooking functions, and discover the full potential of your Ninja Foodi Double Oven. The more you use it, the more confident and creative you'll become in the kitchen.

Cleaning

By incorporating proper care into your routine, you'll maintain the Ninja Foodi Double Oven's performance, longevity, and appearance while ensuring a safe and hygienic cooking environment.

Regular Maintenance

After each use, give the Ninja Foodi Double Oven a quick wipe-down with a damp cloth to remove any crumbs or spills. Regular cleaning prevents buildup and makes deeper cleaning sessions easier.

Cool Down Completely

Always wait for the oven to cool down completely before cleaning. This prevents burns and ensures effective cleaning without damaging any components.

Remove Accessories

Take out all removable accessories like the wire racks, crumb tray, and air fry basket. Wash them separately in warm, soapy water and allow them to dry thoroughly.

Crumb Tray Cleaning

The crumb tray can accumulate debris over time. Empty it regularly and wipe it clean with a damp cloth or sponge. For thorough cleaning, remove the crumb tray and wash it gently with soapy water, then let it dry before placing it back.

Interior Cleaning

Wipe down the interior walls, top, and bottom of the oven with a soft damp cloth or sponge. For stubborn stains, use a mixture of warm water and mild dish soap. Avoid abrasive cleaners or scouring pads to prevent damaging the oven's interior.

Glass Door Cleaning

Thoroughly lean the glass door with a non-abrasive glass cleaner or a mixture of equal parts water and vinegar. Gently wipe away fingerprints, smudges, and grease. Be cautious not to let any liquid seep into the door vents.

Vent Cleaning

Check the oven's vents for any debris or food particles that might have collected. Use a soft brush or a can of compressed air to clear out any obstructions.

Exterior Cleaning

Wipe the exterior surfaces of the oven with a damp cloth. For stainless steel parts, use a mild stainless steel cleaner to maintain their shine. Always follow the manufacturer's instructions for cleaning stainless steel.

Dealing with Stubborn Stains

For stubborn stains or baked-on residues, make a paste using baking soda and water. Apply the paste to the stains, let it sit for a while, and then gently scrub with a soft cloth. Rinse thoroughly and dry.

Avoiding Harsh Chemicals

When cleaning the Ninja Foodi Double Oven, steer clear of harsh chemicals, abrasive cleaners, and scouring pads. These can damage the oven's surfaces and finishes. Stick to gentle, non-abrasive cleaning solutions.

Care and maintenance

Ensuring the longevity and optimal performance of your Ninja Foodi Double Oven goes hand in hand with creating culinary masterpieces. From routine cleaning to storage considerations, these care and maintenance practices are your keys to upholding the artistry and functionality of your appliance for countless meals to come.

Regular Cleaning for Optimal Performance

To ensure the Ninja Foodi Double Oven maintains its peak performance, regular cleaning is essential. Allow the oven to cool down completely before starting the cleaning process. Start by removing the accessories like wire racks, sheet pans, and the crumb tray. Gently wipe down the interior with a soft damp cloth to remove any food particles or residue. For stubborn stains, a mixture of simple dish soap and water can be used, followed by a thorough rinse with clean water.

Cleaning Accessories

The accessories that come with your Ninja Foodi Double Oven, such as wire racks and sheet pans, also require regular cleaning. Wash them with warm soapy water using a non-abrasive sponge or cloth. Avoid using harsh scouring pads that could damage the non-stick surfaces. To prolong the life of these accessories, ensure they are completely dry before placing them back in the oven.

Crumb Tray Maintenance

The removable crumb tray is an essential component of the oven's hygiene. Regularly remove and empty the crumb tray to prevent the buildup of crumbs and debris. Wash the crumb tray with warm soapy water, rinse thoroughly, and allow it to dry completely before reinserting it into the oven. Regular maintenance of the crumb tray not only maintains cleanliness but also prevents potential fire hazards.

Exterior Cleaning

The exterior of the Ninja Foodi Double Oven can accumulate grease, fingerprints, and spills over time. Use a soft cloth or sponge dampened with mild soapy water to gently wipe down the exterior surfaces. Dry the surfaces with a clean, dry cloth afterward to prevent water spots or streaks. Avoid using abrasive cleaners or scouring pads that could scratch the oven's finish.

Avoiding Harsh Chemicals

When cleaning your Ninja Foodi Double Oven, avoid using harsh chemicals, abrasive cleaners, or scouring pads. These can damage the oven's surfaces and finishes. Stick to mild dish soap, warm water, and non-abrasive cleaning tools to maintain the oven's appearance and functionality.

Dealing with Stubborn Stains

For stubborn stains that resist regular cleaning, create a paste using baking soda and water. Apply the paste to the stained area, let it sit for a while, and then gently scrub with a soft cloth or sponge. Rinse thoroughly and dry with a clean cloth. This method is effective for tackling tough stains without causing damage to the oven's surfaces.

Maintaining the FlexDoor

The FlexDoor feature of the Ninja Foodi Double Oven deserves special attention. To keep it operating smoothly, periodically clean the door hinges using a soft cloth or brush to remove any dust or debris. Lubricate the hinges with a small amount of food-grade mineral oil or silicone lubricant to ensure the door opens and closes effortlessly.

Ventilation Maintenance

The Ninja Foodi Double Oven is equipped with ventilation openings to release excess heat. Keep these openings clear of any obstructions, such as crumbs or debris, to ensure proper airflow. Use a soft brush or compressed air to gently clean the ventilation openings and prevent overheating.

Storing Properly

If you plan to store your Ninja Foodi Double Oven for an extended period, make sure it's clean and dry before storing it in a cool, dry place. If possible, cover it with a dust cover or a clean cloth to prevent dust accumulation. Avoid stacking heavy items on top of the oven, as this could damage its components.

Routine Check for Wear and Tear

Regularly inspect the interior, exterior, and accessories of your Ninja Foodi Double Oven for any signs of wear and tear. Check the power cord and plug for damage as well. If you notice any issues, contact the manufacturer's customer service for guidance on repairs or replacements. Addressing minor issues early can prevent them from escalating into major problems down the line.

Professional Servicing

If you encounter any technical issues or problems beyond your expertise, it's best to seek professional servicing. Attempting to disassemble or repair the oven yourself may void the warranty and lead to further damage. Contact Ninja's customer support or a qualified technician to handle complex repairs and ensure the longevity of your appliance.

Following Manufacturer's Guidelines

Above all, follow the care and maintenance guidelines provided in the user manual that accompanies your Ninja Foodi Double Oven. The manufacturer's recommendations are tailored to ensure the oven's optimal performance, safety, and longevity. Adhering to these guidelines will help you enjoy hassle-free cooking and baking for years to come.

FAQs

Can I cook a main course and dessert at the same time in the Ninja Foodi Double Oven?

Absolutely! The Ninja Foodi Double Oven's FlexDoor™ design allows you to cook a savory main course in one oven while simultaneously baking a sweet dessert in the other. The Smart Finish™ technology ensures both dishes are ready to serve at the same time, saving you time and effort in the kitchen.

How does the FlavorSeal technology prevent flavors from mingling in the Ninja Foodi Double Oven?

With FlavorSeal technology, the Ninja Foodi Double Oven's separate ovens keep the aromas and flavors of one dish from mixing with another. This means you can prepare a garlic-infused roast in one oven without worrying about your delicate pastries taking on the garlic scent in the other oven.

Can I trust the Smart Cook System's leave-in thermometer for accurate cooking in the Ninja Foodi Double Oven?

Absolutely! The Smart Cook System's leave-in thermometer is designed for precision. It monitors temperatures accurately, so you can rely on it to achieve consistent cooking results without the need for constant temperature adjustments.

How versatile are the cooking functions in the Ninja Foodi Double Oven?

The Ninja Foodi Double Oven offers a wide range of 12 cooking functions. You can bake, broil, air fry, roast, dehydrate, and more. From pizza making to convection baking, these functions cater to various culinary techniques, giving you the freedom to explore diverse recipes.

Can I host a dinner party using the Ninja Foodi Double Oven?

Absolutely! The Ninja Foodi Double Oven's family-sized capacity makes it ideal for hosting gatherings. With the ability to fit up to 6 pounds of wings or a 12-inch pizza, you can effortlessly cater to your guests and serve delicious meals without compromising on quality.

Is the Ninja Foodi Double Oven suitable for novice cooks?

Certainly! The Ninja Foodi Double Oven's intuitive design and Smart Cook System make it beginner-friendly. The leave-in thermometer eliminates guesswork, ensuring your dishes turn out perfectly cooked every time.

Can I use the Ninja Foodi Double Oven to prepare healthy meals?

Yes, you can! The Ninja Foodi Double Oven's air frying and dehydrating functions offer healthier cooking alternatives. You can enjoy crispy favorites with less oil or create nutritious dehydrated snacks easily.

Can I cook a meal for both kids and adults simultaneously in the Ninja Foodi Double Oven?

Absolutely! The independent ovens allow you to cook a kid-friendly meal in one oven and a more sophisticated dish for adults in the other. This versatility eliminates the need for separate cooking times and lets everyone enjoy their preferred meal at the same time.

Can I sync both ovens to cook multiple components of a single dish in the Ninja Foodi Double Oven?

Definitely! The Smart Finish™ technology lets you sync both ovens, enabling you to cook different components of a dish simultaneously. This means you can have perfectly cooked proteins, sides, and even desserts ready to serve together.

How does the Ninja Foodi Double Oven enhance cooking efficiency?

The Ninja Foodi Double Oven's innovative design eliminates the need for back-to-back cooking. With two separate ovens, you can prepare meals up to 65% faster compared to a traditional oven. This efficiency empowers you to spend less time cooking and more time enjoying delicious meals with your loved ones.

4-Week Meal Plan

Week 1

Day 1:
Breakfast: Beef Kale Omelet Cups
Lunch: Classic Tostones with Peruvian Green Sauce
Snack: Keto Cauliflower Mac & Cheese
Dinner: Chicken Apple Hamburgers
Dessert: Butter Caramelized Pineapple

Day 2:
Breakfast: Cheese Chicken Frittata
Lunch: Cream Potato Side Dish
Snack: Easy Cheese Rounds
Dinner: Lemony London Broil Roast
Dessert: Blackberry Cocoa Cake

Day 3:
Breakfast: Breakfast Spinach Quiche
Lunch: Flavorful Cornbread
Snack: Classic Mozzarella en Carrozza with Puttanesca Sauce
Dinner: Cheese Tuna Burgers
Dessert: Chocolate Raspberry Cake

Day 4:
Breakfast: Air Fried Eggs with Kale-Almond Pesto & Olives
Lunch: Garlicky Zucchini and Sweet Potatoes
Snack: Thai-Style Turkey Bites
Dinner: Spicy Ham and Kale Egg Cups
Dessert: Lemony Apple Turnovers with Raisins

Day 5:
Breakfast: Simple & Healthy Eggs
Lunch: Vegan Buddha Bowl
Snack: Parmesan-Crusted Bell Pepper Chips
Dinner: Ethiopian-Style Spicy Chicken with Cauliflower
Dessert: Crispy Peanut Butter Cookies

Day 6:
Breakfast: Buttered Breakfast Biscuits
Lunch: Sweet Corn and Carrot Fritters
Snack: Bacon & Onion Cheese Bombs
Dinner: Spicy Monkfish with Olives & Vegetables
Dessert: Raspberry Muffins

Day 7:
Breakfast: Buttered Banana Bread
Lunch: Cilantro Zucchini with Kimchi-Herb Sauce
Snack: Chili Shrimp Toasts
Dinner: Herbed Garlic Pork Tenderloin
Dessert: Orange Coconut Cake

Week 2

Day 1:
Breakfast: Cheese Omelet
Lunch: Fried Eggplant with Marinara Sauce
Snack: Spicy Garlic Chicken Wings
Dinner: Cajun Cheese Fish Fritters
Dessert: Coconut Cupcakes with Peanuts

Day 2:
Breakfast: Swiss Chard & Ham Eggs Cups
Lunch: Paprika Sweet Potato Fries
Snack: Mushroom Meatballs with Tzatziki Dip
Dinner: Herbed Chicken with Roma Tomatoes
Dessert: White Chocolate Cookies

Day 3:
Breakfast: Smoked Salmon Egg Cups
Lunch: Corn-Beans Stuffed Avocados
Snack: Savory Cabbage Steaks
Dinner: Italian Onion Rump Roast
Dessert: Vanilla Chocolate Brownies

Day 4:
Breakfast: Chicken Lettuce Sandwich
Lunch: Yummy Toasty Crispy-Bottom Rice with Currants & Pistachios
Snack: Homemade Pizza Bites
Dinner: Hearty Fish Tacos
Dessert: Chocolate Rum Cake

Day 5:
Breakfast: Breakfast Jalapeño Chimichanga
Lunch: Onion Stuffed Mushrooms
Snack: Coconut Garlic Chicken Bites
Dinner: Vinegary Creole Crab
Dessert: Chocolate Blueberry Muffins

Day 6:
Breakfast: Corn-Tomato Frittata with Avocado Dressing
Lunch: Cheesy Eggplant Slices
Snack: Crunchy Cheese Wafers
Dinner: Rosemary Beef Sausage & Vegetable Medley
Dessert: Cranberry Cake with Ricotta Frosting

Day 7:
Breakfast: Vanilla Buttered Blueberry Muffins
Lunch: Cheese Spinach Omelet
Snack: Cheese Tomato Chips
Dinner: Salmon Cucumber Salad
Dessert: Mini Chocolate Cheesecakes

Week 3

Day 1:
Breakfast: Cottage Cheese Stuffed Chicken Rolls
Lunch: Healthy Okra with Peanut Sauce
Snack: Almond Zucchini Chips
Dinner: Herbed Beef with Dinner Rolls
Dessert: Coconut Walnuts Rum Cookies

Day 2:
Breakfast: Spicy Chicken and Egg Cups
Lunch: Tasty Fennel with Shirataki Noodles
Snack: Garlic Cheese Zucchini Fries
Dinner: Spicy Turkey Thighs Casserole
Dessert: Sweet Cream Cheese Cinnamon Cupcake

Day 3:
Breakfast: Chicken Sausage Egg Cups
Lunch: Sweet-Salty Roasted Carrots with Parsley
Snack: Coconut Zucchini and Bacon Cakes Ole
Dinner: Best Classic Pulled Beef
Dessert: Honeyed Balsamic Roasted Strawberry Tart

Day 4:
Breakfast: Egg-in-a-Hole Bacon Toast
Lunch: Garlic Turkey & Potatoes
Snack: Cheese BLT
Dinner: Mustard Turkey Tenderloins with Gravy
Dessert: Lime Caramelized Peach Shortcakes

Day 5:
Breakfast: Buttered Cinnamon Pecan Roll
Lunch: Simple Sweet Potato Fries
Snack: Beef Steak and Onion Sliders
Dinner: Herbed Fish Fingers
Dessert: Almond Monk Fruit Cookies

Day 6:
Breakfast: Vanilla Blueberry Pancake Poppers
Lunch: Herbed Red Potatoes
Snack: Sweet Cinnamon Pita Chips
Dinner: Herbed Beef Medallions with Bell Peppers
Dessert: Vanilla Cream Cheese Cookies

Day 7:
Breakfast: Cheesy Mushroom-Spinach Frittata
Lunch: Easy Cheese Lings
Snack: Cream Cheese Breadsticks
Dinner: Lemony Pork Chops
Dessert: Monk Fruit Pecan Cookies

Week 4

Day 1:
Breakfast: Cheese Chicken Rolls
Lunch: Scrambled Eggs with Spinach & Tomato
Snack: Yummy Mozzarella Snack
Dinner: Parmesan Crusted Chicken
Dessert: Coconut Pound Cake

Day 2:
Breakfast: Cheese Beef Frittata
Lunch: Lemony Brussels Sprout Salad with Pancetta
Snack: Lime Avocado Fries with Salsa Fresca
Dinner: Spicy Garlic Skirt Steak
Dessert: Orange Custard

Day 3:
Breakfast: Creamy Seeds Porridge
Lunch: Crispy Buttermilk Onion Rings
Snack: Spicy Scallops and Bacon Kabobs
Dinner: Maple-Glazed Salmon
Dessert: Chocolate Fudge Brownies

Day 4:
Breakfast: Blackberries Coconut Porridge
Lunch: Simple Potatoes with Yogurt and Chives
Snack: Tasty Fried Brie with Cherry Tomatoes
Dinner: Crispy Cajun Pork Chops
Dessert: Lemon Coconut Cheese Tart

Day 5:
Breakfast: Crispy and Juicy Bacon
Lunch: Maitake Mushroom with Sesame Seeds
Snack: Spinach Chips with Chili Yogurt Dip
Dinner: Turkey Burgers with Bacon
Dessert: Coconut Orange Galettes

Day 6:
Breakfast: Easy Cheesy Eggs
Lunch: Maple Syrup-Garlic Tomatoes
Snack: Healthy Bacon Avocado Wraps
Dinner: Pork-Bacon Kebabs
Dessert: Coconut Sesame Seeds Cookies

Day 7:
Breakfast: Easy Cinnamon Rolls
Lunch: Mayo Corn & Cilantro Salad
Snack: Lime Parmesan Chicken Meatballs
Dinner: Simple Rosemary Scallops
Dessert: Delicious Chocolate-Maple Bacon

Chapter 1 Breakfast Recipes

Cheese Chicken Rolls

Prep Time: 15 minutes | Cook Time: 28 minutes | Serves: 6

2 eggs, well-whisked	paprika
1 cup grated parmesan cheese	½ teaspoon whole grain mustard
1½ tablespoons extra-virgin olive oil	½ teaspoon cumin powder
1½ tablespoons fresh chives, chopped	⅓ teaspoon fine sea salt
3 chicken breasts, halved lengthwise	⅓ cup fresh cilantro, chopped
1½ cup mozzarella cheese	⅓ teaspoon freshly ground black pepper, or more to taste
2 teaspoons sweet	

1. Flatten each chicken breast with a rolling pin. 2. In a bowl, mix together the mozzarella cheese, cumin, cilantro, fresh chives, and mustard. 3. In another bowl, whisk eggs with sweet paprika. In a third bowl, mix up the parmesan cheese, salt and black pepper. 4. Spread the cheese mixture over each chicken breast and roll them up. 5. Brush each chicken roll with the egg mixture and then dredge into the parmesan mixture. Place the rolls onto the Air Fry Basket. Drizzle all rolls with extra-virgin olive oil. 6. Press BOTTOM and turn the dial until AIR FRY is illuminated. Press TEMP and set to 345°F, then press TIME and set to 28 minutes. Press START/STOP to begin preheating. 7. When preheating is complete, insert the Air Fry Basket in LEVEL 2 position of the bottom oven. Close the door to begin cooking. 8. Serve warm, garnished with sour cream if desired.
Per Serving: Calories 398; Fat 21.11g; Sodium 783mg; Carbs 4.21g; Fiber 0.9g; Sugar 0.59g; Protein 46.01g

Creamy Seeds Porridge

Prep Time: 15 minutes | Cook Time: 12 minutes | Serves: 3

1 tablespoon butter	¼ teaspoon salt
¼ teaspoon nutmeg	3 tablespoons sesame seeds
⅓ cup heavy cream	
1 egg	3 tablespoons chia seeds

1. Grease the inside of the sheet pan with butter. Add the

sesame seeds, chia seeds, heavy cream, salt and nutmeg. Gently stir well. Whisk the egg in a small bowl and add to the sheet pan. Stir the mixture with a wooden spatula. 2. Press TOP and turn the dial until BAKE is illuminated. Press TEMP/SHADE and set to 375°F, then press TIME/SLICES and set to 12 minutes. Press START/STOP to begin preheating. 3. When preheating is complete, place the sheet pan on the rack. Close the door to begin cooking. Stir every 4 minutes during the cooking process. 4. Once done, remove the porridge from the oven and serve hot!
Per Serving: Calories 225; Fat 19.7g; Sodium 256mg; Carbs 7.83g; Fiber 6.1g; Sugar 0.47g; Protein 6.28g

Cheese Chicken Frittata

Prep Time: 15 minutes | Cook Time: 8 minutes | Serves: 4

1 cup goat cheese, crumbled	5 medium-sized whisked eggs
1 teaspoon dried rosemary	⅓ teaspoon ground white pepper
2 cups cooked chicken breasts, boneless and shredded	½ cup green onions, chopped
¼ teaspoon mustard seeds	1 green garlic stalk, chopped
1 teaspoon red pepper flakes, crushed	Fine sea salt, to taste
	Nonstick cooking spray

1. Lightly spray the inside of the Air Fry Basket with a nonstick cooking spray. Add in all ingredients except the cheese. Stir to mix well. 2. Press BOTTOM and turn the dial until AIR FRY is illuminated. Press TEMP and set to 335°F, then press TIME and set to 8 minutes. Press START/STOP to begin preheating. 3. When preheating is complete, place the sheet pan on the wire rack in LEVEL 1 position of the bottom oven. Then insert the Air Fry Basket in LEVEL 2 position of the bottom oven. Close the door to begin cooking. 4. When cooking is complete, check for doneness. Spread the crumbled goat cheese on top and serve immediately!
Per Serving: Calories 326; Fat 17.9g; Sodium 524mg; Carbs 2.32g; Fiber 0.3g; Sugar 0.97g; Protein 37.04g

Cottage Cheese Stuffed Chicken Rolls

Prep Time: 15 minutes | Cook Time: 22 minutes | Serves: 2

½ cup Cottage cheese	½ cup parmesan cheese,
2 eggs, beaten	grated
2 medium-sized chicken	⅓ teaspoon freshly
breasts, halved	ground black pepper, to
2 tablespoons fresh	savor
coriander, chopped	3 cloves garlic, finely
1 teaspoon fine sea salt	minced

1. Flatten out the chicken breast with a meat tenderizer. 2. In a medium bowl, mix together the Cottage cheese with garlic, salt, coriander, and black pepper. 3. Divide the cheese mixture evenly between each chicken breast. Roll the chicken around the filling and secure with the toothpicks. 4. Whisk the eggs in a shallow bowl. In another bowl, mix up the salt, black pepper, and parmesan cheese. 5. Coat the chicken breasts with the egg and roll them in the parmesan cheese. 6. Place the rolls onto the Air Fry Basket. 7. Press BOTTOM and turn the dial until AIR FRY is illuminated. Press TEMP and set to 365°F, then press TIME and set to 22 minutes. Press START/STOP to begin preheating. 8. When preheating is complete, insert the Air Fry Basket in LEVEL 2 position of the bottom oven. Close the door to begin cooking. 9. When cooking is complete, serve immediately.
Per Serving: Calories 799; Fat 38.12g; Sodium 2271mg; Carbs 8.78g; Fiber 0.2g; Sugar 2.37g; Protein 98.87g

Spicy Chicken and Egg Cups

Prep Time: 15 minutes | Cook Time: 28 minutes | Serves: 6

6 medium-sized eggs,	2 tablespoons sesame oil
beaten	Hot sauce, for drizzling
1 teaspoon garam masala	1 teaspoon turmeric
1 cup scallions, finely	1 teaspoon mixed
chopped	peppercorns, freshly
3 cloves garlic, finely	cracked
minced	1 teaspoon kosher salt
2 cups leftover chicken,	⅓ teaspoon smoked
shredded	paprika

1. Warm the sesame oil in a skillet over medium heat. Add the scallions with garlic; stir and cook until just fragrant, about 5 minutes. Stir in the leftover chicken and cook until thoroughly warmed. 2. Whisk the eggs with all seasonings in a small bowl. 3. Spray the inside of six heatproof ramekins with a nonstick cooking spray. Divide the egg and chicken mixture among each ramekin. Then place the ramekins in the Air Fry Basket. 4. Press BOTTOM and turn the dial until AIR FRY is illuminated. Press TEMP and set to 355°F, then press TIME and set to 18 minutes. Press START/STOP to begin preheating. 5. When preheating is complete, insert the Air Fry Basket in LEVEL 1 position of the bottom oven. Close the door to begin cooking. 6. When cooking is complete, drizzle with hot sauce and serve warm.
Per Serving: Calories 224; Fat 14.35g; Sodium 517mg; Carbs 2.77g; Fiber 0.7g; Sugar 0.77g; Protein 20.25g

Beef Kale Omelet Cups

Prep Time: 10 minutes | Cook Time: 16 minutes | Serves: 4

Non-stick cooking spray	6 tablespoons sour cream
½ pound leftover beef,	½ teaspoon turmeric
coarsely chopped	powder
2 garlic cloves, pressed	1 teaspoon red pepper
1 cup kale, torn into	flakes
pieces and wilted	Salt and ground black
1 bell pepper, chopped	pepper, to your liking
6 eggs, beaten	

1. Grease the inside of four heatproof ramekins with cooking spray. 2. Combine together all the ingredients in a bowl and stir to mix well. Divide this mixture among the prepared ramekins. Then place the ramekins in the Air Fry Basket. 3. Press BOTTOM and turn the dial until AIR FRY is illuminated. Press TEMP and set to 360°F, then press TIME and set to 16 minutes. Press START/STOP to begin preheating. 4. When preheating is complete, insert the Air Fry Basket in LEVEL 1 position of the bottom oven. Close the door to begin cooking. 5. When cooking time is up, check with a wooden stick and return the eggs to the oven for a few more minutes if needed. Serve immediately.
Per Serving: Calories 238; Fat 13.14g; Sodium 158mg; Carbs 5.04g; Fiber 0.6g; Sugar 1.58g; Protein 24.79g

Cheese Beef Frittata

Prep Time: 15 minutes | Cook Time: 35 minutes | Serves: 2

3 tablespoons goat cheese, crumbled	½ onion, peeled and chopped
2 cups lean ground beef	½ teaspoon paprika
1½ tablespoons olive oil	½ teaspoon kosher salt
½ teaspoon dried marjoram	1 teaspoon ground black pepper
2 eggs	

1. Heat the oil in a skillet over medium heat. Add the onion and cook until soft. Then add the beef and cook until browned; crumble with a fork and set aside, keeping it warm. 2. In a small bowl, whisk the eggs with all the seasonings. 3. Spray the inside of a sheet pan with cooking spray. Pour the egg mixture into the sheet pan, followed by the beef mixture. Then spread the crumbled goat cheese on top. 4. Press TOP and turn the dial until BAKE is illuminated. Press TEMP/SHADE and set to 345°F, then press TIME/SLICES and set to 27 minutes. Press START/STOP to begin preheating. 5. When preheating is complete, place the sheet pan on the rack. Close the door to begin cooking. Serve warm.

Per Serving: Calories 599; Fat 36.15g; Sodium 1207mg; Carbs 6.92g; Fiber 1.1g; Sugar 3.57g; Protein 61.84g

Smoked Salmon Egg Cups

Prep Time: 15 minutes | Cook Time: 16 minutes | Serves: 4

⅓ cup Asiago cheese, grated	1 cup smoked salmon, chopped
⅓ teaspoon dried dill weed	Fine sea salt and freshly cracked black pepper, to taste
½ tomato, chopped	
6 eggs	⅓ teaspoon smoked cayenne pepper
⅓ cup milk	
Cooking spray	

1. In a medium bowl, whisk together the eggs, smoked cayenne pepper, milk, salt, black pepper, and dill weed. 2. Lightly grease 4 ramekins with cooking spray and divide the egg mixture among the prepared ramekins. Then place the

ramekins in the Air Fry Basket. 3. Add the salmon and tomato to each ramekin and top with the grated Asiago cheese. 4. Press BOTTOM and turn the dial until AIR FRY is illuminated. Press TEMP and set to 365°F, then press TIME and set to 16 minutes. Press START/STOP to begin preheating. 5. When preheating is complete, insert the Air Fry Basket in LEVEL 1 position of the bottom oven. Close the door to begin cooking. 6. When cooking is complete, serve immediately.

Per Serving: Calories 189; Fat 10.78g; Sodium 481mg; Carbs 4.37g; Fiber 0.4g; Sugar 2.26g; Protein 17.88g

Chicken Sausage Egg Cups

Prep Time: 15 minutes | Cook Time: 13 minutes | Serves: 6

6 large-sized eggs	as Caprino, crumbled
2 tablespoons butter, melted	1 teaspoon smoked cayenne pepper
3 tablespoons cream	1 teaspoon freshly ground black pepper
1 cup chicken sausage, chopped	½ red onion, peeled and chopped
2 tablespoons roasted garlic, pressed	1 teaspoon fine sea salt
⅓ cup goat cheese such	

1. Coat the inside of six oven safe ramekins with the melted butter. Divide the garlic and red onion among each ramekin. Add chicken sausage and toss until well combined. 2. Whisk an egg with cream into each ramekin and stir to combine well and pale. Then sprinkle with salt, cayenne pepper, and black pepper; stir again. Then place the ramekins in the Air Fry Basket. 3. Press BOTTOM and turn the dial until AIR FRY is illuminated. Press TEMP and set to 355°F, then press TIME and set to 13 minutes. Press START/STOP to begin preheating. 4. When preheating is complete, insert the Air Fry Basket in LEVEL 1 position of the bottom oven. Close the door to begin cooking. 5. When cooking is complete, top with crumbled cheese and serve immediately.

Per Serving: Calories 203; Fat 15.66g; Sodium 728mg; Carbs 4.35g; Fiber 0.5g; Sugar 2.2g; Protein 11.19g

Swiss Chard & Ham Eggs Cups

Prep Time: 15 minutes | Cook Time: 15 minutes | Serves: 2

2 eggs	Chard
¼ teaspoon dried or fresh marjoram	¼ teaspoon dried or fresh rosemary
2 teaspoons chili powder	4 pork ham slices
⅓ teaspoon kosher salt	⅓ teaspoon ground black pepper, or more to taste
½ cup steamed Swiss	

1. Divide the Swiss Chard and ham evenly into 2 heatproof ramekins; crack an egg into each ramekin and sprinkle with the seasonings. Then place the ramekins in the Air Fry Basket. 2. Press BOTTOM and turn the dial until AIR FRY is illuminated. Press TEMP and set to 335°F, then press TIME and set to 15 minutes. Press START/STOP to begin preheating. 3. When preheating is complete, insert the Air Fry Basket in LEVEL 1 position of the bottom oven. Close the door to begin cooking. When cooking is complete, serve with spicy tomato ketchup and pickles if desired.

Per Serving: Calories 548; Fat 23.7g; Sodium 2129mg; Carbs 9.28g; Fiber 1.2g; Sugar 7.34g; Protein 76.6g

Poppy Seed Scones

Prep Time: 15 minutes | Cook Time: 12 minutes | Serves: 4

1 cup all-purpose flour	2 tsp poppy seeds
2 tbsp granulated sugar	Zest of 1 lemon
1½ tsp baking powder	For the Glaze:
⅛ tsp kosher salt	1½ tsp freshly squeezed
2 tbsp coconut oil	lemon juice
¼ cup unsweetened soy milk	3 tbsp powdered sugar

1. Add the flour, baking powder, granulated sugar, and salt to a large bowl and stir to mix well. 2. Using a pastry cutter, add the coconut oil to the flour so that it is evenly distributed throughout the dry ingredients and form the flour into small pea-sized pieces. 3. Add the poppy seeds, soy milk, and lemon zest. Mix with your clean hands, being careful not to overmix. Gently press the dough into the sheet pan. 4. Press TOP and turn the dial until BAKE is illuminated. Press TEMP/

SHADE and set to 320°F, then press TIME/SLICES and set to 12 minutes. Press START/STOP to begin preheating. When preheating is complete, place the sheet pan on the rack. Close the door to begin cooking. Bake until the edges are golden. 5. Remove the sheet pan from the oven. Let the scones cool for 10 minutes. Slice into triangles and transfer to a wire rack. 6. To make the glaze, mix the lemon juice and powdered sugar in a small bowl and beat with a mixer until thick. 7. Drizzle the glaze over the scones. Let stand for 15 minutes before serving.

Per Serving: Calories 231; Fat 8.03g; Sodium 89mg; Carbs 36.86g; Fiber 1.2g; Sugar 11.07g; Protein 3.77g

Breakfast Spinach Quiche

Prep Time: 15 minutes | Cook Time: 21 minutes | Serves: 6

6-ounces cheddar cheese, shredded	¼ cup cream cheese
1 teaspoon olive oil	1 cup spinach
3 eggs	1 teaspoon sea salt
1 teaspoon ground black pepper	4 tablespoons water, boiled
½ yellow onion, diced	½ cup almond flour

1. In a medium bowl, combine the almond flour, salt and water. Mix and knead into dough. Grease the inside of Air Fry Basket with olive oil. 2. Roll the dough and place it the basket in the shape of the crust. 3. Press BOTTOM and turn the dial until AIR FRY is illuminated. Press TEMP and set to 375°F, then press TIME and set to 5 minutes. Press START/STOP to begin preheating. 4. When preheating is complete, insert the Air Fry Basket in LEVEL 2 position of the bottom oven. Close the door to begin cooking. 5. Meanwhile, chop the spinach and toss it with the cream cheese and black pepper. Dice the yellow onion and stir it to the spinach mixture. 6. In a small bowl, whisk in the eggs. 7. When the quiche crust is cooked, spread the spinach- cheese filling and pour the whisked eggs over the top. Air fry the quiche at 350°F for 7minutes. 8. Then lower the heat to300°F and cook the quiche for 9 minutes more. Once done, let the quiche cool thoroughly and then cut it into pieces before serving.

Per Serving: Calories 124; Fat 8.31g; Sodium 779mg; Carbs 4.91g; Fiber 0.4g; Sugar 2.85g; Protein 7.59g

Chicken Lettuce Sandwich

Prep Time: 10 minutes | Cook Time: 16 minutes | Serves: 2

6-ounces ground chicken	½ teaspoon sea salt
2 slices of cheddar cheese	1 egg
2 lettuce leaves	1 teaspoon cayenne pepper
1 tablespoon dill, dried	1 teaspoon tomato puree

1. In a medium bowl, toss the ground chicken with the cayenne pepper and sea salt. Stir in the dried dill. Beat the egg into the ground chicken mixture. Then form this mixture into 2 medium burgers. 2. Grease the Air Fry Basket with olive oil and place the ground chicken burgers inside. 3. Press BOTTOM and turn the dial until AIR FRY is illuminated. Press TEMP and set to 380°F, then press TIME and set to 10 minutes. Press START/STOP to begin preheating. 4. When preheating is complete, insert the Air Fry Basket in LEVEL 2 position of the bottom oven. Close the door to begin cooking. 5. When cooking time is up, flip the burgers and cook for 6 minutes more. Once done, transfer them to the lettuce leaves. 6. Sprinkle with tomato puree and top with a slice of cheddar cheese. Serve immediately!

Per Serving: Calories 338; Fat 24.6g; Sodium 861mg; Carbs 2.43g; Fiber 0.7g; Sugar 0.57g; Protein 26.01g

Cheese Omelet

Prep Time: 15 minutes | Cook Time: 10 minutes | Serves: 4

1 green pepper, chopped	1 teaspoon oregano, dried
5 eggs	1 teaspoon cilantro, dried
½ yellow onion, diced	1 teaspoon olive oil
3-ounces Parmesan cheese, shredded	3 tablespoons cream cheese
1 teaspoon butter	

1. Whisk the eggs in a mixing bowl and add in the oregano, cilantro, cream cheese and shredded parmesan. Stir to mix well. 2. Grease the inside of the sheet pan with butter and pour the egg mixture into the sheet pan. 3. Press TOP and turn the dial until BAKE is illuminated. Press TEMP/SHADE and set to 360°F, then press TIME/SLICES and set to 10 minutes.

Press START/STOP to begin preheating. When preheating is complete, place the sheet pan on the rack. Close the door to begin cooking. 4. In the meantime, heat the olive oil in a skillet over medium heat. Add the chopped green pepper and onion and cook for 8minutes. Stir veggies often. 5. Remove the omelet from the sheet pan and transfer to a serving plate. Add the roasted vegetables and serve warm.

Per Serving: Calories 230; Fat 16.5g; Sodium 520mg; Carbs 6.27g; Fiber 0.5g; Sugar 1.78g; Protein 14.16g

Egg-in-a-Hole Bacon Toast

Prep Time: 15 minutes | Cook Time: 10 minutes | Serves: 1

1 strip of bacon, diced	butter (optional)
1 slice of 1-inch thick bread (such as Texas Toast or hand-sliced bread)	1 egg
	Salt and freshly ground black pepper
1 tablespoon softened	¼ cup grated Colby or Jack cheese

1. Place the bacon in the Air Fry Basket. 2. Press BOTTOM and turn the dial until AIR FRY is illuminated. Press TEMP and set to 400°F, then press TIME and set to 3 minutes. Press START/STOP to begin preheating. 3. When preheating is complete, insert the Air Fry Basket in LEVEL 2 position of the bottom oven. Close the door to begin cooking. Shake the basket halfway through the cooking time. 4. Once cooked, remove the bacon to a paper towel lined plate, set aside. 5. Using a sharp knife, make a large circle in the center of the bread slice, cutting halfway through, but not all the way to the cutting board. Press down on the circle in the center of the bread slice to create an indentation. 6. If desired, spread softened butter around the edges of the bread and in the indentation. Place the slice of bread, hole side up, in the Air Fry Basket. Crack the egg into the center of the bread. Season with salt and black pepper. 7. Air-fry at 380°F for 5 minutes. Sprinkle grated cheese around the edges of the bread, not on the egg in the center. Then top with cooked bacon. Gently press the cheese and bacon into the bread to hold it in place and prevent it from blowing around in the air fryer. 8. Air fryer for another minute or two to melt the cheese and finish cooking the eggs. Serve immediately.

Per Serving: Calories 422; Fat 32.29g; Sodium 1025mg; Carbs 14.15g; Fiber 0.8g; Sugar 2.22g; Protein 18.66g

Air Fried Eggs with Kale-Almond Pesto & Olives

Prep Time: 15 minutes | Cook Time: 11 minutes | Serves: 2

1 cup roughly chopped kale leaves, stems and center ribs removed	Kosher salt and freshly ground black pepper
¼ cup olive oil	4 large eggs
¼ cup grated pecorino cheese	2 tablespoons heavy cream
3 tablespoons whole almonds	3 tablespoons chopped pitted mixed olives
1 garlic clove, peeled	Toast, for serving

1. In a small blender, combine the kale, pecorino, almonds, olive oil, garlic, and salt and pepper and puree until smooth. 2. Crack the eggs into a round cake pan that fits the oven and spoon the kale pesto over the egg whites only, leaving the yolks exposed. Drizzle the cream over the yolks and swirl into the pesto. 3. Press BOTTOM and turn the dial until AIR FRY is illuminated. Press TEMP and set to 300°F, then press TIME and set to 11 minutes. Press START/STOP to begin preheating. 4. When preheating is complete, place the cake pan on the wire rack in LEVEL 1 position of the bottom oven. Close the door to begin cooking. 5. When cooking is complete, sprinkle the olives over the eggs and serve hot with toast.

Per Serving: Calories 529; Fat 48.1g; Sodium 712mg; Carbs 7.48g; Fiber 1.9g; Sugar 1.65g; Protein 18.44g

Cheese Butternut Squash Frittata

Prep Time: 15 minutes | Cook Time: 33 minutes | Serves: 3

1 cup cubed (½-inch) butternut squash (5½ ounces)	4 fresh sage leaves, thinly sliced
2 tablespoons olive oil	6 large eggs, lightly beaten
Kosher salt and freshly ground black pepper	½ cup ricotta cheese
	Cayenne pepper

1. Place the squash in a bowl and toss with the olive oil. Season with salt and black pepper Sprinkle the sage on the bottom of a round cake pan that fits the oven. Place the squash on top. 2. Press BOTTOM and turn the dial until AIR FRY is illuminated.

Press TEMP and set to 400°F, then press TIME and set to 10 minutes. Press START/STOP to begin preheating. 3. When preheating is complete, place the cake pan on the wire rack in LEVEL 1 position of the bottom oven. Close the door to begin cooking. When cooking is complete, stir to incorporate the sage, then air fry for an additional 3 minutes until the squash is tender and lightly caramelized at the edges. 4. Then pour the beaten eggs over the squash, dollop the ricotta all over, and sprinkle with cayenne pepper. Cook at 300°F for 20 minutes more until the eggs are set and the frittata is golden brown. 5. Remove the pan from the oven and cut the frittata into wedges to serve.

Per Serving: Calories 271; Fat 23.63g; Sodium 207mg; Carbs 4.48g; Fiber 0.9g; Sugar 1.18g; Protein 10.64g

Breakfast Jalapeño Chimichanga

Prep Time: 15 minutes | Cook Time: 10 minutes | Serves: 2

2 large (10- to 12-inch) flour tortillas	½ cup grated pepper jack cheese
½ cup canned refried beans (pinto or black work equally well)	12 pickled jalapeño slices
4 large eggs, cooked scrambled	1 tablespoon vegetable oil
4 corn tortilla chips, crushed	Guacamole, salsa, and sour cream, for serving (optional)

1. Divide the refried beans between the two tortillas, laying a rectangle in the center of the tortillas. Spread the scrambled eggs, crushed chips, pepper jack, and jalapeños on top of the beans. Fold one side over the filling, then fold in each short side and roll up the rest like a burrito. 2. Brush the outside of the burritos with vegetable oil. Then place the burritos in the Air Fry Basket, seam-side down. 3. Press BOTTOM and turn the dial until AIR FRY is illuminated. Press TEMP and set to 350°F, then press TIME and set to 10 minutes. Press START/STOP to begin preheating. 4. When preheating is complete, insert the Air Fry Basket in LEVEL 2 position of the bottom oven. Close the door to begin cooking. When cooking is complete, the tortillas should be browned and crisp and the filling is warm throughout. 5. Transfer the chimichangas to serving plates and serve with guacamole, salsa, and sour cream to your liking.

Per Serving: Calories 583; Fat 30.69g; Sodium 696mg; Carbs 49.54g; Fiber 5.6g; Sugar 3.75g; Protein 27.73g

Blackberries Coconut Porridge

Prep Time: 10 minutes | Cook Time: 7 minutes | Serves: 4

1 cup coconut milk	cinnamon
3 tablespoons blackberries	5 tablespoons chia seeds
2 tablespoons walnuts	3 tablespoons coconut flakes
1 teaspoon butter	¼ teaspoon salt
1 teaspoon ground	

1. Pour the coconut milk into the sheet pan. Stir in the coconut, chia seeds, ground cinnamon, salt, and butter. Ground up the walnuts and add them to the sheet pan. Use a fork to mash the blackberries and stir into the sheet pan. 2. Press TOP and turn the dial until BAKE is illuminated. Press TEMP/SHADE and set to 375°F, then press TIME/SLICES and set to 7 minutes. Press START/STOP to begin preheating. When preheating is complete, place the sheet pan on the rack. Close the door to begin cooking. 3. When cooking is complete, transfer the sheet pan to a cooling rack and let rest for 5-minutes. Stir the porridge with a wooden spoon and serve warm.

Per Serving: Calories 161; Fat 10.24g; Sodium 193mg; Carbs 13.91g; Fiber 5.7g; Sugar 6.96g; Protein 5.24g

Corn-Tomato Frittata with Avocado Dressing

Prep Time: 15 minutes | Cook Time: 20 minutes | Serves: 3

½ cup cherry tomatoes, halved	½ cup grated Monterey Jack cheese
Kosher salt	1 avocado, pitted and peeled
½ cup fresh or thawed frozen corn kernels	2 tablespoons fresh lime juice
¼ cup milk	¼ cup olive oil
1 tablespoon finely chopped fresh dill	8 fresh basil leaves, finely chopped
6 large eggs, lightly beaten	1 scallion, finely chopped
Freshly ground black pepper	

1. Place tomatoes in a colander and sprinkle with salt. Let stand for 10 minutes to drain excess water. 2. Place tomatoes

in a bowl and stir in corn, dill, milk, and eggs. Season with salt and pepper and mix well. 3. Pour the egg mixture into a round cake pan that fits the oven. and place the pan in the air fryer. 4. Press BOTTOM and turn the dial until AIR FRY is illuminated. Press TEMP and set to 300°F, then press TIME and set to 15 minutes. Press START/STOP to begin preheating. 5. When preheating is complete, place the round cake pan on the wire rack in LEVEL 2 position of the bottom oven. Close the door to begin cooking. 6. When cooking is complete, sprinkle with the Monterey Jack and cook at 315°F for an additional 5 minutes, until the eggs are set and the cheese has melted. 7. Meanwhile, place the avocado in a medium bowl and mash with the lime juice until smooth, then stir in the basil, olive oil, and scallion. 8. Once done, remove the pan from the oven, cut the frittata into wedges, and serve with some of the avocado dressing.

Per Serving: Calories 384; Fat 33.64g; Sodium 268mg; Carbs 12.55g; Fiber 4.3g; Sugar 2.22g; Protein 10.59g

Simple & Healthy Eggs

Prep Time: 1 minutes | Cook Time: 15 minutes | Serves: 6

6 eggs

1. Press TOP and turn the dial until BAKE is illuminated. Press TEMP/SHADE and set the temperature to 250°F, then press TIME/SLICES and set the time to 15 minutes. Press START/STOP to start preheating. 2. Place the eggs on the sheet pan. When the unit has preheated, immediately put the sheet pan on the wire rack in the Bottom Oven Level 1. Close oven door. Reduce the cook time to 10 minutes for a soft-boiled egg if you like. 3. Meanwhile, fill a medium mixing bowl half full of ice water. 4. When cooking is up, use tongs to remove the eggs and transfer to the ice water bath. 5. Let the eggs sit for 5 minutes in the ice water. 6. Peel and eat on the spot or refrigerate for up to 1 week.

Per Serving: Calories 130; Fat 9.64g; Sodium 102mg; Carbs 1.02g; Fiber 0g; Sugar 0.65g; Protein 8.97g

Buttered Breakfast Biscuits

Prep Time: 5 minutes | Cook Time: 5 minutes | Serves: 6

2 cups all-purpose flour	cold unsalted butter, cut
1 tablespoon baking	into 1-tablespoon slices
powder	¾ cup buttermilk
¼ teaspoon baking soda	4 tablespoons (½ stick)
2 teaspoons sugar	unsalted butter, melted
1 teaspoon salt	(optional)
6 tablespoons (¾ stick)	

1. Spray the sheet pan with olive oil. 2. Combine the flour, baking soda, baking powder, sugar, and salt in a large mixing bowl and mix well. 3. Using a fork to cut in the butter until the mixture resembles coarse meal. 4. Add the buttermilk and mix until smooth. 5. Sprinkle flour on a clean work surface. Turn the dough out onto the work surface and roll it out until it is about ½ inch thick. 6. Using a 2-inch biscuit cutter to cut out the biscuits. 7. Press TOP and turn the dial until BAKE is illuminated. Press TEMP/SHADE and set the temperature to 360°F, then press TIME/SLICES and set the time to 5 minutes. Press START/STOP to start preheating. Place the uncooked biscuits in the greased sheet pan in a single layer. When the unit has preheated, immediately put the sheet pan on the wire rack in the Bottom Oven Level 1. Close oven door. 8. Transfer the cooked biscuits to a platter. Brush the tops with the melted butter if desired. 9. Cut the remaining biscuits. Bake the remaining biscuits. 10. Plate, serve, and enjoy!

Per Serving: Calories 286; Fat 13.54g; Sodium 512mg; Carbs 35.27g; Fiber 1.2g; Sugar 2.39g; Protein 6.09g

Easy Cinnamon Rolls

Prep Time: 5 minutes | Cook Time: 12 minutes | Serves: 8

1 can of cinnamon rolls

1. Spray the sheet pan with olive oil. 2. Press TOP and turn the dial until BAKE is illuminated. Press TEMP/SHADE and set the temperature to 340°F, then press TIME/SLICES and set the time to 6 minutes. Press START/STOP to start preheating. Separate the canned cinnamon rolls and place them on the sheet pan. 3. When the unit has preheated, immediately put the sheet pan on the wire rack in the Bottom Oven Level 1. Close oven door. 4. Using tongs to flip the cinnamon rolls. Bake for another 6 minutes. 5. When the rolls are done cooking, use tongs to remove them and transfer to a platter and spread them with the icing that comes in the package.

Per Serving: Calories 155; Fat 3.57g; Sodium 297mg; Carbs 26.08g; Fiber 2.2g; Sugar 0.92g; Protein 4.88g

Vanilla Blueberry Pancake Poppers

Prep Time: 5 minutes | Cook Time: 8 minutes | Serves: 8

1 cup all-purpose flour	1 large egg
1 tablespoon sugar	1 teaspoon vanilla
1 teaspoon baking soda	extract
½ teaspoon baking	1 teaspoon olive oil
powder	½ cup fresh blueberries
1 cup milk	

1. Combine the baking powder, flour, and sugar in a medium mixing bowl and mix well. 2. Mix in the milk, vanilla, egg, and oil. 3. Coat the inside of the muffin tin with cooking spray. 4. Fill each muffin cup two-thirds full. You may have to bake the poppers in more than one batch. 5. Drop a few blueberries into each muffin cup. 6. Press TOP and turn the dial until BAKE is illuminated. Press TEMP/SHADE and set the temperature to 320°F, then press TIME/SLICES and set the time to 8 minutes. Press START/STOP to start preheating. 7. Place the cups on the sheet pan. When the unit has preheated, immediately put the sheet pan on the wire rack in the Bottom Oven Level 1. Close oven door. 8. Insert a toothpick into the center of a pancake popper. If it comes out clean, they are done. If batter clings to the toothpick, cook the poppers for 2 minutes more and check again. 9. When the poppers are cooked through, use silicone oven mitts to remove the muffin tin. Turn out the poppers onto a wire rack to cool before serving.

Per Serving: Calories 107; Fat 2.33g; Sodium 173mg; Carbs 18.2g; Fiber 0.7g; Sugar 5.91g; Protein 3.02g

Easy Cheesy Eggs

Prep Time: 2 minutes | Cook Time: 6 minutes | Serves: 6

2 large eggs	Cheddar cheese, divided
2 tablespoons half-and-half, divided	Salt
2 teaspoons shredded	Freshly ground black pepper

1. Lightly coat the insides of 2 (8-ounce) ramekins with cooking spray. 2. Break an egg into each ramekin. 3. Add 1 tablespoon of half-and-half and 1 teaspoon of cheese to each ramekin. Season with salt and pepper. 4. Using a fork, to stir the egg mixture. 5. Press TOP and turn the dial until BAKE is illuminated. Press TEMP/SHADE and set the temperature to 330°F, then press TIME/SLICES and set the time to 6 minutes. Press START/STOP to start preheating. 6. Place the ingredients on the sheet pan. When the unit has preheated, immediately put the sheet pan on the wire rack in the Bottom Oven Level 1. Close oven door. 7. Check the eggs to make sure they are cooked. If they are not done, cook for 1 minute more and check again. 8. Using silicone oven mitts to remove the hot ramekins and serve.

Per Serving: Calories 175; Fat 14.32g; Sodium 638mg; Carbs 1.38g; Fiber 0.1g; Sugar 0.38g; Protein 10.12g

Crispy and Juicy Bacon

Prep Time: 5 minutes | Cook Time: 12 minutes | Serves: 5

10 slices bacon

1. Cut the bacon slices in half, so they will fit in the oven. 2. Press BOTTOM and turn the dial until AIR FRY illuminates. Press the TIME/SLICES buttons to set the cook time to 5 minutes. Then press the TEMP button to set the cook temperature to 400°F. Press START/STOP to start preheating. 3. Place the half-slices on the Air Fry Basket in a single layer. When bottom oven is preheated, immediately, place the wire rack in LEVEL 1 position of the bottom oven and place the sheet pan on top. Slide the Basket in LEVEL 2 position of bottom oven. Close door to begin cooking. (You may need to cook the bacon in more than one batch.). 4. Open and check the bacon. 5. Fry for 5 minutes more. 6. When the time has elapsed, check the bacon again. If you like your bacon crispier, cook it for another 1 to 2 minutes.

Per Serving: Calories 212; Fat 20.42g; Sodium 244mg; Carbs 0.43g; Fiber 0g; Sugar 0.43g; Protein 6.52g

Buttered Cinnamon Pecan Roll

Prep Time: 15 minutes | Cook Time: 25 minutes | Serves: 4

8 ounces store-bought pizza dough	1 tablespoon Lyle's Golden Syrup, maple syrup, or dark agave syrup
All-purpose flour, for dusting	
2 tablespoons unsalted butter, melted	½ cup powdered sugar
¼ cup packed dark brown sugar	1 ounce cream cheese, at room temperature
¼ cup chopped pecans	1 tablespoon milk
¼ teaspoon kosher salt	⅛ teaspoon ground cinnamon

1. Using a rolling pin, roll the pizza dough into a rough 12 x 8-inch rectangle on a lightly floured work surface. 2. Brush the dough all over with the melted butter, then sprinkle evenly with the brown sugar, salt, and pecans, then drizzle with the syrup. 3. Cut the rectangle lengthwise into 8 equal strips with a pizza cutter or knife. 4. Roll up one strip like a snail shell, then continue rolling each spiral up in the next strip until one giant spiral forms. 5. Cut a piece of parchment paper or foil to the size of the bottom of the Air Fry Basket and line the bottom with it. 6. Press BOTTOM and turn the dial until AIR FRY illuminates. Press the TIME/SLICES buttons to set the cook time to 15 minutes. Then press the TEMP button to set the cook temperature to 325°F. Press START/STOP to start preheating. 7. Carefully lay the spiral in the Air Fry Basket and cover with a round of foil cut to fit the size of the spiral. When bottom oven is preheated, immediately slide the Basket in LEVEL 2 position. Close door to start cooking. 8. After cooking for 15 minutes, remove the foil round from the top and cook the roll for about 10 minutes more until golden brown and cooked through in the middle. 9. Meanwhile, whisk together the powdered sugar, milk, cream cheese, and cinnamon in a bowl until smooth. 10. Once the roll is cooked, let it cool in the basket for 10 minutes, then carefully lift it out of Basket using the parchment paper bottom as an aid. Transfer the roll to a plate and pour the icing over the roll to cover it completely. Let the roll and icing cool together for at least 10 more minutes to set before cutting into wedges to serve.

Per Serving: Calories 370; Fat 16.18g; Sodium 525mg; Carbs 51.07g; Fiber 1.3g; Sugar 22.4g; Protein 6.54g

Vanilla Buttered Blueberry Muffins

Prep Time: 5 minutes | Cook Time: 14 minutes | Serves: 10

⅔ cup all-purpose flour	extract
1 teaspoon baking powder	⅓ cup low-fat milk
2 tablespoons sugar	3 tablespoons unsalted butter, melted
1 egg	¾ cup fresh blueberries
2 teaspoons vanilla	

1. In a medium mixing bowl, combine the flour, vanilla, baking powder, egg, milk, sugar, and melted butter and mix well. 2. Fold in the blueberries. 3. Coat the inside of the muffin tin with cooking spray. 4. Fill each muffin cup about two-thirds full. 5. Press TOP and turn the dial until BAKE is illuminated. Press TEMP/SHADE and set the temperature to 320°F, then press TIME/SLICES and set the time to 14 minutes. Press START/STOP to start preheating. You may need to cook the muffins in more than one batch. 6. Place the muffin tin on the sheet pan. When the unit has preheated, immediately put the sheet pan on the wire rack in the Bottom Oven Level 1. Close oven door. 7. Insert a toothpick into the center of a muffin; if it comes out clean, they are done. If batter clings to the toothpick, cook the muffins for 2 minutes more and check again. 8. When the muffins are cooked through, use silicone oven mitts to remove the muffin tin. Place the muffins onto a wire rack to cool slightly before serving.

Per Serving: Calories 104; Fat 4.37g; Sodium 47mg; Carbs 12.7g; Fiber 0.5g; Sugar 5.71g; Protein 3.26g

Buttered Banana Bread

Prep Time: 5 minutes | Cook Time: 22 minutes | Serves: 3

3 ripe bananas, mashed	1½ cups all-purpose flour
1 cup sugar	
1 large egg	1 teaspoon baking soda
4 tablespoons (½ stick) unsalted butter, melted	1 teaspoon salt

1. Coat the sheet pan with cooking spray. 2. Mix together the bananas and sugar in a large mixing bowl. 3. Combine the egg, butter, baking soda, flour, and salt in a separate large mixing bowl and mix well. 4. Put the banana mixture into the egg and flour mixture. Mix well. 5. Press TOP and turn the dial until BAKE is illuminated. Press TEMP/SHADE and set the temperature to 310°F, then press TIME/SLICES and set the time to 22 minutes. Press START/STOP to start preheating. 6. Divide the batter in equal thirds evenly into the sheet pan. 7. When the unit has preheated, immediately put the sheet pan on the wire rack in the Bottom Oven Level 1. Close oven door. 8. Insert a toothpick into the center of each loaf; if it comes out clean, they are done. If the batter clings to the toothpick, cook the loaves for 2 minutes more and check again. 9. When the loaves are cooked through, use silicone oven mitts to remove the pans. Turn out the loaves onto a wire rack to cool.

Per Serving: Calories 579; Fat 12.87g; Sodium 1228mg; Carbs 108.02g; Fiber 4.8g; Sugar 47.27g; Protein 10.45g

Cheesy Mushroom-Spinach Frittata

Prep Time: 10 minutes | Cook Time: 23 minutes | Serves: 2

Cooking spray	¼ cup halved grape tomatoes
4 large eggs	
4 ounces baby bella mushrooms, chopped	1 tablespoon 2% milk
	½ teaspoon kosher salt
1 cup (1 ounce) baby spinach, chopped	¼ teaspoon garlic powder
⅓ cup (from 1 large) chopped leek, white part only	¼ teaspoon dried oregano
	Freshly ground black pepper
½ cup (2 ounces) shredded cheddar cheese	

1. Lightly spray the sheet pan with cooking spray. 2. In a large bowl, beat the eggs with a fork until uniform. Add the mushrooms, leek, spinach, garlic powder, tomatoes, cheddar, milk, salt, oregano, and pepper to taste. Mix to combine. 3. Press TOP and turn the dial until BAKE is illuminated. Press TEMP/SHADE and set the temperature to 300°F, then press TIME/SLICES and set the time to 23 minutes. Press START/STOP to start preheating. and pour into the baking dish. 4. Place the mixture on the sheet pan. When the unit has preheated, immediately put the sheet pan on the wire rack in the Bottom Oven Level 1. Close oven door. 5. Cook until the eggs are set in the center. 6. When cooking is up, cut the frittata in half and serve.

Per Serving: Calories 488; Fat 23.09g; Sodium 952mg; Carbs 50.6g; Fiber 7.2g; Sugar 5.62g; Protein 26.71g

Chapter 2 Vegetable and Side Recipes

Crispy Buttermilk Onion Rings

Prep Time: 10 minutes | Cook Time: 23 minutes | Serves: 4

1 medium Vidalia onion (about 9 ounces)	paprika
1½ cups (1½ ounces) cornflakes	½ cup 1% buttermilk
	1 large egg
½ cup seasoned bread crumbs	¼ cup all-purpose flour
	½ teaspoon kosher salt
½ teaspoon sweet	Olive oil spray

1. Trim the ends off the onion, then quarter the onion crosswise (about ⅓-inch-thick slices) and separate into rings. 2. Pulse the cornflakes in a food processor until fine. Transfer to a medium bowl and add the paprika and bread crumbs to stir. 3. Whisk together the buttermilk, flour, egg, and ½ teaspoon salt in another medium bowl until combined. 4. Working in batches, dip the onion rings in the buttermilk batter, then into the cornflake mixture to coat. Set aside on a work surface and spray both sides with oil. 5. Press BOTTOM and turn the dial until AIR FRY illuminates. Press the TIME/SLICES buttons to set the cook time to 10 minutes. Then press the TEMP button to set the cook temperature to 340°F. Press START/STOP to start preheating. 6. Working in batches, place a single layer of the onion rings on the Air Fry Basket. 7. When bottom oven is preheated, immediately slide the Basket in LEVEL 2 position. Close door to start cooking. 8. Flip halfway, until golden brown. 9. When cooking is up, serve immediately.

Per Serving: Calories 312; Fat 5.39g; Sodium 396mg; Carbs 58.71g; Fiber 5.4g; Sugar 3.36g; Protein 9.09g

Simple Potatoes with Yogurt and Chives

Prep Time: 10 minutes | Cook Time: 35 minutes | Serves: 4

4 (7-ounce) russet potatoes, washed and dried	½ cup 2% Greek yogurt
	¼ cup minced fresh chives
Olive oil spray	Freshly ground black pepper
½ teaspoon kosher salt	

1. Use a fork to pierce the potatoes all over. Spray all potatoes with a little oil. Season the potatoes with ¼ teaspoon of the salt. 2. Press BOTTOM and turn the dial until AIR FRY illuminates. Press the TIME/SLICES buttons to set the cook time to 35 minutes. Then press the TEMP button to set the cook temperature to 400°F. Press START/STOP to start preheating. 3. Place the potatoes on the Air Fry Basket. When bottom oven is preheated, immediately, place the wire rack in LEVEL 1 position of the bottom oven and place the sheet pan on top. Slide the Basket in LEVEL 2 position of bottom oven. Close door to begin cooking. 4. Flip halfway through and cook until a knife can easily be inserted into the center of each potato. 5. When cooking is up, split open the potatoes and serve topped with the yogurt, chives, the pepper and remaining ¼ teaspoon salt to taste.

Per Serving: Calories 330; Fat 1.27g; Sodium 327mg; Carbs 68.97g; Fiber 5g; Sugar 3.91g; Protein 13.09g

Paprika Sweet Potato Fries

Prep Time: 10 minutes | Cook Time: 8 minutes | Serves: 2

2 (6-ounce) sweet potatoes, peeled	powder
	¼ teaspoon sweet paprika
2 teaspoons olive oil	
½ teaspoon kosher salt	Freshly ground black pepper
½ teaspoon garlic	

1. Cut the potatoes lengthwise into ¼-inch-thick slices, then cut each slice into ¼-inch-thick fries. Transfer to a large bowl and toss with the oil, salt, paprika, garlic powder, and pepper to taste. 2. Press BOTTOM and turn the dial until AIR FRY illuminates. Press the TIME/SLICES buttons to set the cook time to 8 minutes. Then press the TEMP button to set the cook temperature to 400°F. Press START/STOP to start preheating. 3. Working in batches, arrange a single layer of the fries on the Air Fry Basket. When bottom oven is preheated, immediately, place the wire rack in LEVEL 1 position of the bottom oven and place the sheet pan on top. Slide the Basket in LEVEL 2 position of bottom oven. Close door to begin cooking. 4. Flip halfway and cook until golden brown and crisp on the outside. 5. When cooking is up, serve immediately.

Per Serving: Calories 329; Fat 4.9g; Sodium 604mg; Carbs 65.59g; Fiber 8.4g; Sugar 2.93g; Protein 7.69g

Classic Tostones with Peruvian Green Sauce

Prep Time: 10 minutes | Cook Time: 18 minutes | Serves: 2

1 large green plantain	½ teaspoon kosher salt
Kosher salt	¼ teaspoon freshly
¾ teaspoon garlic	ground black pepper
powder	3 jalapeños, seeded
Olive oil spray	(but keep the ribs) and
Peruvian Green Sauce,	roughly chopped (about
for Serving:	1 cup)
2 tablespoons olive oil	2 cups (2 ounces)
¼ cup chopped red onion	chopped fresh cilantro
½ cup light mayonnaise	(leaves and stems
2 tablespoons distilled	included)
white vinegar	3 garlic cloves, crushed
4 teaspoons yellow	through a garlic press
mustard	

1. Trim the ends of the plantain with a sharp knife to. To make it easier to peel, score a slit along the length of the plantain skin. Slice the plantain crosswise into eight 1-inch pieces and peel the skin off each piece. 2. Combine 1 cup water with 1 teaspoon salt and the garlic powder in a small bowl. 3. Press BOTTOM and turn the dial until AIR FRY illuminates. Press the TIME/SLICES buttons to set the cook time to 6 minutes. Then press the TEMP button to set the cook temperature to 400°F. Press START/STOP to start preheating. 4. Spritz the plantain all over with olive oil and place on the Air Fry Basket. When bottom oven is preheated, immediately, place the wire rack in LEVEL 1 position of the bottom oven and place the sheet pan on top. Slide the Basket in LEVEL 2 position of bottom oven. Close door to begin cooking. 5. Shake halfway and cook until soft. 6. When cooking is up, immediately transfer to a work surface. While they are still hot, use a tostonera or the bottom of a glass jar or measuring cup to flatten each piece. 7. Dip each piece, one at a time, in the seasoned water, then transfer to the work surface (discard the water). Generously spray both sides of the plantain with oil. 8. Set the temperature to 400°F again. Arrange a single layer of the plantain in the Basket. Cook for about 10 minutes and flip halfway until golden and crisp. Work in batches if needed. 9. To make the sauce: In a small skillet, warm 1 teaspoon of the olive oil over medium heat. Pour in the onion to cook for 3 to 4 minutes until soft, stirring occasionally. 10. Transfer the cooked onion to a blender with the vinegar, remaining 1 tablespoon plus 2 teaspoons oil, mustard, salt, mayonnaise,

and black pepper. 11. Add the cilantro, jalapeños, and garlic and blend on high speed for about half minutes until the sauce is smooth and creamy. The sauce can be stored in a sealed container in the refrigerator for up to 1 week. 12. When cooking is done, transfer to a serving dish. Spray lightly with olive oil and season with ⅛ teaspoon salt while still hot. Serve immediately with the green sauce on the side.

Per Serving: Calories 537; Fat 40.59g; Sodium 1753mg; Carbs 38.01g; Fiber 4.8g; Sugar 6.74g; Protein 7.06g

Fried Eggplant with Marinara Sauce

Prep Time: 10 minutes | Cook Time: 8 minutes | Serves: 8

1 large eggplant (about	1⅔ cups seasoned bread
1½ pounds)	crumbs, whole wheat or
¾ teaspoon kosher salt	gluten-free
Freshly ground black	Olive oil spray
pepper	Marinara sauce, for
3 large eggs	dipping (optional)

1. Slice the ends off the eggplant and cut into ¼-inch-thick rounds, 40 to 42 slices. Season both sides with the and salt. 2. On a shallow plate, beat the eggs with 1 teaspoon water. Place the bread crumbs on another plate. 3. Dip all eggplant slices in the egg, then in the bread crumbs, pressing gently to adhere. After shaking off any excess bread crumbs, place on a work surface. Spray both sides of the eggplant with oil. 4. Press BOTTOM and turn the dial until AIR FRY illuminates. Press the TIME/SLICES buttons to set the cook time to 8 minutes. Then press the TEMP button to set the cook temperature to 380°F. Press START/STOP to start preheating. 5. Working in batches, arrange a single layer of the eggplant in the Air Fry Basket. Flip halfway and cook until crisp, golden, and cooked through in the center. 6. When cooking is up, serve warm with the marinara, if desired.

Per Serving: Calories 61; Fat 2.44g; Sodium 263mg; Carbs 8.1g; Fiber 2.3g; Sugar 2.9g; Protein 2.37g

Maitake Mushroom with Sesame Seeds

Prep Time: 10 minutes | Cook Time: 8 minutes | Serves: 2

1 tablespoon soy sauce	the woods) mushrooms
3 teaspoons vegetable oil	½ teaspoon flaky sea salt
2 teaspoons toasted sesame oil	½ teaspoon sesame seeds
1 garlic clove, minced	½ teaspoon finely chopped fresh thyme
7 ounces maitake (hen of	leaves

1. Combine the 1 teaspoon of the vegetable oil, soy sauce, sesame oil, and garlic in a small bowl. 2. Press BOTTOM and turn the dial until AIR FRY illuminates. Press the TIME/SLICES buttons to set the cook time to 10 minutes. Then press the TEMP button to set the cook temperature to 300°F. Press START/STOP to start preheating. 3. Place the maitake mushrooms in more or less a single layer in the Air Fry Basket, then drizzle with the soy sauce mixture. 4. When bottom oven is preheated, immediately, place the wire rack in LEVEL 1 position of the bottom oven and place the sheet pan on top. Slide the Basket in LEVEL 2 position of bottom oven. Close door to begin cooking. 5. Sprinkle with the sesame seeds, sea salt, and thyme, then drizzle with the remaining 2 teaspoons vegetable oil. Cook for about 5 minutes more until browned and crisp at the edges and tender inside. 6. When cooking is up, remove the mushrooms and transfer to plates, and serve hot.

Per Serving: Calories 423; Fat 14.11g; Sodium 715mg; Carbs 77.41g; Fiber 11.7g; Sugar 3.75g; Protein 10.33g

Maple Syrup-Garlic Tomatoes

Prep Time: 10 minutes | Cook Time: 20 minutes | Serves: 2

10 ounces cherry tomatoes, halved	oil
Kosher salt	2 sprigs fresh thyme, stems removed
2 tablespoons maple syrup	1 garlic clove, minced
1 tablespoon vegetable	Freshly ground black pepper

1. Place the tomatoes in a colander and sprinkle liberally with salt. Let stand for 10 minutes to drain. 2. Press TOP and turn the dial until BAKE is illuminated. Press TEMP/SHADE and set the temperature to 325°F, then press TIME/SLICES and set the time to 20 minutes. Press START/STOP to start preheating. 3. Place the tomatoes on the sheet pan, cut-side up. Then drizzle with the maple syrup, followed by the oil. Sprinkle with the thyme leaves and garlic and season with pepper. 4. When the unit has preheated, immediately put the sheet pan on the wire rack in the Bottom Oven Level 1. Close oven door. 5. Cook until the tomatoes are soft, collapsed, and lightly caramelized on top. 6. When cooking is up, serve straight from the pan or transfer the tomatoes to a plate and drizzle with the juices from the pan to serve.

Per Serving: Calories 206; Fat 7.14g; Sodium 584mg; Carbs 37.18g; Fiber 3.3g; Sugar 30.28g; Protein 1.71g

Sweet-Salty Roasted Carrots with Parsley

Prep Time: 10 minutes | Cook Time: 20 minutes | Serves: 2

1½ tablespoons agave syrup or honey	¼ teaspoon freshly ground black pepper
1 tablespoon soy sauce	1 pound carrots, peeled and cut on an angle into
1 tablespoon vegetable oil	½-inch-thick slices
¼ teaspoon crushed red chile flakes	1 tablespoon finely chopped fresh flat-leaf
¼ teaspoon ground coriander	parsley

1. In a bowl, combine the oil, agave syrup, soy sauce, chile flakes, black pepper, coriander, and carrots and toss to coat evenly. 2. Transfer the carrots and dressing to the sheet pan. 3. Press TOP and turn the dial until BAKE is illuminated. Press TEMP/SHADE and set the temperature to 375°F, then press TIME/SLICES and set the time to 20 minutes. Press START/STOP to start preheating. 4. When the unit has preheated, immediately put the sheet pan on the wire rack in the Bottom Oven Level 1. Close oven door. 5. Cook and stir every 5 minutes until the dressing is reduced to a glaze and the carrots are lightly caramelized and tender. 6. When cooking is up, remove the pan, transfer to a bowl, and sprinkle with the parsley before serving.

Per Serving: Calories 227; Fat 8.88g; Sodium 282mg; Carbs 37.22g; Fiber 6.8g; Sugar 25.33g; Protein 2.95g

Mayo Corn & Cilantro Salad

Prep Time: 10 minutes | Cook Time: 10 minutes | Serves: 2

2 ears of corn, shucked (halved crosswise if too large to fit in the oven)
1 tablespoon unsalted butter, at room temperature
1 teaspoon chili powder
¼ teaspoon garlic powder
Kosher salt and freshly ground black pepper
1 cup lightly packed fresh cilantro leaves
1 tablespoon sour cream
1 tablespoon mayonnaise
1 teaspoon adobo sauce (from a can of chipotle peppers in adobo sauce)
2 tablespoons crumbled queso fresco
Lime wedges, for serving

1. Brush the corn all over with the butter, then sprinkle with the garlic powder and chili powder, and season with pepper and salt. 2. Press BOTTOM and turn the dial until AIR FRY illuminates. Press the TIME/SLICES buttons to set the cook time to 10 minutes. Then press the TEMP button to set the cook temperature to 400°F. Press START/STOP to start preheating. 3. Place the corn on the Air Fry Basket. 4. When bottom oven is preheated, immediately slide the Basket in LEVEL 2 position. Close door to start cooking. 5. Turn over halfway through and cook until the kernels are lightly charred and tender. 6. When cooking is up, transfer the ears to a cutting board, let stand 1 minute, then carefully cut the kernels off the cobs and move them to a bowl. Place the cilantro leaves and toss to combine. 7. In a small bowl, stir together the sour cream, mayonnaise, and adobo sauce. 8. Divide the corn and cilantro among plates and spoon the adobo dressing over the top. Sprinkle with the queso fresco and serve with lime wedges on the side.

Per Serving: Calories 187; Fat 10.47g; Sodium 828mg; Carbs 21.74g; Fiber 3.5g; Sugar 3.63g; Protein 5.9g

Cilantro Zucchini with Kimchi-Herb Sauce

Prep Time: 10 minutes | Cook Time: 15 minutes | Serves: 2

2 medium zucchini, ends trimmed (about 6 ounces each)
2 tablespoons olive oil
½ cup kimchi, finely chopped
¼ cup finely chopped fresh cilantro
¼ cup finely chopped fresh flat-leaf parsley,
plus more for garnish
2 tablespoons rice vinegar
2 teaspoons Asian chili-garlic sauce
1 teaspoon grated fresh ginger
Kosher salt and freshly ground black pepper

1. Brush the zucchini with half of the olive oil. 2. Press BOTTOM and turn the dial until AIR FRY illuminates. Press the TIME/SLICES buttons to set the cook time to 15 minutes. Then press the TEMP button to set the cook temperature to 400°F. Press START/STOP to start preheating. 3. Place the zucchini on the Air Fry Basket. 4. When bottom oven is preheated, immediately slide the Basket in LEVEL 2 position. Close door to start cooking. Turn halfway through and cook until lightly charred on the outside and tender. 5. Meanwhile, in a small bowl, combine the remaining 1 tablespoon olive oil, cilantro, kimchi, parsley, chili-garlic sauce, vinegar, and ginger. 6. Once the zucchini is finished cooking, transfer it to a colander and let it cool for 5 minutes. With the fingers, pinch and break the zucchini into bite-size pieces, letting them fall back into the colander. Season with the pepper and salt, toss to combine, and then let sit a further 5 minutes to allow some of its liquid to drain. Pile the zucchini on top of the kimchi sauce on a plate and sprinkle with more parsley to serve.

Per Serving: Calories 148; Fat 14.37g; Sodium 686mg; Carbs 3.51g; Fiber 1.2g; Sugar 0.8g; Protein 2.06g

Healthy Okra with Peanut Sauce

Prep Time: 10 minutes | Cook Time: 22 minutes | Serves: 2

¾ pound okra pods	want a milder sauce)
2 tablespoons vegetable oil	1 tablespoon tomato paste
Kosher salt and freshly ground black pepper	1 cup vegetable stock or water
1 large shallot, minced	2 tablespoons natural peanut butter
1 garlic clove, minced	Juice of ½ lime
½ Scotch bonnet chile, minced (seeded if you	

1. In a bowl, toss the okra with 1 tablespoon of the oil and season with the pepper and salt. 2. Press BOTTOM and turn the dial until AIR FRY illuminates. Press the TIME/SLICES buttons to set the cook time to 16 minutes. Then press the TEMP button to set the cook temperature to 400°F. Press START/STOP to start preheating. 3. Place the okra on the Air Fry Basket. 4. When bottom oven is preheated, immediately, place the wire rack in LEVEL 1 position of the bottom oven and place the sheet pan on top. Slide the Basket in LEVEL 2 position of bottom oven. Close door to begin cooking. 5. Shake the basket halfway through and cook until tender and lightly charred at the edges. 6. Meanwhile, heat the remaining 1 tablespoon oil over medium-high heat in a small skillet. 7. Add the garlic, shallot, and chile to cook for 2 minutes until soft, stirring. 8. Add the tomato paste to stir and cook for 30 seconds, then stir in the vegetable stock and peanut butter. 9. Reduce the temperature to maintain a simmer and cook for 3 to 4 minutes until the sauce is reduced slightly and thickened. Remove the sauce from the heat, add the lime juice to stir, and season with salt and pepper. 10. Place the peanut sauce on a plate. 11. When cooking is up, pile the okra on top of the sauce and serve hot.

Per Serving: Calories 284; Fat 17.17g; Sodium 492mg; Carbs 31.16g; Fiber 7.4g; Sugar 12.77g; Protein 6.21g

Garlic Turkey & Potatoes

Prep Time: 10 minutes | Cook Time: 10 minutes | Serves: 2

3 unsmoked turkey strips	2 tsp. olive oil
6 small potatoes, peeled and cubed	Salt to taste
1 tsp. garlic, minced	Pepper to taste

1. In a large bowl, slice the turkey finely and toss with the garlic, oil, salt and pepper. Add the potatoes to the bowl and stir to mix well. 2. Line the Air Fry Basket with silver aluminum foil and pour the turkey mixture into the basket. 3. Press BOTTOM and turn the dial until AIR FRY is illuminated. Press TEMP and set to 350°F, then press TIME and set to 10 minutes. Press START/STOP to begin preheating. 4. When preheating is complete, insert the Air Fry Basket in LEVEL 2 position of the bottom oven. Close the door to begin cooking. When cooking is complete, serve immediately.

Per Serving: Calories 458; Fat 5.51g; Sodium 529mg; Carbs 90.25g; Fiber 11.3g; Sugar 4.73g; Protein 14.09g

Air Fried Croutons

Prep Time: 5 minutes | Cook Time: 8 minutes | Serves: 4

2 slices friendly bread	1 tbsp. olive oil

1. Press BOTTOM and turn the dial until AIR FRY is illuminated. Press TEMP and set to 390°F, then press TIME and set to 8 minutes. Press START/STOP to begin preheating. 2. Cut the bread slices into medium-sized chunks. Grease the inside of the Air Fry Basket with oil and place the bread inside. 3. When preheating is complete, insert the Air Fry Basket in LEVEL 2 position of the bottom oven. Close the door to begin cooking. When cooking is complete, serve immediately.

Per Serving: Calories 56; Fat 3.71g; Sodium 49mg; Carbs 4.94g; Fiber 0.3g; Sugar 0.57g; Protein 0.89g

Onion Stuffed Mushrooms

Prep Time: 15 minutes | Cook Time: 10 minutes | Serves: 4

6 small mushrooms	1 tbsp. olive oil
1 oz. onion, peeled and diced	1 tsp. garlic, pureed
1 tbsp. friendly bread crumbs	1 tsp. parsley
	Salt and pepper to taste

1. In a bowl, add the bread crumbs, onion, parsley, oil, salt, pepper and garlic and stir to combine. Remove the mushrooms' stalks and stuff each cap with the crumb mixture. Then place the stuffed mushrooms in the Air Fry Basket. 2. Press BOTTOM and turn the dial until AIR FRY is illuminated. Press TEMP and set to 350°F, then press TIME and set to 10 minutes. Press START/STOP to begin preheating. 3. When preheating is complete, insert the Air Fry Basket in LEVEL 2 position of the bottom oven. Close the door to begin cooking. When cooking is complete, serve immediately.

Per Serving: Calories 67; Fat 3.81g; Sodium 134mg; Carbs 6.96g; Fiber 0.6g; Sugar 1.25g; Protein 1.59g

Garlicky Zucchini and Sweet Potatoes

Prep Time: 15 minutes | Cook Time: 20 minutes | Serves: 4

2 large-sized sweet potatoes, peeled and quartered	matchsticks
	¼ cup olive oil
1 medium-sized zucchini, sliced	1½ tbsp. maple syrup
	½ tsp. porcini powder
1 Serrano pepper, deveined and thinly sliced	¼ tsp. mustard powder
	½ tsp. fennel seeds
1 bell pepper, deveined and thinly sliced	1 tbsp. garlic powder
	½ tsp. fine sea salt
1 – 2 carrots, cut into	¼ tsp. ground black pepper
	Tomato ketchup to serve

1. Combine the zucchini, sweet potatoes, peppers, and the carrot in the Air Fry Basket. Drizzle with some olive oil. 2. Press BOTTOM and turn the dial until AIR FRY is illuminated. Press TEMP and set to 350°F, then press TIME and set to 15 minutes. Press START/STOP to begin preheating. 3. When preheating is complete, insert the Air Fry Basket in LEVEL 2 position of the bottom oven. Close the door to begin cooking. 4. Meanwhile, make the sauce by whisking the other ingredients except the tomato ketchup. 5. Lightly grease the sheet pan and transfer the cooked vegetables to the pan. Pour over the sauce and toss until the vegetables are well coated. 6. Turn the temperature to 390°F and air fry for 5 minutes more. 7. Serve warm with a side of ketchup.

Per Serving: Calories 285; Fat 14.08g; Sodium 598mg; Carbs 38.66g; Fiber 4.8g; Sugar 17.34g; Protein 3.73g

Yummy Toasty Crispy-Bottom Rice with Currants & Pistachios

Prep Time: 10 minutes | Cook Time: 25 minutes | Serves: 2

1 tablespoon olive oil	¼ cup roughly chopped pistachios
¼ teaspoon ground turmeric	Kosher salt and freshly ground black pepper
2 cups cooked white basmati, jasmine, or other long-grain rice	1 tablespoon thinly sliced fresh cilantro
¼ cup dried currants	

1. Combine the olive oil and turmeric in the bottom of sheet pan. 2. In a bowl, combine the currants, rice, and pistachios, season with salt and pepper, then spoon the rice over the oil, ensuring to not stir the oil up into the rice. Very gently press the rice into an even layer. 3. Press TOP and turn the dial until BAKE is illuminated. Press TEMP/SHADE and set the temperature to 300°F, then press TIME/SLICES and set the time to 25 minutes. Press START/STOP to start preheating. 4. When the unit has preheated, immediately put the sheet pan on the wire rack in the Bottom Oven Level 1. Close oven door. 5. Cook for 20 to 25 minutes until rice is warmed through and the bottom is toasted and crispy. 6. When cooking is up, remove the pan and invert onto a serving plate. Break up the crust on the bottom of the rice, sprinkle with the cilantro, and serve warm.

Per Serving: Calories 406; Fat 14.43g; Sodium 593mg; Carbs 51.75g; Fiber 13.7g; Sugar 2.84g; Protein 20.85g

Easy Cheese Lings

Prep Time: 15 minutes | Cook Time: minutes | Serves: 6

1 cup flour	1 tsp. butter
Small cubes cheese, grated	Salt to taste
¼ tsp. chili powder	1 tsp. baking powder

1. Combine all the ingredients in a bowl and form the mixture into a dough, add some water if needed. 2. Divide the dough into equal portions and knead each one into a ball. 3. Press BOTTOM and turn the dial until AIR FRY is illuminated. Press TEMP and set to 360°F, then press TIME and set to 5 minutes. Press START/STOP to begin preheating. 4. When preheating is complete, insert the Air Fry Basket in LEVEL 2 position of the bottom oven. Close the door to begin cooking. Flip halfway through the cooking time. 5. When cooking is complete, serve immediately.

Per Serving: Calories 94; Fat 1.82g; Sodium 105mg; Carbs 16.38g; Fiber 0.6g; Sugar 0.07g; Protein 2.86g

Cheese Potatoes & Asparagus

Prep Time: 10 minutes | Cook Time: 20 minutes | Serves: 4

4 medium potatoes	fraiche
1 asparagus bunch	1 tbsp. wholegrain
⅓ cup cottage cheese	mustard
⅓ cup low-fat crème	

1. Grease the Air Fry Basket with some oil and place the potatoes inside. 2. Press BOTTOM and turn the dial until AIR FRY is illuminated. Press TEMP and set to 390°F, then press TIME and set to 20 minutes. Press START/STOP to begin preheating. 3. When preheating is complete, insert the Air Fry Basket in LEVEL 2 position of the bottom oven. Close the door to begin cooking. 4. Meanwhile, fill a pot with salted water and bring to a boil. Add the asparagus and boil for 3 minutes. 5. Transfer the cooked potatoes to a bowl and mash them with the remaining ingredients. Season with salt and pepper. Serve hot.

Per Serving: Calories 338; Fat 3.57g; Sodium 213mg; Carbs 65.51g; Fiber 8.4g; Sugar 3.51g; Protein 12.69g

Cream Potato Side Dish

Prep Time: 10 minutes | Cook Time: 15 minutes | Serves: 2

2 medium potatoes	1 tsp. chives
1 tsp. butter	1½ tbsp. cheese, grated
3 tbsp. sour cream	Salt and pepper to taste

1. Pierce the potatoes with a fork, place in a pot with water and cook until done. 2. Then transfer the potatoes to the Air Fry Basket. 3. Press BOTTOM and turn the dial until AIR FRY is illuminated. Press TEMP and set to 350°F, then press TIME and set to 15 minutes. Press START/STOP to begin preheating. 4. When preheating is complete, insert the Air Fry Basket in LEVEL 2 position of the bottom oven. Close the door to begin cooking. 5. Meanwhile, mix together the cheese, sour cream, and chives in a bowl. Cut the potatoes halfway to open them up and fill with the butter and toppings. Season with salt and pepper. 6. Serve with salad.

Per Serving: Calories 368; Fat 6.63g; Sodium 240mg; Carbs 68.89g; Fiber 8.5g; Sugar 4.91g; Protein 10.45g

Cheese Spinach Omelet

Prep Time: 15 minutes | Cook Time: 13 minutes | Serves: 2

3 tbsp. plain milk	1 green bell pepper, deveined and chopped
4 eggs, whisked	1 white onion, finely chopped
1 tsp. melted butter	½ cup baby spinach leaves, roughly chopped
Kosher salt and freshly ground black pepper, to taste	½ cup Halloumi cheese, shaved
1 red bell pepper, deveined and chopped	

1. Grease the sheet pan with some canola oil. 2. Put all of the ingredients in the pan and stir to mix well. 3. Press TOP and turn the dial until BAKE is illuminated. Press TEMP/SHADE and set to 350°F, then press TIME/SLICES and set to 13 minutes. Press START/STOP to begin preheating. 4. When preheating is complete, place the sheet pan on the rack. Close the door to begin cooking. Serve warm.

Per Serving: Calories 299; Fat 18.7g; Sodium 646mg; Carbs 13.51g; Fiber 2.7g; Sugar 7.1g; Protein 20.19g

Scrambled Eggs with Spinach & Tomato

Prep Time: 15 minutes | Cook Time: 10 minutes | Serves: 2

2 tbsp. olive oil, melted	1 tsp. fresh lemon juice
4 eggs, whisked	½ tsp. coarse salt
5 oz. fresh spinach, chopped	½ tsp. ground black pepper
1 medium-sized tomato, chopped	½ cup of fresh basil, roughly chopped

1. Grease the inside of the sheet pan with the oil. 2. Combine all the ingredients in the sheet pan except the basil leaves, stirring well until well combined. 3. Press TOP and turn the dial until BAKE is illuminated. Press TEMP/SHADE and set to 280°F, then press TIME/SLICES and set to 10 minutes. Press START/STOP to begin preheating. When preheating is complete, place the sheet pan on the rack. Close the door to begin cooking. 4. Top with fresh basil leaves before serving.

Per Serving: Calories 279; Fat 22.34g; Sodium 767mg; Carbs 7g; Fiber 2.6g; Sugar 2.9g; Protein 14.04g

Sweet Corn and Carrot Fritters

Prep Time: 15 minutes | Cook Time: 10 minutes | Serves: 4

1 medium-sized carrot, grated	1 medium-sized egg, whisked
1 yellow onion, finely chopped	2 tbsp. plain milk
4 oz. canned sweet corn kernels, drained	1 cup of Parmesan cheese, grated
1 tsp. sea salt flakes	¼ cup flour
1 heaping tbsp. fresh cilantro, chopped	⅓ tsp. baking powder
	⅓ tsp. sugar

1. Place the grated carrot in a colander and press down to squeeze out excess moisture. Pat dry with a paper towel. 2. Combine the carrots with the rest of the ingredients in a mixing bowl. 3. Shape 1 tablespoon of the mixture into a ball and flatten with your hands or a spoon. Repeat until you have used up the rest of the mixture. 4. Spritz the balls with cooking spray and place in the Air Fry Basket. 5. Press BOTTOM and turn the dial until AIR FRY is illuminated. Press TEMP and

set to 350°F, then press TIME and set to 10 minutes. Press START/STOP to begin preheating. 6. When preheating is complete, insert the Air Fry Basket in LEVEL 2 position of the bottom oven. Close the door to begin cooking. When cooking is complete, serve warm.

Per Serving: Calories 210; Fat 11.11g; Sodium 1117mg; Carbs 17.73g; Fiber 1.7g; Sugar 3.02g; Protein 10.54g

Lemony Brussels Sprout Salad with Pancetta

Prep Time: 15 minutes | Cook Time: 15 minutes | Serves: 4

⅔ pound Brussels sprouts	chopped
1 tablespoon olive oil	Lemon Vinaigrette:
Coarse sea salt and ground black pepper, to taste	2 tablespoons extra virgin olive oil
	2 tablespoons fresh lemon juice
2 ounces baby arugula	1 tablespoon honey
1 shallot, thinly sliced	1 teaspoon Dijon
4 ounces pancetta,	mustard

1. Add the Brussels sprouts to the Air Fry Basket and brush with olive oil. 2. Press BOTTOM and turn the dial until AIR FRY is illuminated. Press TEMP and set to 380°F, then press TIME and set to 15 minutes. Press START/STOP to begin preheating. 3. When preheating is complete, insert the Air Fry Basket in LEVEL 2 position of the bottom oven. Close the door to begin cooking. When cooking is complete, remove the basket and allow it to cool to room temperature about 15 minutes. 4. Then toss the Brussels sprouts with the baby arugula, salt, black pepper, and shallot. 5. Mix all ingredients for the lemon vinaigrette dressing and pour into the vegetables salad. Garnish with pancetta, and serve well chilled. Enjoy!

Per Serving: Calories 177; Fat 9.92g; Sodium 114mg; Carbs 13.73g; Fiber 3.4g; Sugar 7.25g; Protein 10.6g

Flavorful Cornbread

Prep Time: 15 minutes | Cook Time: 1 hour | Serves: 6

1 cup cornmeal	¼ tsp. garlic powder
1½ cups flour	2 tbsp. sugar
½ tsp. baking soda	2 eggs
½ tsp. baking powder	¼ cup melted butter
¼ tsp. kosher salt	1 cup buttermilk
1 tsp. dried rosemary	½ cup corn kernels

1. Combine all of the dry ingredients in a bowl. In a separate bowl, mix all the wet ingredients. Add the dry ingredients to the wet and stir to mix well. 2. Fold in the corn kernels and stir vigorously. 3. Lightly greased round loaf pan that fits the oven and pour the batter inside. 4. Press TOP and turn the dial until BAKE is illuminated. Press TEMP/SHADE and set to 380°F, then press TIME/SLICES and set to 1 hour. Press START/STOP to begin preheating. 5. When preheating is complete, place the loaf pan on the rack. Close the door to begin cooking. Serve warm.

Per Serving: Calories 337; Fat 10.39g; Sodium 389mg; Carbs 51.74g; Fiber 2.2g; Sugar 5.46g; Protein 8.71g

Vegan Buddha Bowl

Prep Time: 15 minutes | Cook Time: 12 minutes | Serves: 3

1 (1-pound) head cauliflower, food-processed into rice-like particles	champagne vinegar
	4 tablespoons mayonnaise
2 bell pepper, spiralized	1 teaspoon yellow mustard
Coarse sea salt and ground black pepper, to taste	4 tablespoons olive oil, divided
3 cups baby spinach	2 tablespoons cilantro leaves, chopped
2 tablespoons	2 tablespoons pine nuts

1. Lightly greased Air Fry Basket and place the cauliflower florets and bell peppers inside. Season with salt and black pepper. 2. Press BOTTOM and turn the dial until AIR FRY is illuminated. Press TEMP and set to 400°F, then press TIME and set to 12 minutes. Press START/STOP to begin preheating.

3. When preheating is complete, insert the Air Fry Basket in LEVEL 2 position of the bottom oven. Close the door to begin cooking. Toss halfway through the cooking process. 4. When cooking is complete, stir in the baby spinach. Add the champagne vinegar, mustard, mayonnaise, and olive oil and mix well. Garnish with fresh cilantro and pine nuts. Enjoy!

Per Serving: Calories 274; Fat 24.94g; Sodium 228mg; Carbs 10.58g; Fiber 3.4g; Sugar 4.34g; Protein 4.73g

Cheesy Eggplant Slices

Prep Time: 15 minutes | Cook Time: 10 minutes | Serves: 4

1-pound eggplant, sliced	4 ounces pork rinds
1 tablespoon sea salt	½ cup mozzarella cheese, grated
½ cup Romano cheese, preferably freshly grated	2 tablespoons fresh Italian parsley, roughly chopped
Sea salt and ground black pepper, to taste	
1 egg, whisked	

1. Place the eggplant in a bowl and toss with 1 tablespoon of salt. Let it sit for 30 minutes. Drain and rinse. 2. In another bowl, mix together the Romano cheese, salt, and black pepper. Then, whisk in the egg. 3. Place the pork rinds in a third bowl. 4. Dip the eggplant slices in the cheese mixture and press to coat on all sides. Then dredge them in pork rinds. Transfer to the lightly greased Air Fry Basket. 5. Press BOTTOM and turn the dial until AIR FRY is illuminated. Press TEMP and set to 370°F, then press TIME and set to 8 minutes. Press START/STOP to begin preheating. 6. When preheating is complete, insert the Air Fry Basket in LEVEL 2 position of the bottom oven. Close the door to begin cooking. When cooking is complete, flip them over and top with the mozzarella. Cook for 2 minutes more or until the cheese melts. 7. Serve garnished with fresh Italian parsley. Enjoy!

Per Serving: Calories 238; Fat 12.06g; Sodium 2291mg; Carbs 9.46g; Fiber 3.9g; Sugar 5.05g; Protein 23.53g

Tasty Fennel with Shirataki Noodles

Prep Time: 15 minutes | Cook Time: 15 minutes | Serves: 3

1 fennel bulb, quartered	2 tablespoons rice wine
Salt and white pepper, to	vinegar
taste	2 tablespoons sesame oil
1 clove garlic, finely	1 teaspoon ginger,
chopped	freshly grated
1 green onion, thinly	1 tablespoon soy sauce
sliced	1⅓ cups Shirataki
1 cup Chinese cabbage,	noodles, boiled
shredded	

1. Lightly grease the Air Fry Basket and place the fennel bulb inside. 2. Press BOTTOM and turn the dial until AIR FRY is illuminated. Press TEMP and set to 370°F, then press TIME and set to 15 minutes. Press START/STOP to begin preheating. 3. When preheating is complete, insert the Air Fry Basket in LEVEL 2 position of the bottom oven. Close the door to begin cooking. Shake the basket halfway through the cooking time. 4. Once cooked, allow it to cool completely and toss with the remaining ingredients. Serve well chilled.

Per Serving: Calories 237; Fat 10.45g; Sodium 308mg; Carbs 31.52g; Fiber 3.2g; Sugar 5.69g; Protein 5.11g

Classic Peperonata

Prep Time: 15 minutes | Cook Time: 20 minutes | Serves: 4

4 tablespoons olive oil	1 large tomato, pureed
4 bell peppers, seeded	Sea salt and black pepper
and sliced	1 teaspoon cayenne
1 serrano pepper, seeded	pepper
and sliced	4 fresh basil leaves
½ cup onion, peeled and	8 Sicilian olives green,
sliced	pitted and sliced
2 garlic cloves, crushed	

1. Grease the sides and bottom of the Air Fry Basket with 1 tablespoon of olive oil. Add the peppers, onions, and garlic to the basket. 2. Press BOTTOM and turn the dial until AIR FRY is illuminated. Press TEMP and set to 380°F, then press TIME and set to 5 minutes. Press START/STOP to begin preheating.

3. When preheating is complete, insert the Air Fry Basket in LEVEL 2 position of the bottom oven. Close the door to begin cooking. Cook until the onion and peppers are tender. 4. Then stir in the tomatoes, salt, cayenne pepper, black pepper and the remaining olive oil. Air fry for 15 minutes more, stirring occasionally. 5. Divide between serving bowls and garnish with basil leaves and olives. Enjoy!

Per Serving: Calories 168; Fat 14.64g; Sodium 92mg; Carbs 9.51g; Fiber 2g; Sugar 4.83g; Protein 1.93g

Corn-Beans Stuffed Avocados

Prep Time: 15 minutes | Cook Time: 7 minutes | Serves: 4

1 cup frozen shoepeg	2 teaspoons lime juice,
corn, thawed	plus extra for serving
1 cup cooked black	Salt and pepper
beans	2 large avocados, split in
¼ cup diced onion	half, pit removed
½ teaspoon cumin	

1. Mix together the beans, onion, corn, cumin, and lime juice in a bowl. Season with salt and pepper. 2. Scoop out some of the flesh from center of each avocado, set aside. Divide the corn mixture evenly among the avocado cavities. 3. Place avocado halves in the Air Fry Basket. 4. Press BOTTOM and turn the dial until AIR FRY is illuminated. Press TEMP and set to 360°F, then press TIME and set to 7 minutes. Press START/STOP to begin preheating. 5. When preheating is complete, insert the Air Fry Basket in LEVEL 2 position of the bottom oven. Close the door to begin cooking. 6. When cooking is complete, season the avocado flesh that you scooped out with some salt, lime juice, and pepper. Spoon it over the cooked halves. Enjoy!

Per Serving: Calories 273; Fat 15.57g; Sodium 53mg; Carbs 30.01g; Fiber 11.8g; Sugar 3g; Protein 7.4g

Herbed Red Potatoes

Prep Time: 10 minutes | Cook Time: 5 minutes | Serves: 4

3 large red potatoes (enough to make 3 cups sliced)	thyme
	⅛ teaspoon salt
	⅛ teaspoon ground black pepper
¼ teaspoon ground rosemary	2 teaspoons extra-light olive oil
¼ teaspoon ground	

1. In a large bowl, toss the potatoes with thyme, rosemary, salt, oil and pepper. Then transfer to the Air Fry Basket. 2. Press BOTTOM and turn the dial until AIR FRY is illuminated. Press TEMP and set to 330°F, then press TIME and set to 4 minutes. Press START/STOP to begin preheating. 3. When preheating is complete, insert the Air Fry Basket in LEVEL 2 position of the bottom oven. Close the door to begin cooking. When cooking time is up, stir and break apart any that have stuck together. 4. Then cook for 1 to 2 minutes more or until fork-tender. Serve warm.

Per Serving: Calories 214; Fat 2.64g; Sodium 127mg; Carbs 44.17g; Fiber 4.7g; Sugar 3.65g; Protein 5.26g

Simple Sweet Potato Fries

Prep Time: 15 minutes | Cook Time: 30 minutes | Serves: 4

2 pounds sweet potatoes, peeled	marjoram
	2 teaspoons olive oil
1 teaspoon dried	Sea salt

1. Cut the potatoes into ¼x4-inch sticks. 2. Place the sweet potatoes in a sealable plastic bag and toss with marjoram and olive oil. Rub seasonings in to coat well. 3. Then pour the sweet potatoes into the Air Fry Basket. 4. Press BOTTOM and turn the dial until AIR FRY is illuminated. Press TEMP and set to 390°F, then press TIME and set to 30 minutes. Press START/STOP to begin preheating. 5. When preheating is complete, insert the Air Fry Basket in LEVEL 2 position of the bottom oven. Close the door to begin cooking. When cooking is complete, season to taste with sea salt and serve immediately.

Per Serving: Calories 195; Fat 2.46g; Sodium 304mg; Carbs 39.71g; Fiber 5.1g; Sugar 1.78g; Protein 4.6g

Crispy Yellow Squash Slices

Prep Time: 15 minutes | Cook Time: 10 minutes | Serves: 4

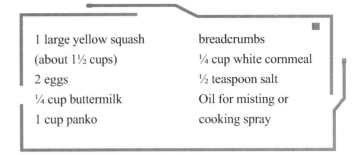

1 large yellow squash (about 1½ cups)	breadcrumbs
	¼ cup white cornmeal
2 eggs	½ teaspoon salt
¼ cup buttermilk	Oil for misting or cooking spray
1 cup panko	

1. Cut the squash into ¼-inch slices. 2. Whisk eggs and buttermilk in a shallow bowl. 3. Mix together the white cornmeal, ¼ cup panko crumbs, and salt in another bowl. 4. Place the remaining ¾ cup panko crumbs in a third shallow bowl. 5. Place all the squash slices into the egg mixture and stir until well coated. 6. Using a slotted spoon, remove squash from the egg mixture and drip off any excess. Transfer to the panko- cornmeal mixture and toss to coat well. 7. Finally dip them in the panko crumbs. 8. Place squash slices in a single layer in the Air Fry Basket and spray with cooking oil. 9. Press BOTTOM and turn the dial until AIR FRY is illuminated. Press TEMP and set to 390°F, then press TIME and set to 5 minutes. Press START/STOP to begin preheating. 10. When preheating is complete, insert the Air Fry Basket in LEVEL 2 position of the bottom oven. Close the door to begin cooking. 11. When cooking time is up, shake the basket and spray with more cooking oil. Cook for an additional 5 minutes until the squash slices are golden brown and crisp. Serve.

Per Serving: Calories 121; Fat 3.33g; Sodium 675mg; Carbs 17.84g; Fiber 2.7g; Sugar 4.82g; Protein 6.04g

Chapter 3 Poultry Recipes

Chicken Rochambeau with Mushroom sauce

Prep Time: 15 minutes | Cook Time: 20 minutes | Serves: 4

1 tablespoon butter	4 slices ham, ¼- to
4 chicken tenders, cut in	⅜-inches thick and large
half crosswise	enough to cover an
Salt and pepper	English muffin
¼ cup flour	2 English muffins, split
Oil for misting	

Sauce:

2 tablespoons butter	1 cup chicken broth
½ cup chopped green	¼ teaspoon garlic
onions	powder
½ cup chopped	1½ teaspoons
mushrooms	Worcestershire sauce
2 tablespoons flour	

1. Add 1 tablespoon of butter to the sheet pan. and cook at 390°F for 2 minutes to melt. 2. Press TOP and turn the dial until BAKE is illuminated. Press TEMP/SHADE and set to 390°F, then press TIME/SLICES and set to 2 minutes. Press START/STOP to begin preheating. When preheating is complete, place the sheet pan on the rack. Close the door to begin cooking. Cook until the butter is melted. 3. Meanwhile, sprinkle chicken tenders with salt and black pepper, then roll in the ¼ cup of flour. 4. Place chicken in the sheet pan and toss to coat with the melted butter. 5. Bake for 5 minutes. Then flip the chicken pieces and lightly spray with olive oil. Cook 5 minutes more or until juices run clear. 6. While chicken is cooking, prepare the sauce: Melt 2 tablespoons of butter in a saucepan over medium heat. Stir in the onions and mushrooms and sauté until tender, about 3 minutes. 7. Stir in the flour and gradually pour in the broth, stirring constantly until smooth. 8. Then turn the heat to low and add garlic powder and Worcestershire sauce, simmer until the sauce thickens, about 5 minutes. 9. When chicken is cooked, remove the sheet pan from the oven and set aside. 10. Place ham slices directly into the Air Fry Basket. Press BOTTOM and turn the dial until AIR FRY is illuminated. Press TEMP and set to 390°F, then press TIME and set to 5 minutes. Press START/STOP to begin preheating. 11. When preheating is complete, insert the Air Fry Basket in LEVEL 2 position of the bottom oven. Close the door to begin cooking. When cooking is complete, remove and set aside on top of the chicken. Air fry the English muffin halves at 390°F for 1 minute. 12. Then place a ham slice on top of each English muffin half. Stack 2 pieces of chicken on top of each ham slice. Air fry at 390°F for 1 to 2 minutes to heat through. 13. Place each English muffin stack on a serving plate and top with plenty of sauce.

Per Serving: Calories 464; Fat 17.12g; Sodium 918mg; Carbs 24.8g; Fiber 2.1g; Sugar 2.36g; Protein 51.21g

Chicken Apple Hamburgers

Prep Time: 15 minutes | Cook Time: 10 minutes | Serves: 4

½ cup flour	pounded thin
½ teaspoon salt	Oil for misting or
1 teaspoon marjoram	cooking spray
1 teaspoon dried parsley	4 whole-grain hotdog
flakes	buns
½ teaspoon thyme	4 slices Gouda cheese
1 egg	1 small Granny Smith
1 teaspoon lemon juice	apple, thinly sliced
1 teaspoon water	½ cup shredded Napa
1 cup breadcrumbs	cabbage
4 chicken tenders,	Coleslaw dressing

1. Add together the flour, salt, parsley, marjoram, and thyme to a shallow bowl. Stir to mix well. 2. Whisk together egg, water and lemon juice in a second shallow bowl. 3. Place breadcrumbs in a third shallow bowl. 4. Cut each of the chicken tenders in half lengthwise. 5. Dip the chicken strips in flour mixture, then egg wash. Drip off any excess and roll in the breadcrumbs. Spray both sides with the oil spray and place in the Air Fry Basket. 6. Press BOTTOM and turn the dial until AIR FRY is illuminated. Press TEMP and set to 390°F, then press TIME and set to 5 minutes. Press START/STOP to begin preheating. 7. When preheating is complete, insert the Air Fry Basket in LEVEL 2 position of the bottom oven. Close the door to begin cooking. When cooking time is up, spray with more oil. Flip them and spray other side. 8. Cook for 3 to 5 minutes longer, until well done and crispy brown. 9. Place 2 schnitzel strips on each hotdog bun. Top with cheese, sliced apple, and cabbage. Drizzle with coleslaw dressing and top with other half of bun. Enjoy!

Per Serving: Calories 605; Fat 23.79g; Sodium 862mg; Carbs 40.96g; Fiber 2.2g; Sugar 14.69g; Protein 53.58g

Cheese Chicken Chimichangas

Prep Time: 15 minutes | Cook Time: 15 minutes | Serves: 4

2 cups cooked chicken, shredded

2 tablespoons chopped green chile

½ teaspoon oregano

½ teaspoon cumin

½ teaspoon onion powder

¼ teaspoon garlic powder

Salt and pepper

8 flour tortillas (6- or 7-inch diameter)

Oil for misting or cooking spray

Chimichanga Sauce:

2 tablespoons butter

2 tablespoons flour

1 cup chicken broth

¼ cup light sour cream

¼ teaspoon salt

2 ounces Monterey Jack cheese, shredded

1. Melt the butter in a saucepan over medium-low heat. Stir in the flour until smooth and slightly bubbly. Carefully pour in the broth and stir constantly until smooth. Sauté for 1 minute, until the mixture thickens slightly. Remove from heat and stir in the sour cream and salt. Set the sauce aside. 2. Add the chicken, chile, cumin, garlic, onion powder, oregano, salt, and pepper to a medium bowl. Stir to mix well. Stir in 3 to 4 tablespoons of the sauce to make the filling moist but not soupy. 3. Divide filling among 8 tortillas. Place filling in center of tortillas, leaving a 1-inch border. Fold one side of the tortilla over the filling, then fold both sides over and roll up. Spray all sides with oil. Place chimichangas in the Air Fry Basket, seam side down. 4. Press BOTTOM and turn the dial until AIR FRY is illuminated. Press TEMP and set to 360°F, then press TIME and set to 9 minutes. Press START/STOP to begin preheating. 5. When preheating is complete, insert the Air Fry Basket in LEVEL 2 position of the bottom oven. Close the door to begin cooking. Cook until heated through and crispy brown outside. 6. Add shredded cheese to remaining sauce. Stir over low heat until the cheese is melted. 7. Drizzle sauce over the chimichangas.

Per Serving: Calories 593; Fat 26.95g; Sodium 1290mg; Carbs 54.25g; Fiber 2.9g; Sugar 4.37g; Protein 31.72g

Sweet & Spicy Chicken Tenders

Prep Time: 15 minutes | Cook Time: 7 minutes | Serves: 4

1-pound chicken tenders

Marinade:

¼ cup olive oil

2 tablespoons water

2 tablespoons honey

2 tablespoons white vinegar

½ teaspoon salt

½ teaspoon crushed red pepper

1 teaspoon garlic powder

1 teaspoon onion powder

½ teaspoon paprika

1. Add all marinade ingredients to a bowl and stir to mix well. 2. Add chicken to the marinade and stir until well coated. Cover and refrigerate for 30 minutes. 3. Then remove tenders from the marinade and place them in a single layer in the Air Fry Basket. 4. Press BOTTOM and turn the dial until AIR FRY is illuminated. Press TEMP and set to 390°F, then press TIME and set to 3 minutes. Press START/STOP to begin preheating. 5. When preheating is complete, insert the Air Fry Basket in LEVEL 2 position of the bottom oven. Close the door to begin cooking. 6. When cooking time is up, flip them and cook for 3 to 5 minutes more or until chicken is done and juices run clear. Serve hot.

Per Serving: Calories 284; Fat 16.61g; Sodium 378mg; Carbs 9.95g; Fiber 0.3g; Sugar 8.76g; Protein 23.32g

Coconut Chicken Bites with Apricot-Ginger Sauce

Prep Time: 15 minutes | Cook Time: 8 minutes | Serves: 4

1½ pounds boneless, skinless chicken tenders, cut in large chunks (about 1¼ inches) salt and pepper ½ cup cornstarch	2 eggs 1 tablespoon milk 3 cups shredded coconut oil for misting or cooking spray

Apricot-Ginger Sauce:

½ cup apricot preserves 2 tablespoons white vinegar ¼ teaspoon ground ginger	¼ teaspoon low-sodium soy sauce 2 teaspoons white or yellow onion, grated or finely minced

1. Mix together all the ingredients for the Apricot-Ginger Sauce in a bowl and let stand for several minutes. 2. Season chicken chunks with salt and black pepper. 3. Place cornstarch in a shallow bowl. 4. Whisk together eggs and milk in another shallow bowl. 5. Place coconut in a third shallow bowl. 6. Grease the Air Fry Basket with cooking oil. 7. Dip each chicken chunk into cornstarch and shake off any excess, then dip in the egg mixture. 8. Shake off excess egg mixture and dredge in the coconut. 9. Place the coated chicken in the air fryer basket in a single layer and spray with oil. Press BOTTOM and turn the dial until AIR FRY is illuminated. Press TEMP and set to 360°F, then press TIME and set to 4 minutes. Press START/STOP to begin preheating. 10. When preheating is complete, insert the Air Fry Basket in LEVEL 2 position of the bottom oven. Close the door to begin cooking. 11. When cooking time is up, flip them cook for 3 to 4 minutes more or until chicken is done inside and coating is crispy brown. Serve warm.

Per Serving: Calories 622; Fat 21.92g; Sodium 875mg; Carbs 71.56g; Fiber 6.3g; Sugar 26g; Protein 33.3g

Spicy Nacho Chicken Fries

Prep Time: 15 minutes | Cook Time: 7 minutes | Serves: 5

1-pound chicken tenders Salt ¼ cup flour 2 eggs ¾ cup panko breadcrumbs	¾ cup crushed organic nacho cheese tortilla chips Oil for misting or cooking spray

Seasoning Mix:

1 tablespoon chili powder 1 teaspoon ground cumin ½ teaspoon garlic	powder ½ teaspoon onion powder

1. In a small bowl, mix together all seasonings ingredients and set aside. 2. Cut chicken tenders in half crosswise and cut into ½-inch wide strips. 3. Place the chicken to taste in large bowl and season with salt. Sprinkle with 1 tablespoon of the seasoning mix and stir to coat evenly. 4. Add flour to chicken and stir until all sides are well coated. 5. Whisk the eggs in a shallow bowl. 6. In a separate shallow bowl, mix together the crushed chips, panko, and the remaining 2 teaspoons of seasoning mix. 7. Dip chicken strips in eggs, then dredge in the crumbs. Spray with cooking oil. 8. Then place the chicken strips in the Air Fry Basket. 9. Press BOTTOM and turn the dial until AIR FRY is illuminated. Press TEMP and set to 390°F, then press TIME and set to 4 minutes. Press START/STOP to begin preheating. 10. When preheating is complete, insert the Air Fry Basket in LEVEL 2 position of the bottom oven. Close the door to begin cooking. 11. When cooking time is up, shake the basket and spray with more oil. Cook for an additional 2 to 3 minutes, until chicken juices run clear and outside is crispy. Serve warm.

Per Serving: Calories 352; Fat 14.11g; Sodium 641mg; Carbs 30.35g; Fiber 2.8g; Sugar 1.49g; Protein 24.77g

Parmesan Crusted Chicken

Prep Time: 15 minutes | Cook Time: 12 minutes | Serves: 4

1½ pounds chicken tenderloins	½ teaspoon garlic powder
2 tablespoons peanut oil	1 teaspoon red pepper flakes
½ cup parmesan cheese, grated	2 tablespoons peanuts, roasted and roughly chopped
Sea salt and ground black pepper, to taste	

1. Brush the chicken tenderloins with peanut oil on all sides. 2. Mix together grated parmesan cheese, black pepper, garlic powder, salt, and red pepper flakes in a bowl. Dredge the chicken in the mixture and shake off any excess. 3. Then place the coated chicken in the Air Fry Basket. 4. Press BOTTOM and turn the dial until AIR FRY is illuminated. Press TEMP and set to 360°F, then press TIME and set to 12 minutes. Press START/STOP to begin preheating. 5. When preheating is complete, insert the Air Fry Basket in LEVEL 2 position of the bottom oven. Close the door to begin cooking. Cook until it is no longer pink in the center. 6. Serve garnished with roasted peanuts. Enjoy!
Per Serving: Calories 333; Fat 17.1g; Sodium 355mg; Carbs 3.88g; Fiber 0.6g; Sugar 0.84g; Protein 39.61g

Honey-Lime Glazed Cornish Hens

Prep Time: 15 minutes | Cook Time: 28 minutes | Serves: 3

1 Cornish game hen (1½–2 pounds)	1 teaspoon poultry seasoning
1 tablespoon honey	Salt and pepper
1 tablespoon lime juice	Cooking spray

1. Cut the hens in half from one side of the breastbone and backbone. 2. In a small bowl, mix together the lime juice, honey, and poultry seasoning. Rub the mixture onto all sides of the hen. Season with salt and black pepper. 3. Spray the Air Fry Basket with cooking spray and place hen halves inside, skin-side down. 4. Press BOTTOM and turn the dial until AIR FRY is illuminated. Press TEMP and set to 330°F, then press TIME and set to 28 minutes. Press START/STOP to begin preheating. 5. When preheating is complete, insert the Air Fry Basket in LEVEL 2 position of the bottom oven. Close the door to begin cooking. 6. The hen is cooked when it is pierced with a fork through the joint of the thigh and the clear juices flow out. Allow to cool for 5 to 10 minutes. Cut and serve.
Per Serving: Calories 287; Fat 7.59g; Sodium 349mg; Carbs 6.52g; Fiber 0.1g; Sugar 5.84g; Protein 45.54g

Chicken Beans Plate

Prep Time: 15 minutes | Cook Time: 15 minutes | Serves: 4

1 pound boneless, skinless chicken breasts (2 large breasts)	½ cup salsa
	2 cups shredded lettuce
2 tablespoons lime juice	1 medium tomato, chopped
1 teaspoon cumin	2 avocados, peeled and sliced
½ teaspoon salt	
½ cup grated Pepper Jack cheese	1 small onion, sliced into thin rings
1 16-ounce can refried beans	Sour cream
	Tortilla chips (optional)

1. Cut each chicken breast in half lengthwise. 2. Mix together ground cumin, lime juice, and salt and brush over the surface of the chicken breasts. 3. Then place the chicken in the Air Fry Basket. 4. Press BOTTOM and turn the dial until AIR FRY is illuminated. Press TEMP and set to 390°F, then press TIME and set to 14 minutes. Press START/STOP to begin preheating. 5. When preheating is complete, insert the Air Fry Basket in LEVEL 2 position of the bottom oven. Close the door to begin cooking. When cooking is up, divide the cheese evenly over chicken breasts and cook for 1 minute longer to melt cheese. 6. Meanwhile, heat the refried beans in microwave. 7. Then divide the beans among 4 plates. Place the chicken breasts on top of the beans and pour the salsa over them. Arrange lettuce, tomatoes and avocados on each plate and sprinkle with onion rings. 8. Serve with sour cream or tortilla chips if desired.
Per Serving: Calories 506; Fat 28.01g; Sodium 1021mg; Carbs 48.5g; Fiber 12.3g; Sugar 10.66g; Protein 20.15g

Tasty Turkey Tenderloins

Prep Time: 15 minutes | Cook Time: 30 minutes | Serves: 6

2 pounds turkey tenderloins	paprika
2 tablespoons olive oil	2 tablespoons dry white wine
Salt and ground black pepper, to taste	1 tablespoon fresh tarragon leaves, chopped
1 teaspoon smoked	

1. Place the turkey tenderloins in a bowl and brush with olive oil. Season with salt, paprika and black pepper. Add the white wine and tarragon. Then place the turkey tenderloins in the Air Fry Basket. 2. Press BOTTOM and turn the dial until AIR FRY is illuminated. Press TEMP and set to 350°F, then press TIME and set to 30 minutes. Press START/STOP to begin preheating. 3. When preheating is complete, insert the Air Fry Basket in LEVEL 2 position of the bottom oven. Close the door to begin cooking. Flip halfway through the cooking time. 4. When cooking is complete, let them cool for 5 to 9 minutes. Slice and serve!

Per Serving: Calories 216; Fat 7.14g; Sodium 1404mg; Carbs 10.55g; Fiber 1.1g; Sugar 5.74g; Protein 26.37g

Herbed Chicken with Roma Tomatoes

Prep Time: 15 minutes | Cook Time: 35 minutes | Serves: 8

2 teaspoons olive oil, melted	2 tablespoons fresh parsley, minced
3 pounds chicken breasts, bone-in	1 teaspoon fresh basil, minced
½ teaspoon black pepper, freshly ground	1 teaspoon fresh rosemary, minced
½ teaspoon salt	4 medium-sized Roma tomatoes, halved
1 teaspoon cayenne pepper	

1. Brush the Air Fry Basket with 1 teaspoon of olive oil. 2. Combine all the seasonings in a bowl and rub all over the chicken breasts. Then place the chicken in the Air Fry Basket. 3. Press BOTTOM and turn the dial until AIR FRY is illuminated. Press TEMP and set to 350°F, then press TIME and set to 25 minutes. Press START/STOP to begin preheating. 4. When preheating is complete, insert the Air Fry Basket in LEVEL 2 position of the bottom oven. Close the door to begin cooking. 5. When cooking time is up, place the tomatoes in the basket and brush with the remaining olive oil. Season with sea salt. 6. Cook the tomatoes at 350°F for 10 minutes, shaking halfway through the cooking process. Serve with chicken breasts. Enjoy!

Per Serving: Calories 315; Fat 17.04g; Sodium 256mg; Carbs 2.76g; Fiber 0.9g; Sugar 1.65g; Protein 36.1g

Thai-Style Spicy Duck Breasts with Candy Onions

Prep Time: 15 minutes | Cook Time: 22 minutes | Serves: 4

1½ pounds duck breasts, skin removed	paprika
1 teaspoon kosher salt	1 tablespoon Thai red curry paste
½ teaspoon cayenne pepper	1 cup candy onions, halved
⅓ teaspoon black pepper	¼ small pack coriander, chopped
½ teaspoon smoked	

1. Place the duck breasts between two sheets of foil, then use a rolling pin to pound the duck breasts to 1-inch thickness. 2. Rub the duck breasts with salt, paprika, cayenne pepper, black pepper, and red curry paste. Arrange the duck breast in the Air Fry Basket. 3. Press BOTTOM and turn the dial until AIR FRY is illuminated. Press TEMP and set to 395°F, then press TIME and set to 12 minutes. Press START/STOP to begin preheating. 4. When preheating is complete, insert the Air Fry Basket in LEVEL 2 position of the bottom oven. Close the door to begin cooking. When cooking time is up, spread the candy onions on the top and cook for 10 minutes more. 5. Serve garnished with coriander and enjoy!

Per Serving: Calories 228; Fat 7.57g; Sodium 681mg; Carbs 4.05g; Fiber 1.6g; Sugar 1.33g; Protein 34.42g

Savory Chicken Legs with Turnip

Prep Time: 15 minutes | Cook Time: 25 minutes | Serves: 3

1-pound chicken legs	pepper
1 teaspoon Himalayan salt	1 teaspoon butter, melted
1 teaspoon paprika	1 turnip, trimmed and sliced
½ teaspoon ground black	

1. Spray the sides and bottom of the Air Fry Basket with nonstick cooking spray. 2. Season the chicken legs with paprika, salt and black pepper. Then place the seasoned chicken in the Air Fry Basket. 3. Press BOTTOM and turn the dial until AIR FRY is illuminated. Press TEMP and set to 370°F, then press TIME and set to 10 minutes. Press START/ STOP to begin preheating. 4. When preheating is complete, insert the Air Fry Basket in LEVEL 2 position of the bottom oven. Close the door to begin cooking. When cooking time is up, turn the temperature to 380°F. 5. Drizzle the sliced turnips with melted butter and add to the cooking basket with the chicken. Cook them for another 15 minutes, flipping halfway through. Serve!

Per Serving: Calories 199; Fat 7.77g; Sodium 935mg; Carbs 1.45g; Fiber 0.5g; Sugar 0.65g; Protein 29.29g

Turkey Burgers with Bacon

Prep Time: 15 minutes | Cook Time: 26 minutes | Serves: 4

2 tablespoons vermouth	1 teaspoon red pepper flakes
2 strips Canadian bacon, sliced	4 tablespoons tomato ketchup
1-pound ground turkey	4 tablespoons mayonnaise
½ shallot, minced	
2 garlic cloves, minced	4 (1-ounce) slices Cheddar cheese
2 tablespoons fish sauce	
Sea salt and ground black pepper, to taste	4 lettuce leaves

1. Brush the Canadian bacon with the vermouth and place in the Air Fry Basket. 2. Press BOTTOM and turn the dial until AIR FRY is illuminated. Press TEMP and set to 400°F, then press TIME and set to 3 minutes. Press START/STOP

to begin preheating. 3. When preheating is complete, insert the Air Fry Basket in LEVEL 2 position of the bottom oven. Close the door to begin cooking. Then flip the bacon and cook for 3 minutes more. 4. Meanwhile, mix together the ground turkey, garlic, shallots, fish sauce, black pepper, salt, and red pepper in a large bowl. Form the mixture into 4 burger patties. 5. Remove the cooked bacon to a plate and set aside. 6. Place the patties in the Air Fry Basket and air fry at 370°F for 10 minutes. Then flip them and cook for 10 minutes more. 7. Serve turkey burgers with the mayonnaise, ketchup, bacon, cheese and lettuce.

Per Serving: Calories 389; Fat 23.54g; Sodium 1407mg; Carbs 7.93g; Fiber 1.5g; Sugar 3.92g; Protein 34.27g

Chicken Sausage & Zucchini Casserole

Prep Time: 15 minutes | Cook Time: 16 minutes | Serves: 4

8 ounces zucchini, spiralized	1 tablespoon Italian seasoning mix
1 pound smoked chicken sausage, sliced	3 tablespoons Romano cheese, grated
1 tomato, pureed	1 tablespoon fresh basil leaves, chiffonade
½ cup Asiago cheese, shredded	

1. Place the zucchini in a bowl and toss with the salt. Let it sit for 30 minutes and then pat dry with kitchen towels. 2. Grease the sheet pan with cooking spray and place the zucchini inside. Stir in the chicken sausage, Asiago cheese, tomato puree, and Italian seasoning mix. 3. Press TOP and turn the dial until BAKE is illuminated. Press TEMP/SHADE and set to 325°F, then press TIME/SLICES and set to 11 minutes. Press START/ STOP to begin preheating. When preheating is complete, place the sheet pan on the rack. Close the door to begin cooking. 4. When cooking time is up, spread the grated Romano cheese on top. Increase the temperature to 390°F and cook for 5 minutes more or until everything is thoroughly heated and the cheese is melted. 5. Garnish with fresh basil leaves. Enjoy!

Per Serving: Calories 362; Fat 21.38g; Sodium 663mg; Carbs 6.63g; Fiber 1.2g; Sugar 1.08g; Protein 34.57g

Roasted Turkey Breasts

Prep Time: 15 minutes | Cook Time: 23 minutes | Serves: 2

½ tablespoon minced fresh parsley	peppercorns, to savor
1½ tablespoons Worcestershire sauce	1½ tablespoons olive oil
Sea salt flakes and cracked black	⅓ turkey breasts, halved
	1½ tablespoons rice vinegar
	½ teaspoon marjoram

1. Place the turkey breasts in a bowl and toss with the remaining ingredients until the turkey is well coated. Set aside and let marinate for at least 3 hours. 2. Press BOTTOM and turn the dial until AIR ROAST is illuminated. Press TEMP and set to 395°F, then press TIME and set to 23 minutes. Press START/STOP to begin preheating. 3. When preheating is complete, insert the sheet pan in LEVEL 1 position of the bottom oven. Close the door to begin cooking. Flip halfway through the cooking time. When cooking is complete, serve immediately.

Per Serving: Calories 319; Fat 14.59g; Sodium 499mg; Carbs 2.74g; Fiber 0.1g; Sugar 1.34g; Protein 44.33g

Herbed Chicken with Bacon & Tomatoes

Prep Time: 15 minutes | Cook Time: 24 minutes | Serves: 4

4 medium-sized skin-on chicken drumsticks	2 garlic cloves, crushed
1½ teaspoons herb de Provence	12 ounces crushed canned tomatoes
Salt and pepper, to your liking	1 small-size leek, thinly sliced
1 tablespoon rice vinegar	2 slices smoked bacon, chopped
2 tablespoons olive oil	

1. Place the chicken drumsticks in the sheet pan and sprinkle with salt, herbs de Provence, and pepper; then, drizzle with rice vinegar and olive oil. Gently stir well. 2. Press TOP and turn the dial until BAKE is illuminated. Press TEMP/SHADE and set to 360°F, then press TIME/SLICES and set to 9 minutes. Press START/STOP to begin preheating. When preheating is complete, place the sheet pan on the rack. Close the door to begin cooking. 3. When cooking time is up, stir in the remaining ingredients and cook for 15 minutes longer. Check them periodically and serve warm.

Per Serving: Calories 357; Fat 24.14g; Sodium 345mg; Carbs 8g; Fiber 2.3g; Sugar 3.98g; Protein 26.4g

Mustard Turkey Tenderloins with Gravy

Prep Time: 15 minutes | Cook Time: 40 minutes | Serves: 4

1-pound turkey tenderloins	seasoning mix
1 tablespoon Dijon-style mustard	1 cup turkey stock
	½ teaspoon xanthan gum
1 tablespoon olive oil	4 tablespoons tomato ketchup
Sea salt and ground black pepper, to taste	4 tablespoons mayonnaise
1 teaspoon Italian	4 pickles, sliced

1. Place the turkey tenderloins in a bowl and rub with the mustard and olive oil. Season with salt, Italian seasoning mix and black pepper. 2. Then transfer the seasoned turkey tenderloins to the Air Fry Basket. 3. Press BOTTOM and turn the dial until AIR FRY is illuminated. Press TEMP and set to 350°F, then press TIME and set to 30 minutes. Press START/STOP to begin preheating. 4. When preheating is complete, insert the Air Fry Basket in LEVEL 2 position of the bottom oven. Close the door to begin cooking. Flip halfway through the cooking time. 5. Let them cool for 5 to 7 minutes before slicing. 6. To make the gravy, place the drippings from the roasted turkey in a saucepan. Pour in the turkey stock and bring to a boil. 7. Whisk in the xanthan gum and let simmer another 5 to 10 minutes just thicken. 8. Serve turkey tenderloins with the gravy, mayonnaise, tomato ketchup, and pickles. Enjoy!

Per Serving: Calories 267; Fat 13.42g; Sodium 1497mg; Carbs 7.37g; Fiber 1.1g; Sugar 5.88g; Protein 28.32g

Roasted Turkey Sausage with Cauliflower

Prep Time: 15 minutes | Cook Time: 28 minutes | Serves: 4

1-pound ground turkey	⅓ cup onions, chopped
1 teaspoon garlic pepper	½ head cauliflower,
1 teaspoon garlic powder	broken into florets
⅓ teaspoon dried	⅓ teaspoon dried basil
oregano	½ teaspoon dried thyme,
½ teaspoon salt	chopped

1. In a bowl, mix together the ground turkey, onion, garlic powder, garlic pepper, salt and oregano. Form the mixture into 4 sausages. 2. Spray a nonstick skillet over medium heat with cooking spray and cook the sausage until they are no longer pink, about 12 minutes. 3. Place the cauliflower florets in the bottom of the sheet pan and sprinkle with thyme and basil. Then spray with cooking spray and add the turkey sausages on top. 4. Press BOTTOM and turn the dial until AIR ROAST is illuminated. Press TEMP and set to 375°F, then press TIME and set to 28 minutes. Press START/STOP to begin preheating. 5. When preheating is complete, insert the sheet pan in LEVEL 1 position of the bottom oven. Close the door to begin cooking. Flip halfway through the cooking time. When cooking is complete, serve immediately.

Per Serving: Calories 187; Fat 8.82g; Sodium 368mg; Carbs 4.26g; Fiber 1.1g; Sugar 1.63g; Protein 23.41g

Garlic Turkey with Indian Mint Sauce

Prep Time: 15 minutes | Cook Time: 32 minutes | Serves: 4

1½ pounds turkey breast, quartered	powder
½ teaspoon hot paprika	2 cloves garlic, peeled and halved
½ cup dry sherry	Freshly cracked pink or
1 teaspoon kosher salt	green peppercorns, to
⅓ teaspoon shallot	taste

For the Indian Mint Sauce:

⅓ cup sour cream	roughly chopped mint
1½ tablespoons fresh	1 cup plain yogurt

1. Place the turkey breast in a bowl and rub with the garlic halves evenly. 2. Stir in the shallot powder, hot paprika, dry

sherry, salt, and cracked peppercorns. Refrigerate to marinate for at least 1½ hours. 3. Then transfer the turkey breast to the Air Fry Basket. 4. Press BOTTOM and turn the dial until AIR FRY is illuminated. Press TEMP and set to 365°F, then press TIME and set to 32 minutes. Press START/STOP to begin preheating. 5. When preheating is complete, insert the Air Fry Basket in LEVEL 1 position of the bottom oven. Close the door to begin cooking. Flip halfway through the cooking time. 6. Meanwhile, prepare the sauce by mixing the sour cream, plain yogurt and chopped mint. 7. When cooking is complete, serve warm the with the sauce. Enjoy!

Per Serving: Calories 310; Fat 8.7g; Sodium 761mg; Carbs 16.34g; Fiber 1.2g; Sugar 12.76g; Protein 42.82g

Spicy Cheese Turkey Meatloaf with Onion

Prep Time: 8 minutes | Cook Time: 47 minutes | Serves: 6

2 pounds turkey breasts, ground	rosemary
½ pound Cheddar cheese, cubed	½ cup yellow onion, chopped
½ cup turkey stock	⅓ cup ground almonds
⅓ teaspoon hot paprika	½ teaspoon black pepper
3 eggs, lightly beaten	A few dashes of Tabasco sauce
1½ tablespoon olive oil	1 teaspoon seasoned salt
2 cloves garlic, pressed	½ cup tomato sauce
1½ teaspoons dried	

1. Heat the olive oil in a medium-sized saucepan that is placed over a moderate flame. 2. Sauté the onions, garlic, and dried rosemary until just tender, or about 3 to 4 minutes. 3. Press BOTTOM and turn the dial until AIR FRY illuminates. Press the TIME/SLICES buttons to set the cook time to 47 minutes. Then press the TEMP button to set the cook temperature to 385°F. Press START/STOP to start preheating. 4. Place all the ingredients, minus the tomato sauce, in the Air Fry Basket together with the sautéed mixture and thoroughly mix to combine. 5. Shape into meatloaf and top with the tomato sauce. 6. When bottom oven is preheated, immediately, place the wire rack in LEVEL 1 position of the bottom oven and place the sheet pan on top. Slide the Basket in LEVEL 2 position of bottom oven. Close door to begin cooking. 7. When cooking is up, serve. Bon appétit!

Per Serving: Calories 406; Fat 13.68g; Sodium 1354mg; Carbs 10.07g; Fiber 1.6g; Sugar 5.5g; Protein 56.83g

Chicken Sausage with Mayo-Dijon Sauce

Prep Time: 7 minutes | Cook Time: 13 minutes | Serves: 4

4 chicken sausages	1 tablespoon balsamic
¼ cup mayonnaise	vinegar
2 tablespoons Dijon	½ teaspoon dried
mustard	rosemary

1. Press TOP and turn the dial until BAKE is illuminated. Press TEMP/SHADE and set the temperature to 350°F, then press TIME/SLICES and set the time to 13 minutes. Press START/STOP to start preheating. 2. Arrange the sausages on the sheet pan. When the unit has preheated, immediately put the sheet pan on the wire rack in the Bottom Oven Level 1. Close oven door. 3. After cooking for 13 minutes, turn them halfway through cooking. 4. Meanwhile, prepare the sauce by merging the remaining ingredients with a wire whisk. 5. When cooking is up, serve the warm sausages with chilled Dijon sauce. Enjoy!

Per Serving: Calories 122; Fat 10.1g; Sodium 382mg; Carbs 2.05g; Fiber 0.5g; Sugar 0.8g; Protein 5.52g

Chicken Sausage, Ham & Cauliflower Gratin

Prep Time: 15 minutes | Cook Time: 40 minutes | Serves: 4

½ pound chicken	grated
sausages, smoked	4 eggs
½ pound ham, sliced	½ cup yogurt
6 ounces cauliflower rice	½ cup milk
2 garlic cloves, minced	Salt and ground black
8 ounces spinach	pepper, to taste
½ cup Ricotta cheese	1 teaspoon smoked
½ cup Asiago cheese,	paprika

1. Place the sausages and ham in the Air Fry Basket. 2. Press BOTTOM and turn the dial until AIR FRY is illuminated. Press TEMP and set to 380°F, then press TIME and set to 10 minutes. Press START/STOP to begin preheating. 3. When preheating is complete, insert the Air Fry Basket in LEVEL 2 position of the bottom oven. Close the door to begin cooking. When cooking is complete, set aside. 4. Meanwhile, add the cauliflower and garlic to a saucepan over medium heat and sauté for 4 minutes, stirring constantly. Then remove from heat, add the spinach and cover the lid. 5. Let the spinach wilt completely. Transfer the sautéed mixture to the sheet pan. Add the reserved sausage and ham. 6. In a bowl, mix together the cheese, yogurt, milk, eggs, pepper, salt, and paprika. Pour the cheese mixture over the hash browns in the sheet pan. 7. Press TOP and turn the dial until BAKE is illuminated. Press TEMP/SHADE and set to 380°F, then press TIME/SLICES and set to 30 minutes. Press START/STOP to begin preheating. 8. When preheating is complete, place the sheet pan on the rack. Close the door to begin cooking. Serve warm.

Per Serving: Calories 493; Fat 32.51g; Sodium 1664mg; Carbs 14.65g; Fiber 2.5g; Sugar 5.41g; Protein 36.41g

Savory Chicken Drumettes with Asparagus

Prep Time: 15 minutes | Cook Time: 22 minutes | Serves: 6

6 chicken drumettes	ends trimmed
1½ pounds asparagus,	
Marinade:	
3 tablespoons canola oil	ginger, peeled and
3 tablespoons soy sauce	minced
3 tablespoons lime juice	1 teaspoon Creole
3 heaping tablespoons	seasoning
shallots, minced	Coarse sea salt and
1 heaping teaspoon fresh	ground black pepper, to
garlic, minced	taste
1 (1-inch) piece fresh	

1. Mix together all the ingredients for the marinade in a large bowl. Add the chicken drumettes to the marinade and toss to coat well. Marinate in the refrigerator for at least 5 hours. 2. Then, drain the chicken drumettes and discard the marinade. Place the chicken drumettes in the Air Fry Basket. 3. Press BOTTOM and turn the dial until AIR FRY is illuminated. Press TEMP and set to 370°F, then press TIME and set to 11 minutes. Press START/STOP to begin preheating. 4. When preheating is complete, insert the Air Fry Basket in LEVEL 2 position of the bottom oven. Close the door to begin cooking. When cooking is up, flip them and cook for 11 minutes more. 5. Meanwhile, heat the reserved marinade in a skillet over medium heat. 6. Stir in the asparagus and cook for about 5 minutes or until cooked through. Serve with the air-fried chicken and enjoy!

Per Serving: Calories 328; Fat 20.57g; Sodium 297mg; Carbs 9.21g; Fiber 2.9g; Sugar 4.63g; Protein 26.93g

Smoked Duck Breasts with Gravy

Prep Time: 15 minutes | Cook Time: 30 minutes | Serves: 4

1½ pounds smoked duck breasts, boneless	8 pearl onions peeled
1 tablespoon yellow mustard	5 ounces chicken broth
2 tablespoons ketchup, low-carb	2 egg yolks, whisked
	1 teaspoon rosemary, finely chopped

1. Arrange the smoked duck breasts in the Air Fry Basket. 2. Press BOTTOM and turn the dial until AIR FRY is illuminated. Press TEMP and set to 365°F, then press TIME and set to 15 minutes. Press START/STOP to begin preheating. 3. When preheating is complete, insert the Air Fry Basket in LEVEL 2 position of the bottom oven. Close the door to begin cooking. 4. When cooking time is up, spread the mustard and ketchup on the duck breast. Top with pearl onions. Cook for an additional 7 minutes until golden brown. 5. Slice the duck breasts and reserve. Drain off the duck fat from the basket. 6. Add the reserved 1 tablespoon of duck fat to a skillet over medium heat. Then pour in the chicken broth and bring to a boil. 7. Whisk in the egg yolks and rosemary. Turn the heat to low and cook until the gravy has thickened slightly. Spoon the warm gravy over the reserved duck breasts. Serve warm and enjoy!

Per Serving: Calories 454; Fat 10.23g; Sodium 334mg; Carbs 50.81g; Fiber 6.1g; Sugar 33.57g; Protein 40.79g

Buttered Piri Piri Chicken

Prep Time: 10 minutes | Cook Time: 40 minutes | Serves: 6

12 chicken wings	½ teaspoon cumin powder
1½ ounces butter, melted	
1 teaspoon onion powder	1 teaspoon garlic paste

For the Sauce:

2 ounces piri piri peppers, stemmed and chopped	1 garlic clove, chopped
	2 tablespoons fresh lemon juice
1 tablespoon pimiento, deveined and minced	⅓ teaspoon sea salt
	½ teaspoon tarragon

1. Steam the chicken wings using a steamer basket that is placed over a saucepan with boiling water and reduce the heat. 2. Now, steam the wings for 10 minutes over a moderate heat. 3. Toss the wings with butter, cumin powder, onion powder, and garlic paste. 4. Let the chicken wings cool to room temperature. Then, refrigerate them for 45 to 50 minutes. 5. Press BOTTOM and turn the dial until AIR ROAST illuminates. Press the TIME/SLICES buttons to set the cook time to 30 minutes. Then press the TEMP button to set the cook temperature to 330°F. Press START/STOP to start preheating. 6. Place the chicken on the sheet pan. When the unit has preheated, immediately put the sheet pan on the wire rack in the Bottom Oven Level 1. Close oven door. Roast and flip them halfway through. 7. While cooking the chicken wings, prepare the sauce by merging all of the sauce ingredients in a food processor. 8. When cooking is up, toss the wings with prepared Piri Piri Sauce and serve.

Per Serving: Calories 147; Fat 8.89g; Sodium 289mg; Carbs 2.53g; Fiber 0.4g; Sugar 1.19g; Protein 13.87g

Rosemary Turkey Breast with Celery

Prep Time: 5 minutes | Cook Time: 45 minutes | Serves: 4

2 ½ pounds turkey breasts	½ teaspoon ground black pepper
1 tablespoon fresh rosemary, chopped	1 onion, chopped
1 teaspoon sea salt	1 celery stalk, chopped

1. Press BOTTOM and turn the dial until AIR FRY illuminates. Press the TIME/SLICES buttons to set the cook time to 30 minutes. Then press the TEMP button to set the cook temperature to 360°F. Press START/STOP to start preheating. Spritz the sides and bottom of the Air Fry Basket with a nonstick cooking spray. 2. Place the turkey in the Basket. Add the salt, rosemary, and black pepper. 3. When bottom oven is preheated, immediately slide the Basket in LEVEL 2 position. Close door to start cooking. 4. After cooking for 30 minutes, add the onion and celery and cook an additional 15 minutes. 5. When cooking is up, serve. Bon appétit!

Per Serving: Calories 338; Fat 6.68g; Sodium 796mg; Carbs 3.31g; Fiber 0.7g; Sugar 1.51g; Protein 66.63g

Herbed Cheese Chicken Breasts

Prep Time: 5 minutes | Cook Time: 32 minutes | Serves: 6

3 boneless and skinless chicken breasts, cut into small pieces	cracked black pepper
	⅓ cup Parmigiano-Reggiano cheese, freshly grated
⅓ cup cooking wine (such as Sauvignon Blanc)	
	3 cloves garlic, minced
	2 tablespoons olive oil
1 teaspoon fresh sage leaves, minced	1 teaspoon seasoned salt
	1 teaspoon fresh rosemary leaves, minced
1 teaspoon freshly	

1. Warm the oil in a sauté pan over a moderate flame. 2. Then, sauté the garlic until just fragrant. 3. Next, remove the pan from the heat and pour in the cooking wine. Add the seasonings and toss until everything is well combined. 4. Pour this mixture into a lightly-oiled sheet dish. Toss in the pieces of chicken breasts. 5. Press BOTTOM and turn the dial until AIR ROAST illuminates. Press the TIME/SLICES buttons to set the cook time to 32 minutes. Then press the TEMP button to set the cook temperature to 325°F. Press START/STOP to start preheating. 6. When the unit has preheated, immediately put the sheet pan on the wire rack in the Bottom Oven Level 1. Close oven door. 7. When cooking is up, scatter the grated cheese over the chicken and serve on individual plates.

Per Serving: Calories 240; Fat 9.64g; Sodium 548mg; Carbs 1.93g; Fiber 0.2g; Sugar 0.02g; Protein 32.33g

Cheesy Pizza Chicken with Pepperoni

Prep Time: 5 minutes | Cook Time: 15 minutes | Serves: 4

4 small-sized chicken breasts, boneless and skinless	16 slices pepperoni
	Salt and pepper, to savor
¼ cup pizza sauce	1½ tablespoons olive oil
½ cup Colby cheese, shredded	1½ tablespoons dried oregano

1. Carefully flatten out the chicken breast with a rolling pin. 2. Divide the ingredients among four chicken fillets. Roll the chicken fillets with the stuffing and seal them using a small skewer or two toothpicks. 3. Press BOTTOM and turn the dial until AIR ROAST illuminates. Press the TIME/SLICES buttons to set the cook time to 15 minutes. Then press the TEMP button to set the cook temperature to 370°F. Press START/STOP to start preheating. 4. Place the chicken on the sheet pan. When the unit has preheated, immediately put the sheet pan on the wire rack in the Bottom Oven Level 1. Close oven door. 5. When cooking is up, serve. Bon appétit!

Per Serving: Calories 262; Fat 16.55g; Sodium 380mg; Carbs 3.63g; Fiber 0.8g; Sugar 1.51g; Protein 23.71g

Ethiopian-Style Spicy Chicken with Cauliflower

Prep Time: 5 minutes | Cook Time: 28 minutes | Serves: 6

2 handful fresh Italian parsleys, roughly chopped	powder
	1½ teaspoons berbere spice
½ cup fresh chopped chives	⅓ teaspoon sweet paprika
	½ teaspoon shallot powder
2 sprigs thyme	
6 chicken drumsticks	1 teaspoon granulated garlic
1½ small-sized head cauliflower, broken into large-sized florets	
	1 teaspoon freshly cracked pink peppercorns
2 teaspoons mustard powder	
	½ teaspoon sea salt
⅓ teaspoon porcini	

1. Simply combine all items for the berbere spice rub mix. 2. After that, coat the chicken drumsticks with this rub mix on all sides. Transfer them to the sheet pan. 3. Now, lower the cauliflower onto the chicken drumsticks. Add chives, thyme, and Italian parsley and spritz everything with a pan spray. 4. Press BOTTOM and turn the dial until AIR ROAST illuminates. Press the TIME/SLICES buttons to set the cook time to 28 minutes. Then press the TEMP button to set the cook temperature to 355°F. Press START/STOP to start preheating. 5. When the unit has preheated, immediately put the sheet pan on the wire rack in the Bottom Oven Level 1. Close oven door. 6. Turn occasionally during cooking. 7. When cooking is up, serve. Bon appétit!

Per Serving: Calories 240; Fat 12.46g; Sodium 382mg; Carbs 6.01g; Fiber 2.4g; Sugar 1.52g; Protein 25.74g

Cumin Chicken with Peppers and Tarragon

Prep Time: 5 minutes | Cook Time: 38 minutes | Serves: 4

2 cups of roasted vegetable broth	1½ tablespoons Worcester sauce
2 chicken breasts, cut into halves	½ cup of spring onions, chopped
¾ teaspoon fine sea salt	1 Serrano pepper, deveined and chopped
¼ teaspoon mixed peppercorns, freshly cracked	1 bell pepper, deveined and chopped
1 teaspoon cumin powder	1 tablespoon tamari sauce
1½ teaspoons sesame oil	½ chopped fresh tarragon

1. Place the vegetable broth and chicken breasts in a deep saucepan and cook for 10 minutes. Then reduce the temperature and let it simmer for additional 10 minutes. 2. After cooking, allow the chicken to cool slightly and shred the chicken with a stand mixer or two forks. 3. Toss the shredded chicken with the salt, cumin, cracked peppercorns, sesame oil and the Worcester sauce. 4. Press BOTTOM and turn the dial until AIR FRY illuminates. Press the TIME/SLICES buttons to set the cook time to 18 minutes. Then press the TEMP button to set the cook temperature to 380°F. Press START/STOP to start preheating. 5. Place the chicken on the Air Fry Basket. When bottom oven is preheated, immediately, place the wire rack in LEVEL 1 position of the bottom oven and place the sheet pan on top. Slide the Basket in LEVEL 2 position of bottom oven. Close door to begin cooking. 6. Check for doneness. 7. Meanwhile, in a non-stick skillet, cook the remaining ingredients over a moderate flame. Cook until the peppers and onions are tender and fragrant. 8. Remove the skillet from the heat, and when the chicken is finished, add the shredded chicken and toss to combine. Serve right away!

Per Serving: Calories 279; Fat 15.31g; Sodium 611mg; Carbs 3.13g; Fiber 0.8g; Sugar 1.39g; Protein 31g

Cheesy Chicken with Cauliflower

Prep Time: 5 minutes | Cook Time: 28 minutes | Serves: 4

2 pounds chicken legs	1 (1-pound) head cauliflower, broken into small florets
2 tablespoons olive oil	
1 teaspoon sea salt	
½ teaspoon ground black pepper	2 garlic cloves, minced
	⅓ cup Pecorino Romano cheese, freshly grated
1 teaspoon smoked paprika	½ teaspoon dried thyme
1 teaspoon dried marjoram	Salt, to taste

1. Toss the chicken legs with the olive oil, salt, paprika, black pepper, and marjoram. 2. Press BOTTOM and turn the dial until AIR FRY illuminates. Press the TIME/SLICES buttons to set the cook time to 11 minutes. Then press the TEMP button to set the cook temperature to 380°F. Press START/STOP to start preheating. 3. Place the chicken legs on the Air Fry Basket. When bottom oven is preheated, immediately, place the wire rack in LEVEL 1 position of the bottom oven and place the sheet pan on top. Slide the Basket in LEVEL 2 position of bottom oven. Close door to begin cooking. 4. Flip the chicken legs and cook for a further 5 minutes. Toss the cauliflower florets with garlic, cheese, thyme, and salt. 5. Increase the temperature to 400°F and add the cauliflower florets to cook for 12 more minutes. 6. When cooking is up, serve warm.

Per Serving: Calories 390; Fat 18.91g; Sodium 1550mg; Carbs 5.89g; Fiber 1.7g; Sugar 1.64g; Protein 47.39g

Cheesy Chicken Vegetable Medley

Prep Time: 5 minutes | Cook Time: 22 minutes | Serves: 4

3 eggs, whisked	2 cups leftover keto
½ teaspoon dried	vegetables
marjoram	½ red onion, thinly
⅓ cup Fontina cheese,	sliced
grated	2 cups cooked chicken,
1 teaspoon sea salt	shredded or chopped
⅓ teaspoon red pepper	3 cloves garlic, finely
flakes, crushed	minced

1. Simply mix all of the above ingredients, except for cheese, with a wide spatula. Scrape the mixture into the previously greased sheet pan. 2. Press BOTTOM and turn the dial until AIR ROAST illuminates. Press the TIME/SLICES buttons to set the cook time to 22 minutes. Then press the TEMP button to set the cook temperature to 365°F. Press START/STOP to start preheating. 3. When the unit has preheated, immediately put the sheet pan on the wire rack in the Bottom Oven Level 1. Close oven door. 4. Cook until everything is bubbling. 5. When cooking is up, serve warm topped with the grated Fontina cheese. Bon appétit!

Per Serving: Calories 370; Fat 19.11g; Sodium 832mg; Carbs 14.09g; Fiber 4.2g; Sugar 3.76g; Protein 33.65g

Coconut Chicken with Green Garlic

Prep Time: 5 minutes | Cook Time: 28 minutes | Serves: 4

½ teaspoon grated fresh	oil
ginger	3 green garlic stalks,
⅓ cup coconut milk	finely chopped
½ teaspoon sea salt	½ cup dry white wine
flakes	½ teaspoon fresh thyme
3 medium-sized boneless	leaves, minced
chicken breasts, cut into	⅓ teaspoon freshly
small pieces	cracked black pepper
1½ tablespoons sesame	

1. Warm the sesame oil in a deep sauté pan over a moderate heat. Then sautée the green garlic until just fragrant. 2. Remove the pan from the heat and pour in the coconut milk and the

white wine. 3. After that, add the sea salt, fresh ginger, thyme, and freshly cracked black pepper. Scrape this mixture into the sheet pan. Stir in the chicken chunks. 4. Press BOTTOM and turn the dial until AIR ROAST illuminates. Press the TIME/SLICES buttons to set the cook time to 28 minutes. Then press the TEMP button to set the cook temperature to 335°F. Press START/STOP to start preheating. 5. When the unit has preheated, immediately put the sheet pan on the wire rack in the Bottom Oven Level 1. Close oven door. 6. When cooking is up, serve on individual plates and eat warm.

Per Serving: Calories 200; Fat 14.19g; Sodium 542mg; Carbs 2.51g; Fiber 0.6g; Sugar 0.94g; Protein 15.75g

Homemade Nacho-Fried Chicken Burgers

Prep Time: 10 minutes | Cook Time: 15 minutes | Serves: 4

1 palmful dried basil	⅓ teaspoon porcini
⅓ cup parmesan cheese,	powder
grated	1 teaspoon sea salt flakes
2 teaspoons dried	1 pound chicken meat,
marjoram	ground
⅓ teaspoon ancho chili	2 teaspoons cumin
powder	powder
2 teaspoons dried parsley	⅓ teaspoon red pepper
flakes	flakes, crushed
½ teaspoon onion	1 teaspoon freshly
powder	cracked black pepper
Toppings, to servel	

1. Generously grease the Air Fry Basket with a thin layer of vegetable oil. 2. Combine chicken meat with all seasonings in a mixing dish. Shape into 4 patties and coat them with the grated parmesan cheese. 3. Press BOTTOM and turn the dial until AIR FRY illuminates. Press the TIME/SLICES buttons to set the cook time to 15 minutes. Then press the TEMP button to set the cook temperature to 345°F. Press START/STOP to start preheating. 4. Place the chicken burgers on the Air Fry Basket. When bottom oven is preheated, immediately slide the Basket in LEVEL 2 position. Close door to start cooking. 5. Work in batches and flip them once. 6. When cooking is up, serve with toppings of choice. Bon appétit!

Per Serving: Calories 223; Fat 11.84g; Sodium 854mg; Carbs 3.02g; Fiber 0.6g; Sugar 0.28g; Protein 25.16g

Authentic Mexican Mole Chicken

Prep Time: 5 minutes | Cook Time: 34 minutes | Serves: 4

8 chicken thighs, skinless, bone-in

1 tablespoon peanut oil

Sea salt and ground black pepper, to taste

Mole sauce:

1 tablespoon peanut oil

1 onion, chopped

1 ounce dried negro chiles, stemmed, seeded, and chopped

2 garlic cloves, peeled and halved

1 large-sized fresh tomatoes, pureed

1½ ounces sugar-free bakers' chocolate, chopped

1 teaspoon dried Mexican oregano

½ teaspoon ground cumin

1 teaspoon coriander seeds

A pinch of ground cloves

¼ cup almonds, slivered and toasted

1. Press BOTTOM and turn the dial until AIR ROAST illuminates. Press the TIME/SLICES buttons to set the cook time to 20 minutes. Then press the TEMP button to set the cook temperature to 380°F. Press START/STOP to start preheating. 2. Toss the chicken thighs with the salt, peanut oil, and black pepper. 3. Place the chicken legs on the sheet pan. When the unit has preheated, immediately put the sheet pan on the wire rack in the Bottom Oven Level 1. Close oven door. 4. Flip them and cook an additional 10 minutes. 5. When cooking is up, reserve. 6. To make the sauce, heat 1 tablespoon of peanut oil in a saucepan over medium-high heat. 7. Now, sauté the chiles, onion, and garlic for about 2 minutes until fragrant. 8. Next, stir in the chocolate, tomatoes, oregano, coriander seeds, cumin, and cloves. 9. Allow it to simmer until the sauce has slightly thickened. 10. Add the reserved chicken to the sheet pan and add the sauce. 11. Cook at 360°F for 10 minutes until thoroughly warmed. 12. When cooking is up, serve garnished with slivered almonds. Enjoy!

Per Serving: Calories 526; Fat 27.46g; Sodium 311mg; Carbs 8.76g; Fiber 2.1g; Sugar 3.16g; Protein 59.71g

Chicken with Creamy Mayo-Rosemary Sauce

Prep Time: 5 minutes | Cook Time: 18 minutes | Serves: 4

½ cup full-fat sour cream

1 teaspoon ground cinnamon

½ teaspoon whole grain mustard

1½ tablespoons mayonnaise

1 pound chicken thighs, boneless, skinless, and cut into pieces

1½ tablespoons olive oil

2 heaping tablespoons fresh rosemary, minced

½ cup white wine

3 cloves garlic, minced

½ teaspoon smoked paprika

Salt and freshly cracked black pepper, to taste

1. Firstly, combine chicken thighs with olive oil and white wine in a mixing dish, then stir to coat. 2. After that, throw in the garlic, ground cinnamon, salt, smoked paprika, and black pepper, then cover and refrigerate for 1 to 3 hours. 3. Press BOTTOM and turn the dial until AIR ROAST illuminates. Press the TIME/SLICES buttons to set the cook time to 18 minutes. Then press the TEMP button to set the cook temperature to 375°F. Press START/STOP to start preheating. 4. Place the chicken thighs on the sheet pan. When the unit has preheated, immediately put the sheet pan on the wire rack in the Bottom Oven Level 1. Close oven door. 5. Turn halfway through and working in batches. 6. To make the sauce, combine the mayonnaise, sour cream, whole grain mustard, and rosemary. 7. When cooking is up, serve the turkey with the mustard/rosemary sauce and enjoy!

Per Serving: Calories 317; Fat 19.18g; Sodium 468mg; Carbs 7.88g; Fiber 0.9g; Sugar 1.12g; Protein 29.2g

Yummy Kung Pao Chicken

Prep Time: 10 minutes | Cook Time: 16 minutes | Serves: 4

1½ pounds chicken breast, halved	1 teaspoon ginger, peeled and grated
1 tablespoon lemon juice	2 garlic cloves, minced
2 tablespoons mirin	½ teaspoon salt
¼ cup milk	½ teaspoon Szechuan
2 tablespoons soy sauce	pepper
1 tablespoon olive oil	½ teaspoon xanthan gum

1. In a large ceramic dish, place the chicken, mirin, lemon juice, milk, soy sauce, ginger, olive oil, and garlic. Let it marinate for 30 minutes in the refrigerator. 2. Spritz the sides and bottom of the Air Fry Basket with a nonstick cooking spray. 3. Arrange the chicken in the Basket. 4. Press BOTTOM and turn the dial until AIR FRY illuminates. Press the TIME/SLICES buttons to set the cook time to 10 minutes. Then press the TEMP button to set the cook temperature to 370°F. Press START/STOP to start preheating. 5. Turn over the chicken, baste with the reserved marinade and cook for 4 minutes longer. 6. When cooking is up, taste for doneness, season with salt and pepper, and reserve. 7. Add the marinade to the preheated skillet over medium heat and add in xanthan gum. Let it cook for 5 to 6 minutes until the sauce thickens. 8. Spoon the sauce over the reserved chicken and serve immediately.

Per Serving: Calories 349; Fat 11.42g; Sodium 544mg; Carbs 4.09g; Fiber 0.3g; Sugar 2.71g; Protein 54.04g

Lime Cheese Chicken Tenders

Prep Time: 8 minutes | Cook Time: 12 minutes | Serves: 6

1 lime	Sea salt and ground
2 pounds chicken tenderloins, cut up	black pepper, to taste
½ cup pork rinds, crushed	1 teaspoon cayenne pepper
½ cup Parmesan cheese, grated	⅓ teaspoon ground cumin
1 tablespoon olive oil	1 teaspoon chili powder
	1 egg

1. Squeeze the lime juice all over the chicken. 2. Spritz the Air Fry Basket with a nonstick cooking spray. 3. In a mixing bowl, thoroughly combine the pork rinds, olive oil, salt, Parmesan, black pepper, cumin, cayenne pepper, and chili powder. 4. In another shallow bowl, whisk the egg until well beaten. Dip the chicken tenders in the egg, then in pork rind mixture. 5. Transfer the breaded chicken to the prepared Basket. 6. Press BOTTOM and turn the dial until AIR FRY illuminates. Press the TIME/SLICES buttons to set the cook time to 12 minutes. Then press the TEMP button to set the cook temperature to 380°F. Press START/STOP to start preheating. 7. When bottom oven is preheated, immediately, place the wire rack in LEVEL 1 position of the bottom oven and place the sheet pan on top. Slide the Basket in LEVEL 2 position of bottom oven. Close door to begin cooking. 8. Turn them over halfway through the cooking time. Work in batches if needed. 9. When cooking is up, serve immediately.

Per Serving: Calories 261; Fat 10.6g; Sodium 299mg; Carbs 3.1g; Fiber 0.4g; Sugar 0.69g; Protein 36.65g

Spicy Turkey Thighs Casserole

Prep Time: 15 minutes | Cook Time: 30 minutes | Serves: 4

2 pounds turkey thighs, skinless and boneless	deveined and minced
	1 carrot, sliced
1 red onion, sliced	1 tablespoon Cajun
2 bell peppers, deveined and sliced	seasoning mix
	1 tablespoon fish sauce
1 habanero pepper,	2 cups chicken broth

1. Spray the bottom and sides of a casserole dish that fits the oven with a nonstick cooking spray. 2. Place the turkey thighs in the casserole dish. Add the onion, peppers and carrot. Sprinkle with the Cajun seasoning. 3. Then pour in the chicken broth and fish sauce. Place the casserole dish in LEVEL 1 position of the bottom oven. Close the door. 4. Press BOTTOM and turn the dial until AIR FRY is illuminated. Press TEMP and set to 360°F, then press TIME and set to 30 minutes. Press START/STOP to begin cooking. 5. When cooking is complete, serve warm.

Per Serving: Calories 316; Fat 11.31g; Sodium 1792mg; Carbs 10.06g; Fiber 1.3g; Sugar 6.03g; Protein 41.52g

Chapter 4 Beef, Pork, and Lamb Recipes

Cheesy Pepper and Pork Meatloaf

Prep Time: 12 minutes | Cook Time: 23 minutes | Serves: 4

1 pound pork, ground	1 leek, chopped
½ cup parmesan cheese, grated	1 serrano pepper, chopped
1½ tablespoons green garlic, minced	2 tablespoons tomato puree
1½ tablespoon fresh cilantro, minced	½ teaspoons dried thyme
½ tablespoon fish sauce	Salt and ground black pepper, to taste
⅓ teaspoon dried basil	

1. Add all ingredients to a large-sized mixing dish and combine everything with the hands. 2. Then, form a meatloaf with a spatula. 3. Press TOP and turn the dial until BAKE is illuminated. Press TEMP/SHADE and set the temperature to 365°F, then press TIME/SLICES and set the time to 23 minutes. Press START/STOP to start preheating. 4. Place the meatloaf on the sheet pan. When the unit has preheated, immediately put the sheet pan on the wire rack in the Bottom Oven Level 1. Close oven door. 5. When cooking is up, allow the meatloaf to sit for 10 minutes before slicing and serving. Bon appétit!

Per Serving: Calories 314; Fat 16.15g; Sodium 1054mg; Carbs 7.26g; Fiber 0.9g; Sugar 1.43g; Protein 33.49g

Tasty Pork Ribs with Bell Peppers

Prep Time: 15 minutes | Cook Time: 35 minutes | Serves: 4

1 pound St. Louis-style pork spareribs, individually cut	1 tablespoon sweet paprika
1 teaspoon seasoned salt	½ teaspoon mustard powder
½ teaspoon ground black pepper	2 tablespoons sesame oil
	4 bell pepper, seeded

1. Mix up the spices in a small bowl and rub all over the pork ribs. Then drizzle with 1 tablespoon of sesame oil. 2. Place the pork ribs in the Air Fry Basket. 3. Place the bell peppers in the sheet pan and toss with the remaining 1 tablespoon of oil; season with salt. 4. Press BOTTOM and turn the dial until AIR FRY is illuminated. Press TEMP and set to 390°F, then press TIME and set to 35 minutes. 5. Press TOP and turn the dial until BROIL is illuminated. Press TEMP/SHADE and set to 390°F, then press TIME/SLICES and set to 15 minutes. Press SMART FINISH, then press START/STOP to begin preheating. 6. When preheating is complete, place the sheet pan on the top oven rack. Then insert wire rack in LEVEL 1 position of the bottom oven, place the air fry basket on the rack. Close the door to begin cooking. Flip the pork ribs halfway through the cooking time. 7. Serve the warm spareribs with the peppers on the side. Enjoy!

Per Serving: Calories 325; Fat 23.91g; Sodium 658mg; Carbs 5.74g; Fiber 1.4g; Sugar 2.76g; Protein 21.94g

Pork-Bacon Kebabs

Prep Time: 15 minutes | Cook Time: 35 minutes | Serves: 6

1 cup cream of celery soup	½ teaspoon cayenne pepper
1 (13.5-ounce) can coconut milk, unsweetened	½ teaspoon chili powder
2 tablespoons tamari sauce	1 teaspoon curry powder
1 teaspoon yellow mustard	2 pounds pork tenderloin, cut into bite-sized cubes
Salt and freshly ground white pepper, to taste	4 ounces bacon, cut into pieces
	12 bamboo skewers, soaked in water

1. Add the cream of the celery soup, coconut milk, mustard, tamari sauce, salt, white pepper, chili powder, cayenne pepper, and curry powder to a large pot and bring to a boil. 2. Reduce the heat to low and simmer; cook until the sauce is heated through, about 13 minutes. 3. Gently stir in the pork and refrigerate for 2 hours. 4. Thread the pork onto the skewers, alternating the cubes of meat with the pieces of bacon. Then arrange the skewers in the Air Fry Basket. 5. Press BOTTOM and turn the dial until AIR FRY is illuminated. Press TEMP and set to 370°F, then press TIME and set to 15 minutes. Press START/STOP to begin preheating. 6. When preheating is complete, insert the Air Fry Basket in LEVEL 2 position of the bottom oven. Close the door to begin cooking. Flip them a couple of times. When cooking is complete, serve immediately.

Per Serving: Calories 450; Fat 28.07g; Sodium 730mg; Carbs 7.27g; Fiber 2.5g; Sugar 2.54g; Protein 43.63g

Crispy Cajun Pork Chops

Prep Time: 15 minutes | Cook Time: 18 minutes | Serves: 6

⅓ cup pork rinds	meal
Roughly chopped fresh	1 teaspoon seasoned salt
cilantro, to taste	Garlic & onion spice
2 teaspoons Cajun	blend, to taste
seasonings	6 pork chops
Nonstick cooking spray	⅓ teaspoon freshly
2 eggs, beaten	cracked black pepper
3 tablespoons almond	

1. Rub the pork chops with salt, pepper, Cajun seasonings, and the spice blend on all sides. 2. Place the almond meal in a plate. Whisk the egg until pale and smooth in a shallow bowl. Place the pork rinds in a third bowl. 3. Dredge each pork piece in the almond meal; then, dip them with the egg and finally coat with the pork rinds. Spritz them with cooking spray on both sides and place in the Air Fry Basket. 4. Press BOTTOM and turn the dial until AIR FRY is illuminated. Press TEMP and set to 345°F, then press TIME and set to 18 minutes. Press START/STOP to begin preheating. 5. When preheating is complete, insert the Air Fry Basket in LEVEL 2 position of the bottom oven. Close the door to begin cooking. Flip halfway through the cooking time. 6. When cooking is complete, garnish with fresh cilantro. Serve hot!

Per Serving: Calories 386; Fat 16.91g; Sodium 682mg; Carbs 1.89g; Fiber 0.3g; Sugar 0.57g; Protein 52.82g

Flavorful Pork Burgers with Blue Cheese

Prep Time: 15 minutes | Cook Time: 41 minutes | Serves: 6

1 cup blue cheese, sliced	2 small-sized onions,
2 teaspoons dried basil	peeled and chopped
1 teaspoon smoked	½ teaspoon ground black
paprika	pepper
2 pounds ground pork	3 garlic cloves, minced
2 tablespoons tomato	1 teaspoon fine sea salt
puree	

1. In a large bowl, mix together the pork, tomato puree, garlic, onion, and seasonings. 2. Form the pork mixture into

six patties and place them in the Air Fry Basket. 3. Press BOTTOM and turn the dial until AIR FRY is illuminated. Press TEMP and set to 385°F, then press TIME and set to 23 minutes. Press START/STOP to begin preheating. 4. When preheating is complete, insert the Air Fry Basket in LEVEL 2 position of the bottom oven. Close the door to begin cooking. 5. When cooking time is up, reduce the temperature to 365°F and cook for an additional 18 minutes. 6. Transfer the cooked burgers to a serving platter; top with blue cheese and serve warm.

Per Serving: Calories 545; Fat 37.98g; Sodium 759mg; Carbs 4.34g; Fiber 0.8g; Sugar 1.6g; Protein 44.28g

Lemony Pork Chops

Prep Time: 15 minutes | Cook Time: 27 minutes | Serves: 5

5 pork chops	½ lemon, cut into
⅓ cup vermouth	wedges
½ teaspoon paprika	1 teaspoon freshly
2 sprigs thyme, only	cracked black pepper
leaves, crushed	3 tablespoons lemon
½ teaspoon dried	juice
oregano	3 cloves garlic, minced
Fresh parsley, to serve	2 tablespoons canola oil
1 teaspoon garlic salt	

1. In a sauté pan over low heat, warm the canola oil. Add the garlic and sauté until just fragrant. 2. Remove the pan from the heat and stir in the lemon juice and vermouth. 3. Add the seasonings and stir to mix well. Pour the sauce into the sheet pan along with the pork chops. 4. Tuck the lemon wedges among the pork chops. 5. Press BOTTOM and turn the dial until AIR FRY is illuminated. Press TEMP and set to 345°F, then press TIME and set to 27 minutes. Press START/STOP to begin preheating. 6. When preheating is complete, place the sheet pan on the wire rack in LEVEL 2 position of the bottom oven. Close the door to begin cooking. When cooking is complete, serve immediately.

Per Serving: Calories 413; Fat 23.08g; Sodium 89mg; Carbs 4.69g; Fiber 0.5g; Sugar 1.62g; Protein 40.6g

Spicy Herbed Filet Mignon

Prep Time: 15 minutes | Cook Time: 14 minutes | Serves: 4

1½ pounds filet mignon	1 teaspoon cayenne
2 tablespoons olive oil	pepper
2 cloves garlic, pressed	Kosher salt and freshly
1 tablespoon Italian herb	ground black pepper, to
mix	taste

1. Place the beef in a bowl and toss with the remaining ingredients. Then place the beef in the Air Fry Basket. 2. Press BOTTOM and turn the dial until AIR FRY is illuminated. Press TEMP and set to 400°F, then press TIME and set to 14 minutes. Press START/STOP to begin preheating. 3. When preheating is complete, insert the Air Fry Basket in LEVEL 2 position of the bottom oven. Close the door to begin cooking. Flip halfway through the cooking time. 4. When cooking is complete, serve immediately.

Per Serving: Calories 290; Fat 14.76g; Sodium 307mg; Carbs 0.83g; Fiber 0.2g; Sugar 0.06g; Protein 38.69g

Mustard Skirt Steak Sliders

Prep Time: 15 minutes | Cook Time: 15 minutes | Serves: 4

1½ pounds skirt steak	black pepper, to taste
1 teaspoon steak dry rub	2 tablespoons olive oil
½ teaspoon cayenne	2 tablespoons Dijon
pepper	mustard
Sea salt and ground	8 Hawaiian buns

1. Place the beef in a bowl and toss with the spices and olive oil. Then place the beef in the Air Fry Basket. 2. Press BOTTOM and turn the dial until AIR FRY is illuminated. Press TEMP and set to 400°F, then press TIME and set to 15 minutes. Press START/STOP to begin preheating. 3. When preheating is complete, insert the Air Fry Basket in LEVEL 2 position of the bottom oven. Close the door to begin cooking. Flip halfway through the cooking time. 4. Slice the beef and serve with mustard and Hawaiian buns. Enjoy!

Per Serving: Calories 709; Fat 44.29g; Sodium 629mg; Carbs 27.79g; Fiber 3.7g; Sugar 1.59g; Protein 48.04g

Rosemary Garlic Ribeye Steak

Prep Time: 10 minutes | Cook Time: 15 minutes | Serves: 4

1-pound ribeye steak,	Sea salt and ground
bone-in	black pepper, to taste
2 tablespoons butter,	2 rosemary sprigs, leaves
room temperature	picked, chopped
2 garlic cloves, minced	

1. Place the ribeye steak in a bowl and toss with the butter, salt, black pepper, garlic, and rosemary. 2. Then place the steak in the Air Fry Basket. 3. Press BOTTOM and turn the dial until AIR FRY is illuminated. Press TEMP and set to 400°F, then press TIME and set to 15 minutes. Press START/STOP to begin preheating. 4. When preheating is complete, insert the Air Fry Basket in LEVEL 2 position of the bottom oven. Close the door to begin cooking. Flip halfway through the cooking time. 5. When cooking is complete, serve immediately.

Per Serving: Calories 271; Fat 18.77g; Sodium 147mg; Carbs 3.72g; Fiber 0.3g; Sugar 0.59g; Protein 22.48g

Herbed Roast Beef

Prep Time: 15 minutes | Cook Time: 50 minutes | Serves: 4

1½ pounds bottom round	1 teaspoon parsley
roast	1 teaspoon oregano
2 tablespoons olive oil	Sea salt and freshly
2 garlic cloves, minced	ground black pepper
1 teaspoon rosemary	

1. Place the beef in a bowl and toss with the spices, garlic, and olive oil. Then place the beef in the Air Fry Basket. 2. Press BOTTOM and turn the dial until AIR FRY is illuminated. Press TEMP and set to 390°F, then press TIME and set to 50 minutes. Press START/STOP to begin preheating. 3. When preheating is complete, insert the Air Fry Basket in LEVEL 2 position of the bottom oven. Close the door to begin cooking. Flip halfway through the cooking time. 4. Cut the beef into slices and serve them with dinner rolls. Enjoy!

Per Serving: Calories 350; Fat 15.85g; Sodium 211mg; Carbs 0.72g; Fiber 0.2g; Sugar 0.03g; Protein 48.25g

Garlic Herbed Filet Mignon

Prep Time: 6 minutes | Cook Time: 15 minutes | Serves: 4

1½ pounds filet mignon	1 teaspoon cayenne pepper
2 tablespoons olive oil	Kosher salt and freshly ground black pepper, to taste
2 cloves garlic, pressed	
1 tablespoon Italian herb mix	

1. Toss the beef with the remaining ingredients and place the beef in the Air Fry Basket. 2. Press BOTTOM and turn the dial until AIR FRY illuminates. Press the TIME/SLICES buttons to set the cook time to 14 minutes. Then press the TEMP button to set the cook temperature to 400°F. Press START/STOP to start preheating. 3. When bottom oven is preheated, immediately, place the wire rack in LEVEL 1 position of the bottom oven and place the sheet pan on top. Slide the Basket in LEVEL 2 position of bottom oven. Close door to begin cooking. 4. Turn over halfway through the cooking time. 5. When cooking is up, serve. Enjoy!

Per Serving: Calories 304; Fat 14.85g; Sodium 764mg; Carbs 3.95g; Fiber 0.4g; Sugar 0.49g; Protein 39.16g

Rosemary Butter Ribeye Steak

Prep Time: 5 minutes | Cook Time: 15 minutes | Serves: 4

1 pound ribeye steak, bone-in	Sea salt and ground black pepper, to taste
2 tablespoons butter, room temperature	2 rosemary sprigs, leaves picked, chopped
2 garlic cloves, minced	

1. Toss the ribeye steak with the butter, salt, garlic, black pepper, and rosemary, then place the steak in the Air Fry Basket. 2. Press BOTTOM and turn the dial until AIR FRY illuminates. Press the TIME/SLICES buttons to set the cook time to 15 minutes. Then press the TEMP button to set the cook temperature to 400°F. Press START/STOP to start preheating. 3. When bottom oven is preheated, immediately, place the wire rack in LEVEL 1 position of the bottom oven and place the sheet pan on top. Slide the Basket in LEVEL 2 position of bottom oven. Close door to begin cooking. 4. Turn

over halfway through the cooking time. 5. When cooking is up, serve. Bon appétit!

Per Serving: Calories 268; Fat 18.76g; Sodium 727mg; Carbs 3.03g; Fiber 0.3g; Sugar 0.02g; Protein 22.31g

Mustard Steak Sliders with Hawaiian Buns

Prep Time: 5 minutes | Cook Time: 15 minutes | Serves: 4

1½ pounds skirt steak	black pepper, to taste
1 teaspoon steak dry rub	2 tablespoons olive oil
½ teaspoon cayenne pepper	2 tablespoons Dijon mustard
Sea salt and ground	8 Hawaiian buns

1. Toss the beef with the spices and olive oil and place the beef in the Air Fry Basket. 2. Press BOTTOM and turn the dial until AIR FRY illuminates. Press the TIME/SLICES buttons to set the cook time to 15 minutes. Then press the TEMP button to set the cook temperature to 400°F. Press START/STOP to start preheating. 3. When bottom oven is preheated, immediately, place the wire rack in LEVEL 1 position of the bottom oven and place the sheet pan on top. Slide the Basket in LEVEL 2 position of bottom oven. Close door to begin cooking. 4. Turn over halfway through the cooking time. 5. When cooking is up, cut the beef into slices and serve them with mustard and Hawaiian buns. Bon appétit!

Per Serving: Calories 706; Fat 44.29g; Sodium 1210mg; Carbs 27.09g; Fiber 3.6g; Sugar 1.02g; Protein 47.87g

Herbed Beef with Dinner Rolls

Prep Time: 5 minutes | Cook Time: 50 minutes | Serves: 4

1½ pounds bottom round roast	1 teaspoon parsley
2 tablespoons olive oil	1 teaspoon oregano
2 garlic cloves, minced	Sea salt and freshly
1 teaspoon rosemary	ground black pepper

1. Toss the beef with the garlic, spices, and olive oil and place the beef in the Air Fry Basket. 2. Press BOTTOM and turn the dial until AIR FRY illuminates. Press the TIME/ SLICES buttons to set the cook time to 50 minutes. Then press the TEMP button to set the cook temperature to 390°F. Press START/STOP to start preheating. 3. When bottom oven is preheated, immediately, place the wire rack in LEVEL 1 position of the bottom oven and place the sheet pan on top. Slide the Basket in LEVEL 2 position of bottom oven. Close door to begin cooking. 4. Turn over halfway through the cooking time. 5. When cooking is up, cut the beef into slices and serve them with dinner rolls. Bon appétit!

Per Serving: Calories 352; Fat 15.87g; Sodium 647mg; Carbs 1.09g; Fiber 0.3g; Sugar 0.03g; Protein 48.31g

Tasty Beef Brisket

Prep Time: 5 minutes | Cook Time: 70 minutes | Serves: 4

1½ pounds beef brisket	black pepper, to taste
2 tablespoons olive oil	1 teaspoon dried parsley
1 teaspoon onion powder	flakes
1 teaspoon garlic powder	1 teaspoon dried thyme
Sea salt and ground	

1. Toss the beef with the remaining ingredients and place the beef in the Air Fry Basket. 2. Press BOTTOM and turn the dial until AIR FRY illuminates. Press the TIME/SLICES buttons to set the cook time to 15 minutes. Then press the TEMP button to set the cook temperature to 390°F. Press START/ STOP to start preheating. 3. When bottom oven is preheated, immediately, place the wire rack in LEVEL 1 position of the bottom oven and place the sheet pan on top. Slide the Basket in LEVEL 2 position of bottom oven. Close door to begin

cooking. 4. Turn the beef over and turn the temperature to 360°F. Continue to cook the beef for 55 minutes more. 5. When cooking is up, serve. Bon appétit!

Per Serving: Calories 403; Fat 32.13g; Sodium 2653mg; Carbs 1.71g; Fiber 0.3g; Sugar 0.07g; Protein 25.24g

Best Classic Pulled Beef

Prep Time: 5 minutes | Cook Time: 70 minutes | Serves: 4

1½ pounds beef brisket	flakes, crushed
2 tablespoons olive oil	2 tablespoons tomato
3 garlic cloves, pressed	ketchup
Sea salt and ground	2 tablespoons Dijon
black pepper, to taste	mustard
1 teaspoon red pepper	

1. Toss the beef brisket with the olive oil, salt, garlic, black pepper, and red pepper and place the beef brisket in the Air Fry Basket. 2. Press BOTTOM and turn the dial until AIR FRY illuminates. Press the TIME/SLICES buttons to set the cook time to 15 minutes. Then press the TEMP button to set the cook temperature to 390°F. Press START/STOP to start preheating. 3. When bottom oven is preheated, immediately, place the wire rack in LEVEL 1 position of the bottom oven and place the sheet pan on top. Slide the Basket in LEVEL 2 position of bottom oven. Close door to begin cooking. 4. Turn the beef over and reduce the temperature to 360°F. Continue to cook the beef brisket for approximately 55 minutes or until cooked through. 5. When cooking is up, serve. Shred the beef with two forks and stir in the ketchup and mustard to combine well. Bon appétit!

Per Serving: Calories 411; Fat 32.44g; Sodium 2742mg; Carbs 2.8g; Fiber 0.7g; Sugar 0.77g; Protein 25.71g

Simple Spicy Top Round Roast

Prep Time: 5 minutes | Cook Time: 55 minutes | Serves: 5

2 pounds top round roast	parsley, chopped
2 tablespoons extra-virgin olive oil	1 teaspoon red chili powder
2 cloves garlic, pressed	Kosher salt and freshly ground black pepper, to taste
1 tablespoon fresh rosemary, chopped	
1 tablespoon fresh	

1. Toss the beef with the remaining ingredients and place the beef in the A Air Fry Basket. 2. Press BOTTOM and turn the dial until AIR FRY illuminates. Press the TIME/SLICES buttons to set the cook time to 55 minutes. Then press the TEMP button to set the cook temperature to 390°F. Press START/STOP to start preheating. 3. When bottom oven is preheated, immediately, place the wire rack in LEVEL 1 position of the bottom oven and place the sheet pan on top. Slide the Basket in LEVEL 2 position of bottom oven. Close door to begin cooking. 4. Turn over halfway through the cooking time. 5. When cooking is up, serve. Enjoy!

Per Serving: Calories 237; Fat 6.97g; Sodium 629mg; Carbs 1.08g; Fiber 0.4g; Sugar 0.06g; Protein 43.05g

Spicy Onion Beef Burgers

Prep Time: 5 minutes | Cook Time: 15 minutes | Serves: 3

¾ pound ground beef	pepper
2 tablespoons onion, minced	Sea salt and ground black pepper, to taste
1 teaspoon garlic, minced	1 teaspoon red chili powder
1 teaspoon cayenne	3 hamburger buns

1. Mix the beef, garlic, onion, salt, cayenne pepper, black pepper, and red chili powder until everything is well combined. Form the mixture into three patties. 2. Press BOTTOM and turn the dial until AIR FRY illuminates. Press the TIME/SLICES buttons to set the cook time to 15 minutes. Then press the TEMP button to set the cook temperature to 380°F. Press START/STOP to start preheating. 3. Place the burgers on the

Air Fry Basket. When bottom oven is preheated, immediately, place the wire rack in LEVEL 1 position of the bottom oven and place the sheet pan on top. Slide the Basket in LEVEL 2 position of bottom oven. Close door to begin cooking. 4. Cook until cooked through and turn them over halfway through the cooking time. 5. When cooking is up, serve your burgers on the prepared buns and enjoy!

Per Serving: Calories 414; Fat 20.17g; Sodium 700mg; Carbs 23.04g; Fiber 1.6g; Sugar 3.1g; Protein 33.15g

Lemony London Broil Roast

Prep Time: 5 minutes | Cook Time: 28 minutes | Serves: 4

1 pound London broil	3 cloves garlic, minced
Kosher salt and ground black pepper, to taste	1 tablespoon fresh parsley, chopped
2 tablespoons olive oil	1 tablespoon fresh coriander, chopped
1 small lemon, freshly squeezed	

1. Toss the beef with the remaining ingredients and let it marinate for an hour. 2. Place the beef in a lightly oiled Air Fry Basket and discard the marinade. 3. Press BOTTOM and turn the dial until AIR FRY illuminates. Press the TIME/SLICES buttons to set the cook time to 28 minutes. Then press the TEMP button to set the cook temperature to 400°F. Press START/STOP to start preheating. 4. When bottom oven is preheated, immediately, place the wire rack in LEVEL 1 position of the bottom oven and place the sheet pan on top. Slide the Basket in LEVEL 2 position of bottom oven. Close door to begin cooking. 5. Turn over halfway through the cooking time. 6. When cooking is up, serve. Bon appétit!

Per Serving: Calories 299; Fat 17.02g; Sodium 629mg; Carbs 2.01g; Fiber 0.3g; Sugar 0.34g; Protein 35.06g

Rosemary Onion Meatloaf

Prep Time: 5 minutes | Cook Time: 25 minutes | Serves: 4

1½ pounds ground chuck	1 tablespoon fresh
1 egg, beaten	rosemary, chopped
2 tablespoons olive oil	1 tablespoon fresh
4 tablespoons crackers,	thyme, chopped
crushed	Sea salt and ground
½ cup shallots, minced	black pepper, to taste
2 garlic cloves, minced	

1. Thoroughly combine all ingredients until everything is well combined. 2. Scrape the beef mixture into a lightly oiled Air Fry Basket. 3. Press BOTTOM and turn the dial until AIR FRY illuminates. Press the TIME/SLICES buttons to set the cook time to 25 minutes. Then press the TEMP button to set the cook temperature to 390°F. Press START/STOP to start preheating. 4. When bottom oven is preheated, immediately, place the wire rack in LEVEL 1 position of the bottom oven and place the sheet pan on top. Slide the Basket in LEVEL 2 position of bottom oven. Close door to begin cooking. 5. When cooking is up, serve.

Per Serving: Calories 355; Fat 21.74g; Sodium 721mg; Carbs 4.59g; Fiber 0.7g; Sugar 1.01g; Protein 35.46g

Spicy Garlic Skirt Steak

Prep Time: 5 minutes | Cook Time: 12 minutes | Serves: 4

1½ pounds skirt steak	pepper
Kosher salt and freshly	¼ teaspoon cumin
cracked black pepper, to	powder
taste	2 tablespoons olive oil
1 teaspoon cayenne	2 garlic cloves, minced

1. Toss the steak with the other ingredients and place the steak in the Air Fry Basket. 2. Press BOTTOM and turn the dial until AIR FRY illuminates. Press the TIME/SLICES buttons to set the cook time to 12 minutes. Then press the TEMP button to set the cook temperature to 400°F. Press START/STOP to start preheating. 3. When bottom oven is preheated, immediately, place the wire rack in LEVEL 1 position of the bottom oven and place the sheet pan on top. Slide the Basket in LEVEL 2

position of bottom oven. Close door to begin cooking. 4. Turn over halfway through the cooking time. 5. When cooking is up, serve. Bon appétit!

Per Serving: Calories 414; Fat 23.99g; Sodium 711mg; Carbs 1.17g; Fiber 0.3g; Sugar 0.07g; Protein 45.58g

Classic French Chateaubriand

Prep Time: 5 minutes | Cook Time: 14 minutes | Serves: 4

1 pound beef filet	3 tablespoons olive oil
mignon	1 tablespoon Dijon
Sea salt and ground	mustard
black pepper, to taste	4 tablespoons dry French
1 teaspoon cayenne	wine
pepper	

1. Toss the filet mignon with the rest of the ingredients and place the filet mignon in the Air Fry Basket. 2. Press BOTTOM and turn the dial until AIR FRY illuminates. Press the TIME/SLICES buttons to set the cook time to 14 minutes. Then press the TEMP button to set the cook temperature to 400°F. Press START/STOP to start preheating. 3. When bottom oven is preheated, immediately, place the wire rack in LEVEL 1 position of the bottom oven and place the sheet pan on top. Slide the Basket in LEVEL 2 position of bottom oven. Close door to begin cooking. 4. Turn over halfway through the cooking time. 5. When cooking is up, serve. Enjoy!

Per Serving: Calories 246; Fat 15.64g; Sodium 701mg; Carbs 1.05g; Fiber 0.4g; Sugar 0.25g; Protein 26.03g

Authentic Montreal Ribeye Steak

Prep Time: 5 minutes | Cook Time: 15 minutes | Serves: 4

1½ pounds ribeye steak, bone-in	mix
2 tablespoons butter	Sea salt and ground black pepper, to taste
1 Montreal seasoning	

1. Toss the ribeye steak with the remaining ingredients and place the ribeye steak in a lightly oiled Air Fry Basket. 2. Press BOTTOM and turn the dial until AIR FRY illuminates. Press the TIME/SLICES buttons to set the cook time to 15 minutes. Then press the TEMP button to set the cook temperature to 400°F. Press START/STOP to start preheating. 3. When bottom oven is preheated, immediately, place the wire rack in LEVEL 1 position of the bottom oven and place the sheet pan on top. Slide the Basket in LEVEL 2 position of bottom oven. Close door to begin cooking. 4. Turn over halfway through the cooking time. 5. When cooking is up, serve. Bon appétit!

Per Serving: Calories 373; Fat 25.17g; Sodium 829mg; Carbs 3.77g; Fiber 0.2g; Sugar 0.09g; Protein 33.25g

Italian Onion Rump Roast

Prep Time: 5 minutes | Cook Time: 55 minutes | Serves: 4

1½ pounds rump roast	seasoning mix
2 tablespoons olive oil	1 onion, sliced
Sea salt and ground black pepper, to taste	2 cloves garlic, peeled
1 teaspoon Italian	¼ cup red wine

1. Toss the rump roast with the rest of the ingredients and place the rump roast in a lightly oiled Air Fry Basket. 2. Press BOTTOM and turn the dial until AIR FRY illuminates. Press the TIME/SLICES buttons to set the cook time to 55 minutes. Then press the TEMP button to set the cook temperature to 390°F. Press START/STOP to start preheating. 3. When bottom oven is preheated, immediately, place the wire rack in LEVEL 1 position of the bottom oven and place the sheet pan on top. Slide the Basket in LEVEL 2 position of bottom oven. Close door to begin cooking. 4. Cook the rump roast and turn over halfway through the cooking time. 5. When cooking is up,

serve. Bon appétit!

Per Serving: Calories 265; Fat 13.06g; Sodium 2086mg; Carbs 2.62g; Fiber 0.3g; Sugar 0.69g; Protein 31.89g

Spicy Coconut Pork Curry

Prep Time: 15 minutes | Cook Time: 30 minutes | Serves: 4

2 cardamom pods, only the seeds, crushed	freshly grated
1 teaspoon fennel seeds	1-pound pork loin, cut into bite-sized cubes
1 teaspoon cumin seeds	1 cup coconut milk
1 teaspoon coriander seeds	1 cup chicken broth
2 teaspoons peanut oil	1 teaspoon turmeric powder
2 scallions, chopped	1 tablespoon tamarind paste
2 garlic cloves, smashed	1 tablespoon fresh lime juice
2 jalapeno peppers, minced	
½ teaspoon ginger,	

1. Heat cardamom, cumin seeds, fennel seeds and coriander seeds in a nonstick skillet over medium-high heat. Stir for 6 minutes, until the spices become fragrant and begin to brown. Stir frequently to prevent the spices from burning. Transfer to a bowl for later use. 2. Heat the peanut oil in the skillet for 2 minutes. Then add the scallions and sauté for 2 to 3 minutes until tender. 3. Stir in the peppers, garlic, and ginger. Cook for 1 minute more, stirring frequently. 4. Stir in the pork and cook for 3 to 4 minutes. Pour in the coconut milk and broth. Add the reserved seeds, turmeric, and tamarind paste. Transfer the mixture to the sheet pan. 5. Press BOTTOM and turn the dial until AIR FRY is illuminated. Press TEMP and set to 370°F, then press TIME and set to 15 minutes. Press START/STOP to begin preheating. 6. When preheating is complete, plate the sheet pan on the wire rack on LEVEL 2 position of the bottom oven. Close the door to begin cooking. 7. When cooking is complete, divide between individual bowls. Drizzle with the fresh lime juice and serve immediately.

Per Serving: Calories 307; Fat 15.93g; Sodium 324mg; Carbs 7.69g; Fiber 1.4g; Sugar 4.52g; Protein 32.22g

Spicy Ham and Kale Egg Cups

Prep Time: 5 minutes | Cook Time: 15 minutes | Serves: 4

2 eggs	¼ teaspoon dried or
¼ teaspoon dried or	fresh rosemary
fresh marjoram	4 pork ham slices
2 teaspoons chili powder	⅓ teaspoon ground black
⅓ teaspoon kosher salt	pepper, or more to taste
½ cup steamed kale	

1. Divide the kale and ham among 2 ramekins. Then crack an egg into each ramekin. Sprinkle with seasonings. 2. Press BOTTOM and turn the dial until AIR FRY illuminates. Press the TIME/SLICES buttons to set the cook time to 15 minutes. Then press the TEMP button to set the cook temperature to 335°F. Press START/STOP to start preheating. 3. Place the ramekins on the Air Fry Basket. When bottom oven is preheated, immediately slide the Basket in LEVEL 2 position. Close door to start cooking. 4. Cook until the eggs reach desired texture. 5. When cooking is up, serve warm with spicy tomato ketchup and pickles. Bon appétit!

Per Serving: Calories 579; Fat 17.29g; Sodium 3449mg; Carbs 3.91g; Fiber 0.6g; Sugar 2.94g; Protein 102.54g

Spicy Pork Gratin

Prep Time: 15 minutes | Cook Time: 22 minutes | Serves: 4

2 tablespoons olive oil	ground pepper
2 pounds pork tenderloin,	¼ teaspoon chili powder
cut into serving-size	1 teaspoon dried
pieces	marjoram
1 teaspoon coarse sea	1 tablespoon mustard
salt	1 cup Ricotta cheese
½ teaspoon freshly	1½ cups chicken broth

1. In a pan over medium-high heat, warm the oil and add the pork. Cook for 6 to 7 minutes, stirring frequently. 2. Lightly grease a casserole dish that fits the oven with cooking oil. Place the pork inside and season with salt, chili powder, black pepper, and marjoram. 3. Mix together the cheese, mustard, and chicken broth in a bowl and pour the mixture over the pork chops in the casserole dish. 4. Press BOTTOM and turn the

dial until CONVECTION BAKE is illuminated. Press TEMP and set to 350°F, then press TIME and set to 15 minutes. Press START/STOP to begin preheating. 5. When preheating is complete, place the casserole dish in LEVEL 1 position of the bottom oven. Close the door to begin cooking. When cooking is complete, serve warm.

Per Serving: Calories 511; Fat 23.48g; Sodium 1102mg; Carbs 2.85g; Fiber 0.4g; Sugar 0.31g; Protein 68.38g

Parmesan-Crusted Meatballs

Prep Time: 15 minutes | Cook Time: 7 minutes | Serves: 3

1-pound ground pork	2 tablespoons spring
1 tablespoon coconut	onions, finely chopped
aminos	½ cup pork rinds
1 teaspoon garlic,	½ cup parmesan cheese,
minced	preferably freshly grated

1. In a medium bowl, mix together the ground pork, garlic, coconut aminos, and spring onions until everything is well combined. 2. Form the mixture into small meatballs. 3. Combine the pork rinds and grated parmesan cheese in a shallow bowl. Dredge the meatballs in the parmesan mixture and place in the Air Fry Basket. 4. Press BOTTOM and turn the dial until AIR FRY is illuminated. Press TEMP and set to 380°F, then press TIME and set to 3 minutes. Press START/STOP to begin preheating. 5. When preheating is complete, insert the Air Fry Basket in LEVEL 2 position of the bottom oven. Close the door to begin cooking. 6. When cooking time is up, shake the basket and cook for 4 minutes longer or until meatballs are browned on all sides. Enjoy!

Per Serving: Calories 572; Fat 43.39g; Sodium 413mg; Carbs 3.11g; Fiber 0.2g; Sugar 0.24g; Protein 39.9g

Herbed Garlic Pork Tenderloin

Prep Time: 15 minutes | Cook Time: 16 minutes | Serves: 4

1-pound pork tenderloin	oregano
4-5 garlic cloves, peeled and halved	½ teaspoon dried rosemary
1 teaspoon kosher salt	½ teaspoon dried marjoram
⅓ teaspoon ground black pepper	2 tablespoons cooking wine
1 teaspoon dried basil	
½ teaspoon dried	

1. Place the pork in a bowl and rub with garlic halves. Then sprinkle with the seasoning and drizzle with the cooking wine. Make a slit completely through the pork tenderloin. Stuff the remaining garlic into the slit. 2. Wrap pork tenderloin with foil and refrigerate to marinate overnight. 3. Then place the marinated pork tenderloin in the Air Fry Basket. 4. Press BOTTOM and turn the dial until AIR FRY is illuminated. Press TEMP and set to 360°F, then press TIME and set to 16 minutes. Press START/STOP to begin preheating. 5. When preheating is complete, insert the Air Fry Basket in LEVEL 2 position of the bottom oven. Close the door to begin cooking. When cooking is complete, serve immediately.

Per Serving: Calories 170; Fat 4.03g; Sodium 648mg; Carbs 1.78g; Fiber 0.3g; Sugar 0.31g; Protein 30.07g

Aromatic Beef with Cotija Cheese

Prep Time: 15 minutes | Cook Time: 21 minutes | Serves: 3

2 ounces Cotija cheese, cut into sticks	stock
2 teaspoons paprika	2 tablespoons olive oil
2 teaspoons dried thyme	3 cloves garlic, minced
½ cup shallots, peeled and chopped	1½ cups tomato puree, no sugar added
3 beef tenderloins, cut in half lengthwise	1 teaspoon ground black pepper, or more to taste
2 teaspoons dried basil	1 teaspoon fine sea salt, or more to taste
⅓ cup homemade bone	

1. Season the beef tenderloin with salt, black pepper and

paprika and place a piece of cotija cheese in the middle of each piece of beef. 2. Tie each tenderloin with kitchen string and drizzle with olive oil; set aside. 3. Combine the shallots, garlic, bone broth and tomato paste in an oven-safe bowl. Place the bowl in LEVEL 1 position of the bottom oven. Close the oven door. 4. Press BOTTOM and turn the dial until AIR FRY is illuminated. Press TEMP and set to 375°F, then press TIME and set to 7 minutes. Press START/STOP to begin cooking. 5. When cooking time is up, add the reserved beef along with basil and thyme to the bowl. Cook for 14 minutes more. Serve warm.

Per Serving: Calories 453; Fat 24.01g; Sodium 1240mg; Carbs 17.92g; Fiber 3.8g; Sugar 8.68g; Protein 42.31g

Rosemary Beef Sausage &Vegetable Medley

Prep Time: 15 minutes | Cook Time: 32 minutes | Serves: 4

1-pound beef sausage	wedges
2 red bell peppers, cut lengthwise	2 garlic cloves, minced
1 poblano pepper, minced	½ pound broccoli, cut into chunks
1 sprig rosemary, chopped	½ celery stalk, sliced
2 shallots, cut into	½ teaspoon caraway seeds
	1 teaspoon salt

1. Combine all the ingredients in the Air Fry Basket. Stir until well combined. 2. Press BOTTOM and turn the dial until AIR FRY is illuminated. Press TEMP and set to 385°F, then press TIME and set to 32 minutes. Press START/STOP to begin preheating. 3. When preheating is complete, insert the Air Fry Basket in LEVEL 2 position of the bottom oven. Close the door to begin cooking. Flip halfway through the cooking time. 4. When cooking is complete, serve immediately.

Per Serving: Calories 325; Fat 21.07g; Sodium 1613mg; Carbs 17.45g; Fiber 5.6g; Sugar 2.42g; Protein 23.76g

Roasted Beef with Garlic-Mayo Sauce

Prep Time: 15 minutes | Cook Time: 18 minutes | Serves: 4

1½ pounds beef, cubed	1 teaspoon sweet paprika
½ cup white wine	2 tablespoons extra-virgin olive oil
2 teaspoons dried rosemary	2 teaspoons dried basil
1½ tablespoons herb vinegar	Salt and ground black pepper, to taste
Sauce:	
1 tablespoon mayonnaise	3 cloves garlic, minced
½ cup full fat sour cream	

1. Mix together the beef, oil and wine in a large bowl. Stir in the seasonings and herb vinegar. Cover and allow them to marinate for at least 50 minutes. 2. Then place the marinated beef in the sheet pan. 3. Press BOTTOM and turn the dial until AIR ROAST is illuminated. Press TEMP and set to 375°F, then press TIME and set to 18 minutes. Press START/STOP to begin preheating. 4. When preheating is complete, place the sheet pan on the wire rack on Level 1 in the bottom oven. Close the door to begin cooking. Flip halfway through the cooking time. 5. Meanwhile, prepare the sauce by mixing the sour cream, mayonnaise and garlic in a small bowl. Serve the warm beef with the garlic sauce and enjoy!

Per Serving: Calories 300; Fat 14.05g; Sodium 280mg; Carbs 7.33g; Fiber 0.6g; Sugar 1.15g; Protein 36.73g

Herbed Beef Medallions with Bell Peppers

Prep Time: 15 minutes | Cook Time: 26 minutes | Serves: 4

2 tablespoons olive oil	2 sprigs thyme
2 small bunch parsley, roughly chopped	1 sprig rosemary
1½ pounds beef medallions	Umami dust seasoning, to taste
3 bell peppers, seeded and sliced	Salt and ground black pepper, to taste

1. Place the vegetables in the bottom of the Air Fry Basket. Sprinkle with the seasonings and drizzle with the olive oil. 2. Press BOTTOM and turn the dial until AIR FRY is illuminated.

Press TEMP and set to 375°F, then press TIME and set to 8 minutes. Press START/STOP to begin preheating. 3. When preheating is complete, insert the Air Fry Basket in LEVEL 2 position of the bottom oven. Close the door to begin cooking. 4. When cooking time is up, place the beef medallions on top of the vegetables. Cook for an additional 18 minutes, stirring once halfway through. Sprinkle with umami dust seasoning and enjoy!

Per Serving: Calories 336; Fat 17.91g; Sodium 137mg; Carbs 6.42g; Fiber 1.8g; Sugar 2.57g; Protein 36.72g

Tuscan Beef Chops

Prep Time: 10 minutes | Cook Time: 16 minutes | Serves: 3

3 sprigs fresh thyme, chopped	3 beef chops
⅓ cup herb vinegar	2 teaspoons garlic powder
2 teaspoons Tuscan seasoning	Kosher salt and ground black pepper, to taste

1. Place the beef chops in the sheet pan and toss with the other ingredients. 2. Press BOTTOM and turn the dial until AIR ROAST is illuminated. Press TEMP and set to 395°F, then press TIME and set to 16 minutes. Press START/STOP to begin preheating. 3. When preheating is complete, place the sheet pan on the wire rack on Level 1 in the bottom oven. Close the door to begin cooking. Flip halfway through the cooking time. 4. Season to taste with the seasonings to your liking and serve warm. Bon appétit!

Per Serving: Calories 198; Fat 15.18g; Sodium 179mg; Carbs 4.46g; Fiber 0.8g; Sugar 1.13g; Protein 10.01g

Flavorful Beef Brisket

Prep Time: 15 minutes | Cook Time: 1 hour and 10 minutes | Serves: 4

1½ pounds beef brisket	black pepper, to taste
2 tablespoons olive oil	1 teaspoon dried parsley
1 teaspoon onion powder	flakes
1 teaspoon garlic powder	1 teaspoon dried thyme
Sea salt and ground	

1. Place the beef in a bowl and toss with the remaining ingredients. Then place the beef in the Air Fry Basket. 2. Press BOTTOM and turn the dial until AIR FRY is illuminated. Press TEMP and set to 390°F, then press TIME and set to 15 minutes. Press START/STOP to begin preheating. 3. When preheating is complete, insert the Air Fry Basket in LEVEL 2 position of the bottom oven. Close the door to begin cooking. When cooking time is up, flip the beef over and lower the temperature to 360°F. Cook for an additional 55 minutes. Enjoy!

Per Serving: Calories 406; Fat 32.14g; Sodium 1872mg; Carbs 2.41g; Fiber 0.4g; Sugar 0.64g; Protein 25.41g

Delicious Pulled Beef

Prep Time: 15 minutes | Cook Time: 1 hour and 10 minutes | Serves: 4

1½ pounds beef brisket	flakes, crushed
2 tablespoons olive oil	2 tablespoons tomato
3 garlic cloves, pressed	ketchup
Sea salt and ground	2 tablespoons Dijon
black pepper, to taste	mustard
1 teaspoon red pepper	

1. Place the beef brisket in a bowl and toss with the garlic, olive oil, black pepper, salt, and red pepper. 2. Then place the beef brisket in the Air Fry Basket. 3. Press BOTTOM and turn the dial until AIR FRY is illuminated. Press TEMP and set to 390°F, then press TIME and set to 15 minutes. Press START/STOP to begin preheating. 4. When preheating is complete, insert the Air Fry Basket in LEVEL 2 position of the bottom oven. Close the door to begin cooking. When cooking time is up, turn the beef over and lower the temperature to 360°F.

Cook for 55 minutes longer. 5. Transfer the beef to a serving plate and shred with two forks. Stir in the ketchup and mustard. Enjoy!

Per Serving: Calories 414; Fat 32.44g; Sodium 2161mg; Carbs 3.49g; Fiber 0.8g; Sugar 1.34g; Protein 25.88g

Spicy Herbed Top Round Roast

Prep Time: 15 minutes | Cook Time: 55 minutes | Serves: 5

2 pounds top round roast	parsley, chopped
2 tablespoons extra-	1 teaspoon red chili
virgin olive oil	powder
2 cloves garlic, pressed	Kosher salt and freshly
1 tablespoon fresh	ground black pepper, to
rosemary, chopped	taste
1 tablespoon fresh	

1. Place the beef in a bowl and toss with the remaining ingredients. 2. Then place the beef in the Air Fry Basket. 3. Press BOTTOM and turn the dial until AIR FRY is illuminated. Press TEMP and set to 390°F, then press TIME and set to 55 minutes. Press START/STOP to begin preheating. 4. When preheating is complete, insert the Air Fry Basket in LEVEL 2 position of the bottom oven. Close the door to begin cooking. 5. Flip halfway through the cooking time. Serve warm.

Per Serving: Calories 236; Fat 6.95g; Sodium 280mg; Carbs 0.78g; Fiber 0.3g; Sugar 0.06g; Protein 43.01g

Spicy Beef Burgers

Prep Time: 15 minutes | Cook Time: 15 minutes | Serves: 3

¾ pound ground beef	pepper
2 tablespoons onion, minced	Sea salt and ground black pepper, to taste
1 teaspoon garlic, minced	1 teaspoon red chili powder
1 teaspoon cayenne	3 hamburger buns

1. In a medium bowl, mix together the beef, garlic, onion, black pepper, cayenne pepper, salt, and red chili powder until well combined. Form the mixture into three equal patties and place in the Air Fry Basket. 2. Press BOTTOM and turn the dial until AIR FRY is illuminated. Press TEMP and set to 380°F, then press TIME and set to 15 minutes. Press START/ STOP to begin preheating. 3. When preheating is complete, insert the Air Fry Basket in LEVEL 2 position of the bottom oven. Close the door to begin cooking. Flip halfway through the cooking time. 4. When cooking is complete, serve the burgers on the prepared buns!

Per Serving: Calories 596; Fat 35.91g; Sodium 302mg; Carbs 34.73g; Fiber 1.6g; Sugar 17.89g; Protein 32.15g

Lemony London Broil

Prep Time: 15 minutes | Cook Time: 28 minutes | Serves: 4

1 pound London broil	3 cloves garlic, minced
Kosher salt and ground black pepper, to taste	1 tablespoon fresh parsley, chopped
2 tablespoons olive oil	1 tablespoon fresh coriander, chopped
1 small lemon, freshly squeezed	

1. Place the beef in a bowl and toss with the remaining ingredients. Allow it to marinate for an hour. 2. Then discard the marinade and lightly grease the Air Fry Basket with oil. Place the beef inside. 3. Press BOTTOM and turn the dial until AIR FRY is illuminated. Press TEMP and set to 400°F, then press TIME and set to 28 minutes. Press START/STOP to begin preheating. 4. When preheating is complete, insert the Air Fry Basket in LEVEL 2 position of the bottom oven. Close

the door to begin cooking. Flip halfway through the cooking time. 5. When cooking is complete, serve immediately.

Per Serving: Calories 302; Fat 17.03g; Sodium 49mg; Carbs 2.71g; Fiber 0.3g; Sugar 0.91g; Protein 35.22g

Savory Meatloaf

Prep Time: 15 minutes | Cook Time: 25 minutes | Serves: 4

1½ pounds ground chuck	1 tablespoon fresh rosemary, chopped
1 egg, beaten	1 tablespoon fresh thyme, chopped
2 tablespoons olive oil	Sea salt and ground black pepper, to taste
4 tablespoons crackers, crushed	
½ cup shallots, minced	
2 garlic cloves, minced	

1. Place all ingredients in a bowl and mix until everything is well combined. 2. Lightly grease the Air Fry Basket with oil and place the beef mixture inside. 3. Press BOTTOM and turn the dial until AIR FRY is illuminated. Press TEMP and set to 390°F, then press TIME and set to 25 minutes. Press START/STOP to begin preheating. 4. When preheating is complete, insert the Air Fry Basket in LEVEL 2 position of the bottom oven. Close the door to begin cooking. Flip halfway through the cooking time. 5. When cooking is complete, serve immediately.

Per Serving: Calories 429; Fat 26.48g; Sodium 211mg; Carbs 5.65g; Fiber 0.7g; Sugar 1.76g; Protein 41.87g

Chapter 5 Fish and Seafood Recipes

Pine Nuts & Veggie Stuffed Flounder

Prep Time: 20 minutes | Cook Time: 16 minutes | Serves: 4

¼ cup pine nuts	2 tablespoons unsalted
2 tablespoons olive oil	butter, divided
½ cup chopped tomatoes	4 flounder filets (about
1 (6-ounce) bag spinach,	1½ pounds)
coarsely chopped	Dash of paprika
2 cloves garlic, chopped	½ lemon, sliced into 4
Salt and freshly ground	wedges
black pepper	

1. Place the pine nuts in the sheet pan. 2. Mix together the oil, spinach, tomatoes, and garlic in a bowl and transfer to the Air Fry Basket. 3. Press BOTTOM and turn the dial until AIR FRY is illuminated. Press TEMP and set to 400°F, then press TIME and set to 5 minutes. 4. Press TOP and turn the dial until BAKE is illuminated. Press TEMP/SHADE and set to 400°F, then press TIME/SLICES and set to 4 minutes. Press SMART FINISH. Press START/STOP to begin preheating. 5. When preheating is complete, place the sheet pan with pine nuts on the wire rack of the top oven. 6. Then insert the Air Fry Basket in LEVEL 2 position of the bottom oven. Close the door to begin cooking. 7. Once done, remove the sheet pan from the oven, transfer the nuts onto a plate and let them cool completely. Then chop them into fine pieces. 8. Transfer the vegetables to a bowl and stir in the toasted pine nuts. Season to taste with salt and f black pepper. 9. Coat the bottom of the sheet pan with 1 tablespoon of the butter. 10. Place the flounder on a clean work surface. Sprinkle both sides with salt and black pepper. Divide the vegetable mixture evenly among the halibut fillets, roll them up carefully, and secure with toothpicks. 11. Place the fillets, seam side down, in the sheet pan with 1 tablespoon water. Spread remaining 1 tablespoon butter on the fillets and sprinkle with a little paprika. Cover loosely with foil. 12. Press BOTTOM and turn the dial until AIR FRY is illuminated. Press TEMP and set to 350°F, then press TIME and set to 12 minutes. Press START/STOP to begin preheating. 13. When preheating is complete, place the sheet pan on the wire rack in LEVEL 2 position of the bottom oven. Close the door to begin cooking. When cooking is complete, remove the toothpicks before serving with the lemon wedges.

Per Serving: Calories 266; Fat 19.29g; Sodium 701mg; Carbs 12.19g; Fiber 2.3g; Sugar 4.99g; Protein 13.08g

Potato-Fish Cakes

Prep Time: 15 minutes | Cook Time: 18 minutes | Serves: 4

¾ cup mashed potatoes	1 large egg
(about 1 large russet	¼ cup potato starch
potato), peeled	½ cup panko
12 ounces cod or other	breadcrumbs
white fish	1 tablespoon fresh
Salt and pepper	chopped chives
Oil for misting or	2 tablespoons minced
cooking spray	onion

1. Season the raw fish with salt and pepper. Spray with cooking oil and place in the Air Fry Basket. 2. Press BOTTOM and turn the dial until AIR FRY is illuminated. Press TEMP and set to 360°F, then press TIME and set to 7 minutes. Press START/STOP to begin preheating. 3. When preheating is complete, insert the Air Fry Basket in LEVEL 2 position of the bottom oven. Close the door to begin cooking. 4. Once cooked, transfer the fish to a plate and break apart to cool. 5. When the fish is cooking, cut the potatoes into cubes and cook on stovetop till soft. Then drain in colander and rinse with cold water. 6. In a shallow bowl, whisk in the egg. 7. Place potato starch in a second shallow bowl, and panko crumbs in a third bowl. 8. Mash the potatoes in a large bowl and stir in the chives and onion. Season with salt and pepper, then stir in the fish. You can add a tablespoon of the beaten egg to help bind the mixture if needed. 9. Shape the mixture into 8 small patties. Dust lightly with potato starch, then dip in egg, and finally roll in the panko crumbs. Spray both sides with cooking oil and arrange them in the Air Fry Basket in a single layer. 10. Press BOTTOM and turn the dial until AIR FRY is illuminated. Press TEMP and set to 360°F, then press TIME and set to 11 minutes. Press START/STOP to begin preheating. 11. When preheating is complete, insert the Air Fry Basket in LEVEL 2 position of the bottom oven. Close the door to begin cooking. Cook until golden brown and crispy. Serve warm.

Per Serving: Calories 205; Fat 9.51g; Sodium 131mg; Carbs 11.11g; Fiber 1.3g; Sugar 1.66g; Protein 17.89g

Sesame Seeds-Crusted Salmon

Prep Time: 15 minutes | Cook Time: 10 minutes | Serves: 4

¼ cup mixed black and brown sesame seeds	4 (6-ounce) salmon filets, skin removed
1 tablespoon reduced-sodium soy sauce	2 tablespoons chopped fresh marjoram, for garnish (optional)
1 teaspoon sesame oil	
1 teaspoon honey	

1. Place the sesame seeds in a small shallow bowl. 2. Mix up the sesame oil, soy sauce, and honey in a second small bowl. 3. Brush the soy sauce mixture all over the salmon with the until thoroughly coated. Press each fillet into the sesame seeds Until well coated. 4. Place the fish in a single layer in the Air Fry Basket, seed-side up. 5. Press BOTTOM and turn the dial until AIR FRY is illuminated. Press TEMP and set to 360°F, then press TIME and set to 10 minutes. Press START/STOP to begin preheating. 6. When preheating is complete, insert the Air Fry Basket in LEVEL 2 position of the bottom oven. Close the door to begin cooking. Top with the marjoram if desired before serving.

Per Serving: Calories 304; Fat 15.13g; Sodium 193mg; Carbs 4.07g; Fiber 1.5g; Sugar 2.31g; Protein 37.18g

Salmon Cucumber Salad

Prep Time: 15 minutes | Cook Time: 9 minutes | Serves: 2

1-pound salmon filet	thinly sliced
1½ tablespoons olive oil, divided	¼ Vidalia onion, thinly sliced
1 tablespoon sherry vinegar	2 tablespoons chopped fresh parsley
1 tablespoon capers, rinsed and drained	Salt and freshly ground black pepper
1 seedless cucumber,	

1. Brush the salmon with ½ tablespoon of the olive oil and place in the Air Fry Basket, skin-side down. 2. Press BOTTOM and turn the dial until AIR FRY is illuminated. Press TEMP and set to 400°F, then press TIME and set to 9 minutes. Press START/STOP to begin preheating. 3. When preheating is complete, insert the Air Fry Basket in LEVEL 2 position of the bottom oven. Close the door to begin cooking. 4. When cooking is complete, transfer the salmon to a plate and let it cool to room temperature. Remove the skin and flake the fish into bite-size chunks. 5. Whisk together the remaining olive oil and the vinegar in a small bowl. Stir in the flaked fish, cucumber, onion, capers, and parsley. Season with salt and black pepper. Serve immediately or cover and refrigerate for up to 4 hours.

Per Serving: Calories 454; Fat 26.52g; Sodium 1380mg; Carbs 3.72g; Fiber 0.7g; Sugar 2.21g; Protein 47.36g

Air Fried Tuna Steaks with Olive Tapenade

Prep Time: 15 minutes | Cook Time: 10 minutes | Serves: 4

4 (6-ounce) ahi tuna steaks	black pepper
1 tablespoon olive oil	½ lemon, sliced into 4 wedges
Salt and freshly ground	
Olive Tapenade:	
½ cup pitted kalamata olives	1 clove garlic
1 tablespoon olive oil	2 teaspoons red wine vinegar
1 tablespoon chopped fresh parsley	1 teaspoon capers, drained

1. Place the tuna steaks in a bowl and drizzle with olive oil and sprinkle with salt and black pepper. 2. Place the tuna steaks in a single layer in the Air Fry Basket. 3. Press BOTTOM and turn the dial until AIR FRY is illuminated. Press TEMP and set to 400°F, then press TIME and set to 10 minutes. Press START/STOP to begin preheating. 4. When preheating is complete, insert the Air Fry Basket in LEVEL 2 position of the bottom oven. Close the door to begin cooking. Flip halfway through the cooking time. 5. Meanwhile, prepare the tapenade. Pulse the olives, parsley, garlic, olive oil, vinegar, and capers in a food processor until the mixture is finely chopped. 6. Spoon the dressing over the tuna steaks and serve with lemon wedges.

Per Serving: Calories 269; Fat 9.53g; Sodium 407mg; Carbs 1.91g; Fiber 0.7g; Sugar 0.18g; Protein 41.8g

Crispy Fish Sticks

Prep Time: 15 minutes | Cook Time: 7 minutes | Serves: 8

8 ounces fish fillets (pollock or cod)	½ cup plain breadcrumbs
Salt (optional)	Oil for misting or cooking spray

1. Cut the fish fillets into "fingers" about ½ x 3 inches. Season with salt to taste. 2. Roll the fish in the breadcrumbs until well coated. Spray all sides with cooking oil and place in the Air Fry Basket. 3. Press BOTTOM and turn the dial until AIR FRY is illuminated. Press TEMP and set to 390°F, then press TIME and set to 7 minutes. Press START/STOP to begin preheating. 4. When preheating is complete, insert the Air Fry Basket in LEVEL 2 position of the bottom oven. Close the door to begin cooking. Cook until golden brown and crispy. Serve warm.

Per Serving: Calories 73; Fat 3.07g; Sodium 141mg; Carbs 4.87g; Fiber 0.3g; Sugar 0.42g; Protein 6.14g

Maple-Glazed Salmon

Prep Time: 15 minutes | Cook Time: 22 minutes | Serves: 4

½ cup maple syrup substitute, such as ChocZero sugar-free maple syrup	squeezed lemon juice
1 tablespoon grated fresh ginger	1 teaspoon minced garlic
	Sea salt
2 tablespoons coconut aminos	Freshly ground black pepper
2 tablespoons freshly	1 pound (1½-inch-thick) salmon fillets
	Avocado oil spray

1. In a small heatproof dish that fits the oven, mix together the maple syrup substitute, ginger, lemon juice, coconut aminos, and garlic. Season with salt and black pepper. 2. Place the dish in the Air Fry Basket. 3. Press BOTTOM and turn the dial until AIR FRY is illuminated. Press TEMP and set to 300°F, then press TIME and set to 15 minutes. Press START/STOP to begin preheating. 4. When preheating is complete, insert the Air Fry Basket in LEVEL 2 position of the bottom oven. Close the door to begin cooking, stirring every 5 minutes. 5. When cooking is complete, divide the glaze between 2 bowls and let cool slightly. Brush the salmon with the glaze from one bowl, and spray both sides of the fillets with oil. Place the fillets in a single layer in the air fry basket, skin-side up. Insert the basket in LEVEL 2 position of the bottom oven. Air fry at 400°F for 7 minutes. Flip and cook for 1 more minute. 6. Let rest for 5 minutes, then serve with the reserved sauce from the second bowl.

Per Serving: Calories 202; Fat 9.34g; Sodium 645mg; Carbs 4.81g; Fiber 0.4g; Sugar 3.34g; Protein 23.7g

Spicy Tuna Patties

Prep Time: 15 minutes | Cook Time: 10 minutes | Serves: 4

2 (6-ounce) cans tuna packed in oil, drained	mayonnaise
	1 teaspoon dried dill
3 tablespoons almond flour	½ teaspoon onion powder
2 tablespoons	Pinch of salt and pepper
Spicy Sriracha Sauce:	
¼ cup mayonnaise	sauce
1 tablespoon sriracha	1 teaspoon garlic powder

1. Line the Air Fry Basket with parchment paper. 2. Mix together the tuna, almond flour, dill, mayonnaise, and onion powder in a large bowl. Season with salt and black pepper. 3. Form the tuna mixture into patties and place the patties in a single layer on the parchment paper in the basket. 4. Using the bottom of a spoon, gently press the patty into a circle about ½-inch thick. 5. Press BOTTOM and turn the dial until AIR FRY is illuminated. Press TEMP and set to 380°F, then press TIME and set to 10 minutes. Press START/STOP to begin preheating. 6. When preheating is complete, insert the Air Fry Basket in LEVEL 2 position of the bottom oven. Close the door to begin cooking. Flip halfway through the cooking time. 7. Meanwhile, prepare the sriracha sauce: Mix together the sriracha, mayonnaise, and garlic powder in a small bowl. Serve the tuna patties topped with the sriracha sauce.

Per Serving: Calories 247; Fat 14.6g; Sodium 587mg; Carbs 3.39g; Fiber 0.9g; Sugar 1.25g; Protein 24.57g

Spicy Fish Sticks

Prep Time: 15 minutes | Cook Time: 8 minutes | Serves: 4

1-pound fish fillets	¾ cup panko
½ teaspoon hot sauce	breadcrumbs
1 tablespoon coarse	¼ cup stone-ground
brown mustard	cornmeal
1 teaspoon	¼ teaspoon salt
Worcestershire sauce	Oil for misting or
Salt	cooking spray
Crumb Coating:	

1. Cut the fish fillets crosswise into slices 1-inch wide. 2. In a small bowl, mix together the mustard, hot sauce, and Worcestershire sauce and rub on all sides of the fish. Season with salt. 3. In another bowl, mix together the crumb coating ingredients. 4. Roll the fish fillets in the crumb mixture. 5. Spray all sides of the fillets with olive oil and place in the Air Fry Basket in a single layer. 6. Press BOTTOM and turn the dial until AIR FRY is illuminated. Press TEMP and set to 390°F, then press TIME and set to 8 minutes. Press START/ STOP to begin preheating. 7. When preheating is complete, insert the Air Fry Basket in LEVEL 2 position of the bottom oven. Close the door to begin cooking. When cooking is complete, serve immediately.

Per Serving: Calories 298; Fat 18.41g; Sodium 538mg; Carbs 8.64g; Fiber 1.8g; Sugar 0.67g; Protein 24.52g

Crunchy Flounder Fillets

Prep Time: 15 minutes | Cook Time: 6 minutes | Serves: 4

1 egg white	4 (4-ounce) flounder
1 tablespoon water	fillets
1 cup panko	Salt and pepper
breadcrumbs	Oil for misting or
2 tablespoons extra-light	cooking spray
virgin olive oil	

1. In a shallow bowl, whisk the egg white and water together. 2. In separate shallow bowl, mix together the panko crumbs and oil until crumbly. 3. Season the flounder fillets with salt and pepper. Dip each fillet into egg mixture and then dredge in

the panko crumbs, pressing in crumbs until the fillets are well coated. 4. Grease the Air Fry Basket with nonstick cooking spray and place the fillets inside. 5. Press BOTTOM and turn the dial until AIR FRY is illuminated. Press TEMP and set to 390°F, then press TIME and set to 3 minutes. Press START/ STOP to begin preheating. 6. When preheating is complete, insert the Air Fry Basket in LEVEL 2 position of the bottom oven. Close the door to begin cooking. 7. When cooking time is up, spray the fish fillets with more cooking oil and cook for 2 to 5 minutes more or until golden brown and crispy. Serve warm.

Per Serving: Calories 199; Fat 9.99g; Sodium 858mg; Carbs 6.75g; Fiber 0.5g; Sugar 1.5g; Protein 19.76g

Herbed Fish Fingers

Prep Time: 15 minutes | Cook Time: 9 minutes | Serves: 4

1-pound tilapia fillet	paprika
½ cup coconut flour	1 teaspoon dried oregano
2 eggs, beaten	1 teaspoon avocado oil
½ teaspoon ground	

1. Cut the tilapia fillets into fingers. Sprinkle them with the paprika and dried oregano. 2. Whisk the eggs in a shallow bowl and place the coconut flour in another bowl. 3. Dip the tilapia fingers in the eggs and then roll in the coconut flour. 4. Sprinkle fish fingers with avocado oil and arrange them in the Air Fry basket. 5. Press BOTTOM and turn the dial until AIR FRY is illuminated. Press TEMP and set to 370°F, then press TIME and set to 9 minutes. Press START/STOP to begin preheating. 6. When preheating is complete, insert the Air Fry Basket in LEVEL 2 position of the bottom oven. Close the door to begin cooking. Shake the basket halfway through the cooking process. Serve warm.

Per Serving: Calories 191; Fat 7.98g; Sodium 142mg; Carbs 1.95g; Fiber 0.5g; Sugar 1.15g; Protein 27.54g

Hearty Fish Tacos

Prep Time: 15 minutes | Cook Time: 10 minutes | Serves: 4

Fish Tacos:

1-pound fish fillets	¼ teaspoon smoked
¼ teaspoon cumin	paprika
¼ teaspoon coriander	1 teaspoon oil
⅛ teaspoon ground red	Cooking spray
pepper	6–8 corn or flour tortillas
1 tablespoon lime zest	(6-inch size)

Jalapeño-Lime Sauce:

½ cup sour cream	½ teaspoon minced
1 tablespoon lime juice	jalapeño (flesh only)
¼ teaspoon grated lime	¼ teaspoon cumin
zest	

Napa Cabbage Garnish:

1 cup shredded Napa	green bell pepper
cabbage	¼ cup slivered onion
¼ cup slivered red or	

1. Slice the fish fillets into ½-inch thick strips. 2. Place the strips, cumin, red pepper, smoked paprika, lime zest, coriander, and oil in a sealable plastic bag. Massage the seasonings into the fish until evenly distributed. 3. Lightly grease the Air Fry Basket with nonstick cooking spray and place the seasoned fish inside. 4. Press BOTTOM and turn the dial until AIR FRY is illuminated. Press TEMP and set to 390°F, then press TIME and set to 5 minutes. Press START/STOP to begin preheating. 5. When preheating is complete, insert the Air Fry Basket in LEVEL 2 position of the bottom oven. Close the door to begin cooking. When cooking time is up, flip them and cook for 2 to 5 minutes longer, until fish flakes easily. 6. Meanwhile, mix together the sour cream, jalapeño, lime juice, lime zest, and cumin in a small bowl to make a smooth sauce. Set aside. 7. In a medium bowl, combine the cabbage, onion and bell pepper, set aside. 8. To serve, spoon some of fish into a warm tortilla. Add one or two tablespoons Napa Cabbage Garnish and drizzle with Jalapeño-Lime Sauce. Enjoy!

Per Serving: Calories 328; Fat 16.09g; Sodium 119mg; Carbs 21.66g; Fiber 2.6g; Sugar 1.24g; Protein 24.64g

Juicy Lime Lobster Tails

Prep Time: 10 minutes | Cook Time: 6 minutes | Serves: 4

4 lobster tails, peeled	½ teaspoon coconut oil,
2 tablespoons lime juice	melted
½ teaspoon dried basil	

1. Place the lobster tails in a bowl and toss with lime juice, dried basil, and coconut oil. 2. Place the lobster tails in the Air Fry Basket. Press BOTTOM and turn the dial until AIR FRY is illuminated. Press TEMP and set to 380°F, then press TIME and set to 6 minutes. Press START/STOP to begin preheating. 3. When preheating is complete, insert the Air Fry Basket in LEVEL 2 position of the bottom oven. Close the door to begin cooking. When cooking is complete, serve immediately.

Per Serving: Calories 123; Fat 1.71g; Sodium 635mg; Carbs 0.69g; Fiber 0.1g; Sugar 0.13g; Protein 24.83g

Cream Shrimp and Swiss Chard Bowl

Prep Time: 10 minutes | Cook Time: 10 minutes | Serves: 4

1-pound shrimp, peeled	chopped
and deveined	2 tablespoons apple cider
½ teaspoon smoked	vinegar
paprika	1 tablespoon coconut oil
½ cup Swiss chard,	¼ cup heavy cream

1. Place the shrimps in a bowl and toss with smoked paprika and apple cider vinegar. 2. Put the shrimps in the in the Air Fry Basket and brush with coconut oil. 3. Press BOTTOM and turn the dial until AIR FRY is illuminated. Press TEMP and set to 350°F, then press TIME and set to 10 minutes. Press START/STOP to begin preheating. 4. When preheating is complete, insert the Air Fry Basket in LEVEL 2 position of the bottom oven. Close the door to begin cooking. 5. When cooking is complete, mix the cooked shrimps with remaining ingredients and enjoy.

Per Serving: Calories 155; Fat 6.8g; Sodium 148mg; Carbs 0.61g; Fiber 0.2g; Sugar 0.32g; Protein 23.07g

Simple Rosemary Scallops

Prep Time: 10 minutes | Cook Time: 6 minutes | Serves: 4

12 oz. scallops	½ teaspoon pink salt
1 tablespoon dried rosemary	1 tablespoon avocado oil

1. Place the scallops in a bowl and sprinkle with pink salt, dried rosemary, and avocado oil. 2. Then place the scallops in the Air Fry Basket in one layer. 3. Press BOTTOM and turn the dial until AIR FRY is illuminated. Press TEMP and set to 400°F, then press TIME and set to 6 minutes. Press START/STOP to begin preheating. 4. When preheating is complete, insert the Air Fry Basket in LEVEL 2 position of the bottom oven. Close the door to begin cooking. When cooking is complete, serve immediately.

Per Serving: Calories 90; Fat 3.94g; Sodium 624mg; Carbs 2.79g; Fiber 0.1g; Sugar 0g; Protein 10.27g

Cheese Tuna Burgers

Prep Time: 10 minutes | Cook Time: 8 minutes | Serves: 4

2 cans canned tuna fish	mustard
2 celery stalks, trimmed and finely chopped	½ teaspoon sea salt
1 egg, whisked	¼ teaspoon freshly cracked black
½ cup parmesan cheese, grated	peppercorns
1 teaspoon whole-grain	1 teaspoon paprika

1. In a large bowl, mix together all of the ingredients and shape into four cakes; refrigerate for 50 minutes. 2. Then place the cakes in the Air Fry Basket and spray with non-stick cooking spray on all sides. 3. Press BOTTOM and turn the dial until AIR FRY is illuminated. Press TEMP and set to 360°F, then press TIME and set to 5 minutes. Press START/STOP to begin preheating. 4. When preheating is complete, insert the Air Fry Basket in LEVEL 2 position of the bottom oven. Close the door to begin cooking. 5. When cooking time is up, flip them and cook for an additional 3 minutes. Serve warm.

Per Serving: Calories 161; Fat 6.79g; Sodium 753mg; Carbs 3.06g; Fiber 0.4g; Sugar 0.36g; Protein 22.03g

Fried Shrimp with Mayo-Chipotle Sauce

Prep Time: 10 minutes | Cook Time: 7 minutes | Serves: 4

12 jumbo shrimp	cracked mixed peppercorns
½ teaspoon garlic salt	
¼ teaspoon freshly	
For the Sauce:	
1 teaspoon Dijon mustard	grated
4 tablespoons mayonnaise	1 teaspoon chipotle powder
1 teaspoon lemon rind,	½ teaspoon cumin powder

1. Season the shrimp with garlic salt and cracked peppercorns. Then place them in the Air Fry Basket. 2. Press BOTTOM and turn the dial until AIR FRY is illuminated. Press TEMP and set to 395°F, then press TIME and set to 5 minutes. Press START/STOP to begin preheating. 3. When preheating is complete, insert the Air Fry Basket in LEVEL 2 position of the bottom oven. Close the door to begin cooking. When cooking time is up, flip them and cook for 2 more minutes. 4. In the meantime, combine all of the sauce ingredients in a bowl and stir to mix well. Serve with the warm shrimps. Enjoy!

Per Serving: Calories 69; Fat 5.26g; Sodium 253mg; Carbs 1.53g; Fiber 0.3g; Sugar 0.23g; Protein 3.94g

Delicious Italian-Style Shrimp

Prep Time: 15 minutes | Cook Time: minutes | Serves: 4

1-pound shrimp, peeled	1 tablespoon Italian seasonings
1 tablespoon avocado oil	

1. Place the shrimps in the Air Fry Basket and sprinkle with the avocado oil and Italian seasonings. 2. Press BOTTOM and turn the dial until AIR FRY is illuminated. Press TEMP and set to 400°F, then press TIME and set to 5 minutes. Press START/STOP to begin preheating. 3. When preheating is complete, insert the Air Fry Basket in LEVEL 2 position of the bottom oven. Close the door to begin cooking. When cooking is complete, serve immediately.

Per Serving: Calories 134; Fat 4.08g; Sodium 290mg; Carbs 1.25g; Fiber 0.3g; Sugar 0.23g; Protein 22.89g

Cajun Cheese Fish Fritters

Prep Time: 15 minutes | Cook Time: 15 minutes | Serves: 4

2 catfish fillets	½ cup buttermilk
1 cup parmesan cheese	1 teaspoon Cajun seasoning
3 ounces butter	
1 teaspoon baking powder	1 cup Swiss cheese, shredded
1 teaspoon baking soda	

1. Bring a pot of salted water to a boil. Add the fish fillets and boil for 5 minutes or until it is opaque. Then place the fish in a bowl and flake into small pieces. 2. Stir the remaining ingredients to the bowl and toss until the mixture is well combined. Shape the fish mixture into 12 patties and arrange them in the Air Fry Basket in a single layer. 3. Press BOTTOM and turn the dial until AIR FRY is illuminated. Press TEMP and set to 380°F, then press TIME and set to 15 minutes. Press START/STOP to begin preheating. 4. When preheating is complete, insert the Air Fry Basket in LEVEL 2 position of the bottom oven. Close the door to begin cooking. When cooking is complete, serve immediately.

Per Serving: Calories 474; Fat 35.91g; Sodium 937mg; Carbs 7.74g; Fiber 0.1g; Sugar 2.01g; Protein 30.24g

Parmesan-Crusted Crab Burgers

Prep Time: 15 minutes | Cook Time: 14 minutes | Serves: 3

2 eggs, beaten	10 ounces crab meat
1 shallot, chopped	1 teaspoon smoked paprika
2 garlic cloves, crushed	
1 tablespoon olive oil	½ teaspoon ground black pepper
1 teaspoon yellow mustard	
	Sea salt, to taste
1 teaspoon fresh cilantro, chopped	¾ cup parmesan cheese

1. In a bowl, whisk together the eggs, garlic, shallot, mustard, cilantro, crab meat, black pepper, olive oil, paprika, and salt until well combined. 2. Shape the mixture into 6 patties and roll them in the grated parmesan cheese, coating well on all sides. Refrigerate for 2 hours. 3. Then spray the crab patties with cooking oil on both sides and place in the Air Fry Basket. 4. Press BOTTOM and turn the dial until AIR FRY is illuminated. Press TEMP and set to 360°F, then press TIME and set to 14 minutes. Press START/STOP to begin preheating. 5. When preheating is complete, insert the Air Fry Basket in LEVEL 2 position of the bottom oven. Close the door to begin cooking. When cooking is complete, serve on dinner rolls if desired. Enjoy!

Per Serving: Calories 468; Fat 28.07g; Sodium 1133mg; Carbs 6.67g; Fiber 0.6g; Sugar 1g; Protein 44.94g

Spicy Monkfish with Olives & Vegetables

Prep Time: 15 minutes | Cook Time: 12 minutes | Serves: 2

2 teaspoons olive oil	1 tablespoon soy sauce
1 cup celery, sliced	2 tablespoons lime juice
2 bell peppers, sliced	Coarse salt and ground black pepper, to taste
1 teaspoon dried thyme	
½ teaspoon dried marjoram	1 teaspoon cayenne pepper
½ teaspoon dried rosemary	½ cup Kalamata olives, pitted and sliced
2 monkfish fillets	

1. Place the fish fillets in a bowl and toss with the lime juice, soy sauce, black pepper, salt, and cayenne pepper. Lightly grease the Air Fry Basket with cooking oil and place the seasoned fillets inside. 2. Press BOTTOM and turn the dial until AIR FRY is illuminated. Press TEMP and set to 390°F, then press TIME and set to 8 minutes. Press START/STOP to begin preheating. 3. When preheating is complete, insert the Air Fry Basket in LEVEL 2 position of the bottom oven. Close the door to begin cooking. When cooking time is up, flip and add the olives, and cook for 4 minutes longer. 4. Meanwhile, heat the olive oil in a nonstick skillet over medium heat for 1 minute. Then add the celery and peppers and sauté for 4 minutes until tender. Sprinkle with marjoram, thyme, and rosemary, set aside. 5. Serve the fish fillets with the sautéed vegetables on the side. Bon appétit!

Per Serving: Calories 187; Fat 10.81g; Sodium 424mg; Carbs 13.99g; Fiber 3.5g; Sugar 6.01g; Protein 10.98g

Snapper Fish Packets

Prep Time: 15 minutes | Cook Time: 15 minutes | Serves: 2

2 snapper fillets	1 tomato, sliced
1 shallot, peeled and sliced	1 tablespoon olive oil
2 garlic cloves, halved	¼ teaspoon freshly ground black pepper
1 bell pepper, sliced	½ teaspoon paprika
1 small-sized serrano pepper, sliced	Sea salt, to taste
	2 bay leaves

1. Lay out two sheets of parchment paper on your work surface. Place the fish in the center of one side of the parchment paper. 2. Add the shallot, garlic, peppers, and tomato on top. Then drizzle with the olive oil. Season with black pepper, paprika, and salt. Spread the bay leaves on top. 3. Fold over the other half of the parchment paper. Now, fold the edges of the parchment tightly to make a half moon shape and seal the fish inside and arrange in the Air Fry Basket. 4. Press BOTTOM and turn the dial until AIR FRY is illuminated. Press TEMP and set to 390°F, then press TIME and set to 15 minutes. Press START/STOP to begin preheating. 5. When preheating is complete, insert the Air Fry Basket in LEVEL 2 position of the bottom oven. Close the door to begin cooking. When cooking is complete, serve immediately.

Per Serving: Calories 301; Fat 9.9g; Sodium 434mg; Carbs 5.42g; Fiber 1.2g; Sugar 1.95g; Protein 45.76g

Lemony Sea Bass and Olives Mix

Prep Time: 5 minutes | Cook Time: 20 minutes | Serves: 2

2 sea bass, fillets	1 tablespoon olive oil
1 fennel bulb, sliced	A pinch of salt and black pepper
Juice of 1 lemon	¼ cup basil, chopped
¼ cup black olives, pitted and sliced	

1. In the sheet pan, combine all the ingredients. 2. Press TOP and turn the dial until BAKE is illuminated. Press TEMP/SHADE and set the temperature to 280°F, then press TIME/SLICES and set the time to 20 minutes. Press START/STOP to start preheating. 3. When the unit has preheated, immediately

put the sheet pan on the wire rack in the Bottom Oven Level 1. Close oven door. 4. Shake the fryer halfway. 5. When cooking is up, divide between plates and serve.

Per Serving: Calories 236; Fat 9.7g; Sodium 151mg; Carbs 12.41g; Fiber 4.1g; Sugar 6.36g; Protein 25.85g

Vinegary Creole Crab

Prep Time: 15 minutes | Cook Time: 6 minutes | Serves: 6

1 teaspoon Creole seasonings	¼ teaspoon onion powder
4 tablespoons almond flour	1 teaspoon dried dill
¼ teaspoon baking powder	1 teaspoon ghee
1 teaspoon apple cider vinegar	13 oz crab meat, finely chopped
	1 egg, beaten
	Cooking spray

1. In the mixing bowl, mix up the egg, crab meat, ghee, dried dill, onion powder, baking powder, apple cider vinegar, and Creole seasonings. Then add almond flour and stir the mixture with the fork until it is homogenous. 2. Make the small balls (hushpuppies). Press BOTTOM and turn the dial until AIR FRY illuminates. Press the TIME/SLICES buttons to set the cook time to 3 minutes. Then press the TEMP button to set the cook temperature to 390°F. Press START/STOP to start preheating. 3. Place the hushpuppies on the Air Fry Basket and spray with cooking spray. When bottom oven is preheated, immediately, place the wire rack in LEVEL 1 position of the bottom oven and place the sheet pan on top. Slide the Basket in LEVEL 2 position of bottom oven. Close door to begin cooking. 4. Cook for 3 minutes later, then flip them on another side and cook for 3 minutes more until the hushpuppies are golden brown. 5. When cooking is up, serve.

Per Serving: Calories 233; Fat 5.13g; Sodium 58mg; Carbs 24.54g; Fiber 11g; Sugar 0.21g; Protein 25.16g

Cheesy Tarragon Sea Bass and Risotto

Prep Time: 5 minutes | Cook Time: 25 minutes | Serves: 4

4 sea bass fillets, boneless	1 tablespoon parmesan, grated
A pinch of salt and black pepper	1 tablespoon chervil, chopped
1 tablespoon ghee, melted	1 tablespoon parsley, chopped
1 garlic clove, minced	1 tablespoon tarragon, chopped
1 cup cauliflower rice	
½ cup chicken stock	

1. In the sheet pan, mix the cauliflower rice with the stock, chervil, tarragon, parmesan, and parsley and toss. 2. Press TOP and turn the dial until BAKE is illuminated. Press TEMP/SHADE and set the temperature to 380°F, then press TIME/SLICES and set the time to 12 minutes. Press START/STOP to start preheating. 3. When the unit has preheated, immediately put the sheet pan on the wire rack in the Bottom Oven Level 1. Close oven door. 4. In a bowl, mix the fish with pepper, salt, garlic, and melted ghee and toss gently. Put the fish over the cauliflower rice and cook   for 12 minutes more. 5. When cooking is up, divide everything between plates and serve.
Per Serving: Calories 246; Fat 13.36g; Sodium 155mg; Carbs 4.72g; Fiber 0.8g; Sugar 1.59g; Protein 26.06g

Delicious Taco Lobster

Prep Time: 10 minutes | Cook Time: 6 minutes | Serves: 4

4 lettuce leaves	cumin
½ teaspoon taco seasonings	½ teaspoon chili flakes
4 lobster tails	1 tablespoon ricotta cheese
1 teaspoon Splenda	1 teaspoon avocado oil
½ teaspoon ground	

1. Peel the lobster tails and sprinkle with taco seasonings, ground cumin, and chili flakes.2. Arrange the lobster tails in the Air Fry Basket and sprinkle with avocado oil. 3. Press BOTTOM and turn the dial until AIR FRY illuminates. Press the TIME/SLICES buttons to set the cook time to 6 minutes.

Then press the TEMP button to set the cook temperature to 380°F. Press START/STOP to start preheating. 4. When bottom oven is preheated, immediately, place the wire rack in LEVEL 1 position of the bottom oven and place the sheet pan on top. Slide the Basket in LEVEL 2 position of bottom oven. Close door to begin cooking. 5. After cooking, remove the cooked lobster tails from the Basket and chop them roughly. Transfer the lobster tails into the bowl. Add ricotta cheese and Splenda. Mix them up. Place the lobster mixture on the lettuce leaves and fold them.
Per Serving: Calories 149; Fat 2.88g; Sodium 674mg; Carbs 4.2g; Fiber 0.3g; Sugar 3.16g; Protein 25.43g

Lemony Tuna Roast

Prep Time: 15 minutes | Cook Time: 24 minutes | Serves: 8

Cooking spray	1 teaspoon lemon juice
1 tablespoon Italian seasoning	1 tuna loin (approximately 2 pounds, 3 to 4 inches thick, large enough to fill a 6 x 6-inch baking dish)
⅛ teaspoon ground black pepper	
1 tablespoon extra-light olive oil	

1. Spray the sheet pan with cooking spray. Press TOP and turn the dial until BAKE is illuminated. Press TEMP/SHADE and set the temperature to 390°F, then press TIME/SLICES and set the time to 20 minutes. Press START/STOP to start preheating. 2. Mix together the Italian seasoning, oil, pepper, and lemon juice. 3. With a dull table knife or butter knife to pierce top of tuna about every half inch: Insert knife into top of tuna roast and pierce almost all the way to the bottom. 4. Spoon oil mixture into each of the holes and use the knife to push seasonings into the tuna as deeply as possible. 5. Spread any remaining oil mixture on all outer surfaces of tuna. 6. Place the tuna roast on the sheet pan. When the unit has preheated, immediately put the sheet pan on the wire rack in the Bottom Oven Level 1. Close oven door. 7. Check the temperature with a meat thermometer. Cook for an additional 1 to 4 minutes until temperature reaches 145°F. 8. When cooking is up, remove the Basket and let tuna sit in the Basket for 10 minutes.
Per Serving: Calories 71; Fat 2.61g; Sodium 218mg; Carbs 0.74g; Fiber 0.2g; Sugar 0.17g; Protein 11.09g

Keto Hot Cod

Prep Time: 5 minutes | Cook Time: 15 minutes | Serves: 4

4 cod fillets, boneless	1 tablespoon avocado oil
1 tablespoon keto hot sauce	½ teaspoon ground cinnamon

1. Sprinkle the cod fillets with the avocado oil, hot sauce, and ground cinnamon. 2. Press BOTTOM and turn the dial until AIR FRY illuminates. Press the TIME/SLICES buttons to set the cook time to 15 minutes. Then press the TEMP button to set the cook temperature to 350°F. Press START/STOP to start preheating. 3. Place the fish on the Air Fry Basket. When bottom oven is preheated, immediately, place the wire rack in LEVEL 1 position of the bottom oven and place the sheet pan on top. Slide the Basket in LEVEL 2 position of bottom oven. Close door to begin cooking. 4. When cooking is up, serve.
Per Serving: Calories 279; Fat 18.82g; Sodium 512mg; Carbs 7.97g; Fiber 5.4g; Sugar 0.73g; Protein 19.58g

Yummy Popcorn Crawfish

Prep Time: 15 minutes | Cook Time: 20 minutes | Serves: 4

½ cup flour, plus 2 tablespoons	crawfish tail meat, thawed and drained
½ teaspoon garlic powder	oil for misting or cooking spray
1½ teaspoons Old Bay Seasoning	Coating:
½ teaspoon onion powder	1½ cups panko crumbs
½ cup beer, plus 2 tablespoons	1 teaspoon Old Bay Seasoning
12-ounce package frozen	½ teaspoon ground black pepper

1. In a large bowl, mix together the flour, Old Bay Seasoning, garlic powder, and onion powder. Stir in beer to blend. 2. Add the crawfish meat to batter and stir to coat. 3. Combine the coating ingredients in a food processor and pulse to finely crush the crumbs. Transfer crumbs to shallow dish. 4. Press BOTTOM and turn the dial until AIR FRY illuminates. Press the TIME/SLICES buttons to set the cook time to 5 minutes.

Then press the TEMP button to set the cook temperature to 390°F. Press START/STOP to start preheating. 5. Pour the crawfish and batter into a colander to drain. Stir with a spoon to drain excess batter. 6. Working with a handful of crawfish at a time, roll in crumbs and place on a cookie sheet. 7. Spray the breaded crawfish with oil or cooking spray and place all at once into the Air Fry Basket. 8. Shake the Basket or stir and mist again with olive oil or spray. Cook for 5 more minutes, shake basket again, and mist lightly again. Continue cooking for 3 to 5 more minutes, until browned and crispy. 9. When cooking is up, serve.
Per Serving: Calories 295; Fat 10.28g; Sodium 387mg; Carbs 21.68g; Fiber 1.1g; Sugar 1.36g; Protein 28.39g

Ketchup Salmon

Prep Time: 35 minutes | Cook Time: 10 minutes | Serves: 4

3 tablespoons low-sodium soy sauce	1 teaspoon garlic powder
3 tablespoons rice vinegar	½ teaspoon ground ginger
3 tablespoons ketchup	4 salmon fillets (½-inch thick, 3 to 4 ounces each)
3 tablespoons olive oil	
3 tablespoons brown sugar	Cooking spray

1. Mix all marinade ingredients until well blended. 2. Place salmon in a sealable plastic bag or shallow container with lid. Pour marinade over fish and turn to coat well. Refrigerate for 30 minutes. 3. Drain the marinade, and spray the Air Fry Basket with cooking spray. 4. Place the salmon in Basket, skin-side down. 5. Press BOTTOM and turn the dial until AIR FRY illuminates. Press the TIME/SLICES buttons to set the cook time to 10 minutes. Then press the TEMP button to set the cook temperature to 360°F. Press START/STOP to start preheating. 6. When bottom oven is preheated, immediately, place the wire rack in LEVEL 1 position of the bottom oven and place the sheet pan on top. Slide the Basket in LEVEL 2 position of bottom oven. Close door to begin cooking. Watch closely to avoid overcooking. Salmon is done when just beginning to flake and still very moist. 7. When cooking is up, serve.
Per Serving: Calories 464; Fat 26.34g; Sodium 1189mg; Carbs 11.07g; Fiber 0.2g; Sugar 8.77g; Protein 43.88g

Crispy Salmon Croquettes

Prep Time: 10 minutes | Cook Time: 8 minutes | Serves: 4

1 tablespoon oil	crackers)
½ cup breadcrumbs	½ teaspoon Old Bay
1 14.75-ounce can	Seasoning
salmon, drained and all	½ teaspoon onion
skin and fat removed	powder
1 egg, beaten	½ teaspoon
⅓ cup coarsely crushed	Worcestershire sauce
saltine crackers (about 8	

1. Press BOTTOM and turn the dial until AIR FRY illuminates. Press the TIME/SLICES buttons to set the cook time to 8 minutes. Then press the TEMP button to set the cook temperature to 390°F. Press START/STOP to start preheating. 2. In a shallow dish, mix oil and breadcrumbs until crumbly. 3. Combine the salmon, egg, Old Bay, cracker crumbs, onion powder, and Worcestershire in a large bowl. Mix well and shape into 8 small patties about ½-inch thick. 4. Gently dip each patty into the breadcrumb mixture and turn to coat well on all sides. 5. Place the salmon on the Air Fry Basket. When bottom oven is preheated, immediately, place the wire rack in LEVEL 1 position of the bottom oven and place the sheet pan on top. Slide the Basket in LEVEL 2 position of bottom oven. Close door to begin cooking. Cook until outside is crispy and browned. 6. When cooking is up, serve.

Per Serving: Calories 248; Fat 13.99g; Sodium 540mg; Carbs 3.04g; Fiber 0.2g; Sugar 0.51g; Protein 25.72g

Cheesy Seafood Salad

Prep Time: 10 minutes | Cook Time: 8 minutes | Serves: 4

1½ pounds sea scallops	½ cup plain breadcrumbs
Salt and pepper	Oil for misting or
2 eggs	cooking spray
½ cup flour	

1. Rinse the scallops and remove the tough side muscle. Sprinkle to taste with salt and pepper. 2. Beat eggs together in a shallow dish. Place flour in a second shallow dish and breadcrumbs in a third. 3. Press BOTTOM and turn the dial until AIR FRY illuminates. Press the TIME/SLICES buttons to set the cook time to 8 minutes. Then press the TEMP button to set the cook temperature to 390°F. Press START/STOP to start preheating. 4. Dip the scallops in flour, then eggs, and then roll in breadcrumbs. Mist with oil or cooking spray. 5. Place scallops in the Air Fry Basket in a single layer, leaving some space between. You should be able to cook about a dozen at a time. 6. When bottom oven is preheated, immediately, place the wire rack in LEVEL 1 position of the bottom oven and place the sheet pan on top. Slide the Basket in LEVEL 2 position of bottom oven. Close door to begin cooking. Watch carefully so as not to overcook. Scallops are done when they turn opaque all the way through. They will feel slightly firm when pressed with tines of a fork. 7. Repeat step 6 to cook remaining scallops. 8. When cooking is up, serve.

Per Serving: Calories 451; Fat 19.05g; Sodium 1277mg; Carbs 28.26g; Fiber 3.9g; Sugar 2.92g; Protein 45.07g

Cheesy Sea Scallops

Prep Time: 10 minutes | Cook Time: 5 minutes | Serves: 4

½ cup mozzarella,	1 cup lettuce, chopped
shredded	1-pound shrimps, peeled
1 tablespoon apple cider	1 teaspoon avocado oil
vinegar	1 teaspoon chili powder
1 teaspoon white pepper	

1. Mix the shrimps with white pepper and apple cider vinegar. 2. Press BOTTOM and turn the dial until AIR FRY illuminates. Press the TIME/SLICES buttons to set the cook time to 5 minutes. Then press the TEMP button to set the cook temperature to 400°F. Press START/STOP to start preheating. 3. Place the shrimps on the Air Fry Basket. When bottom oven is preheated, immediately, place the wire rack in LEVEL 1 position of the bottom oven and place the sheet pan on top. Slide the Basket in LEVEL 2 position of bottom oven. Close door to begin cooking. 4. When cooking is up, put the shrimps in the salad bowl. Add all remaining ingredients and shake the salad.

Per Serving: Calories 133; Fat 1.84g; Sodium 260mg; Carbs 1.58g; Fiber 0.8g; Sugar 0.4g; Protein 27.61g

Simple Cajun Shrimps

Prep Time: 10 minutes | Cook Time: 6 minutes | Serves: 4

1-pound shrimps, peeled
1 teaspoon Cajun
seasonings

1 teaspoon mascarpone
½ teaspoon salt
1 teaspoon olive oil

1. Mix the shrimps with Cajun seasonings, salt, and olive oil. 2. Press BOTTOM and turn the dial until AIR FRY illuminates. Press the TIME/SLICES buttons to set the cook time to 6 minutes. Then press the TEMP button to set the cook temperature to 395°F. Press START/STOP to start preheating. 3. Place the shrimps on the Air Fry Basket. When bottom oven is preheated, immediately, place the wire rack in LEVEL 1 position of the bottom oven and place the sheet pan on top. Slide the Basket in LEVEL 2 position of bottom oven. Close door to begin cooking. 4. When cooking is up, transfer the shrimps in the bowl and sprinkle with mascarpone.
Per Serving: Calories 109; Fat 1.7g; Sodium 478mg; Carbs 0.42g; Fiber 0.1g; Sugar 0.08g; Protein 22.83g

Crunchy Coconut Shrimps

Prep Time: 5 minutes | Cook Time: 12 minutes | Serves: 4

1-pound shrimp, peeled
3 tablespoons coconut
shred

2 eggs, beaten
1 teaspoon salt

1. Mix the shrimps with salt. 2. Then dip every shrimp in the eggs and coat in the coconut shred. 3. Press BOTTOM and turn the dial until AIR FRY illuminates. Press the TIME/SLICES buttons to set the cook time to 12 minutes. Then press the TEMP button to set the cook temperature to 375°F. Press START/STOP to start preheating. 4. Place the shrimps on the Air Fry Basket. When bottom oven is preheated, immediately, place the wire rack in LEVEL 1 position of the bottom oven and place the sheet pan on top. Slide the Basket in LEVEL 2 position of bottom oven. Close door to begin cooking. 5. When cooking is up, serve.
Per Serving: Calories 163; Fat 5.42g; Sodium 779mg; Carbs 0.92g; Fiber 0.1g; Sugar 0.62g; Protein 27.36g

Coconut Tilapia Fritters

Prep Time: 15 minutes | Cook Time: 12 minutes | Serves: 4

1-pound tilapia fillet,
diced
3 tablespoons coconut
flour
¼ cup cauliflower,
shredded

1 egg, beaten
1 teaspoon ground black
pepper
¼ teaspoon ground
paprika

1. In the mixing bowl, mix diced tilapia fillet, cauliflower, ground black pepper, coconut flour, egg, ground paprika. 2. Make the fritters from the tilapia mixture. 3. Press BOTTOM and turn the dial until AIR FRY illuminates. Press the TIME/SLICES buttons to set the cook time to 6 minutes. Then press the TEMP button to set the cook temperature to 365°F. Press START/STOP to start preheating. 4. Place the fritters on the Air Fry Basket in one layer. When bottom oven is preheated, immediately, place the wire rack in LEVEL 1 position of the bottom oven and place the sheet pan on top. Slide the Basket in LEVEL 2 position of bottom oven. Close door to begin cooking. 5. When cooking is up, serve.
Per Serving: Calories 147; Fat 4.42g; Sodium 99mg; Carbs 1.55g; Fiber 0.5g; Sugar 0.6g; Protein 25.32g

Chapter 6 Snack and Appetizer Recipes

Lime Avocado Fries with Salsa Fresca

Prep Time: 10 minutes | Cook Time: 6 minutes | Serves: 4-6

½ cup flour	bottle
2 teaspoons salt	Quick Salsa Fresca
2 eggs, lightly beaten	1 cup cherry tomatoes
1 cup panko	1 tablespoon-sized chunk
breadcrumbs	of shallot or red onion
⅛ teaspoon cayenne	2 teaspoons fresh lime
pepper	juice
¼ teaspoon smoked	1 teaspoon chopped
paprika (optional)	fresh cilantro or parsley
2 large avocados, just	Salt and freshly ground
ripe	black pepper
Vegetable oil, in a spray	

1. Set up a dredging station with three shallow dishes. Add the flour and salt in the first shallow dish. Place the eggs into the second dish. Combine the cayenne pepper, breadcrumbs, and paprika (if using) in the third dish. 2. Press BOTTOM and turn the dial until AIR FRY illuminates. Press the TIME/SLICES buttons to set the cook time to 6 minutes. Then press the TEMP button to set the cook temperature to 400°F. Press START/STOP to start preheating. 3. Cut the avocado in half around the pit and separate the two sides. Slice the avocados into long strips while still in their skin. Run a spoon around the slices, separating them from the avocado skin. Try to keep the slices whole, but don't worry if they break – you can still coat and air-fry the pieces. 4. Coat the avocado slices by dredging them first in the flour, then the egg and then the breadcrumbs, pressing the crumbs on gently with your hands. Set the coated avocado fries on a tray and spray them on all sides with vegetable oil. 5. Place the coated avocado fries on the Air Fry Basket. When bottom oven is preheated, immediately, place the wire rack in LEVEL 1 position of the bottom oven and place the sheet pan on top. Slide the Basket in LEVEL 2 position of bottom oven. Close door to begin cooking. Cook the avocado fries, one layer at a time, turn them over halfway through the cooking time, and spray lightly again if necessary. When the fries are nicely browned on all sides, season with salt and remove. 6. While the avocado fries are cooking, make the salsa fresca by combining everything in a food processor. Pulse several times until the salsa is a chunky purée. Serve the fries warm with the salsa on the side for dipping.

Per Serving: Calories 277; Fat 14.24g; Sodium 1429mg; Carbs 31.67g; Fiber 6.3g; Sugar 5.43g; Protein 7.78g

Tasty Fried Brie with Cherry Tomatoes

Prep Time: 10 minutes | Cook Time: 15 minutes | Serves: 8

1 baguette	fresh parsley
2 pints red and yellow	1 (8-ounce) wheel of
cherry tomatoes	Brie cheese
1 tablespoon olive oil	Olive oil
Salt and freshly ground	½ teaspoon Italian
black pepper	seasoning (optional)
1 teaspoon balsamic	1 tablespoon chopped
vinegar	fresh basil
1 tablespoon chopped	

1. Press BOTTOM and turn the dial until AIR FRY illuminates. Press the TIME/SLICES buttons to set the cook time to 6 minutes. Then press the TEMP button to set the cook temperature to 350°F. Press START/STOP to start preheating. 2. Start by making the crostini. Slice the baguette diagonally into ½-inch slices and brush the both sides of slices with olive oil. Place the baguette slices on the Air Fry Basket. When bottom oven is preheated, immediately slide the Basket in LEVEL 2 position. Close door to start cooking. Cook the baguette slices in batches for 6 minutes or until lightly browned on all sides. After cooking, set the bread aside on the serving platter. 3. Toss the cherry tomatoes in a bowl with the salt, olive oil, and pepper. Cook the cherry tomatoes in the oven for 3 to 5 minutes, shaking the basket a few times during the cooking process. The tomatoes should be soft and some of them will burst open. Toss the warm tomatoes with the balsamic vinegar and fresh parsley and set aside. 4. Cut a circle of parchment paper the same size as the wheel of Brie cheese. Brush the Brie wheel with olive oil on both sides and sprinkle with Italian seasoning if using. Place the circle of parchment paper on one side of the Brie and transfer the Brie to the Basket, parchment side down. Cook for 8 to 10 minutes at 350°F until the Brie is slightly puffed and soft to the touch. 5. Watch carefully and remove the Brie before the rind cracks and the cheese starts to leak out. Transfer the wheel to the serving platter and top with the roasted tomatoes. Sprinkle with basil and serve with the toasted bread slices.

Per Serving: Calories 557; Fat 38.34g; Sodium 1306mg; Carbs 23.07g; Fiber 1.5g; Sugar 6.82g; Protein 30.54g

Classic Mozzarella en Carrozza with Puttanesca Sauce

Prep Time: 10 minutes | Cook Time: 8 minutes | Serves: 6-8

Puttanesca Sauce	parsley, chopped
2 teaspoons olive oil	8 slices of thinly sliced
1 anchovy, chopped	white bread (Pepperidge
(optional)	Farm®)
2 cloves garlic, minced	8 ounces mozzarella
1 (14-ounce) can petite	cheese, cut into ¼-inch
diced tomatoes	slices
½ cup chicken stock or	½ cup all-purpose flour
water	3 eggs, beaten
⅓ cup Kalamata olives,	1½ cups seasoned panko
chopped	breadcrumbs
2 tablespoons capers	½ teaspoon garlic
½ teaspoon dried	powder
oregano	½ teaspoon salt
¼ teaspoon crushed red	Freshly ground black
pepper flakes	pepper
Salt and freshly ground	Olive oil, in a spray
black pepper	bottle
1 tablespoon fresh	

1. Start by making the puttanesca sauce. Heat the olive oil in a medium saucepan on the stovetop. Add the garlic and anchovies if using and sauté for 3 minutes until the anchovies have "melted" into the oil. Add the tomatoes, olives, chicken stock, oregano, capers, and crushed red pepper flakes and simmer the sauce for 20 minutes. Season with salt and freshly ground black pepper and stir in the fresh parsley. 2. Cut the crusts off the slices of bread. Place four slices of the bread on a cutting board. Divide the cheese between the four slices of bread. Top the cheese with the remaining four slices of bread to make little sandwiches and cut each sandwich into 4 triangles. 3. Set up a dredging station using three shallow dishes. Place the flour in the first shallow dish, the eggs in the second dish and in the third dish, combine the panko breadcrumbs, salt, garlic powder, and black pepper. Dredge each little triangle in the flour first (you might think this is redundant, but it helps to get the coating to adhere to the edges of the sandwiches) and then dip them into the egg, making sure both the sides and the edges are coated. Let the excess egg drip off and then press the triangles into the breadcrumb mixture, pressing the crumbs on with the hands so they adhere. Place the coated triangles in the freezer for 2 hours, until the cheese is frozen. 4. Press BOTTOM and turn the dial until AIR FRY illuminates. Press the TIME/SLICES buttons to set the cook time to 5 minutes. Then press the TEMP button to set the cook temperature to 390°F. Press START/STOP to start preheating. Spray all sides of the mozzarella triangles with oil and transfer a single layer of triangles to the Air Fry Basket. 5. When bottom oven is preheated, immediately, place the wire rack in LEVEL 1 position of the bottom oven and place the sheet pan on top. Slide the Basket in LEVEL 2 position of bottom oven. Close door to begin cooking. Turn the triangles over and cook for an additional 3 minutes. 6. When cooking is up, serve the mozzarella triangles immediately with the warm puttanesca sauce.

Per Serving: Calories 301; Fat 6.62g; Sodium 2708mg; Carbs 37.9g; Fiber 8.2g; Sugar 6.39g; Protein 18.18g

Coconut Garlic Chicken Bites

Prep Time: 5 minutes | Cook Time: 20 minutes | Serves: 4

2 teaspoons garlic	¾ cup coconut flakes
powder	Cooking spray
2 eggs	1 pound chicken breasts,
Salt and black pepper to	skinless, boneless and
the taste	cubed

1. Put the coconut in a bowl and mix the eggs with salt, garlic powder, and pepper in a second one. 2. Dredge the chicken cubes in eggs and then in coconut and arrange them all in the Air Fry Basket and grease with cooking spray. 3. Press BOTTOM and turn the dial until AIR FRY illuminates. Press the TIME/SLICES buttons to set the cook time to 20 minutes. Then press the TEMP button to set the cook temperature to 370°F. Press START/STOP to start preheating. 4. When bottom oven is preheated, immediately, place the wire rack in LEVEL 1 position of the bottom oven and place the sheet pan on top. Slide the Basket in LEVEL 2 position of bottom oven. Close door to begin cooking. 5. When cooking is up, arrange the chicken bites on a platter and serve as an appetizer.

Per Serving: Calories 338; Fat 14.12g; Sodium 763mg; Carbs 10.27g; Fiber 1.9g; Sugar 6.32g; Protein 40.48g

Homemade Pizza Bites

Prep Time: 15 minutes | Cook Time: 3 minutes | Serves: 10

10 Mozzarella cheese slices	10 pepperoni slices

1. Press TOP and turn the dial until BAKE is illuminated. Press TEMP/SHADE and set the temperature to 400°F, then press TIME/SLICES and set the time to 3 minutes. Press START/STOP to start preheating. 2. Line the sheet pan with baking paper and put Mozzarella in it in one layer. 3. When the unit has preheated, immediately put the sheet pan on the wire rack in the Bottom Oven Level 1. Close oven door. Cook the cheese for 3 minutes until it is melted. 4. After cooking, remove the cheese and cool it to room temperature. Then remove the melted cheese from the baking paper and put the pepperoni slices on it. Fold the cheese in the shape of turnovers.

Per Serving: Calories 88; Fat 5.66g; Sodium 40mg; Carbs 0.87g; Fiber 0g; Sugar 0.34g; Protein 8.16g

Almond Zucchini Chips

Prep Time: 5 minutes | Cook Time: 15 minutes | Serves: 6

3 zucchinis, thinly sliced	2 eggs, whisked
Salt and black pepper to the taste	1 cup almond flour

1. In a bowl, mix the eggs with salt and pepper. 2. Put the flour in a second bowl. Dredge the zucchinis in flour and then in eggs. 3. Press BOTTOM and turn the dial until AIR FRY illuminates. Press the TIME/SLICES buttons to set the cook time to 15 minutes. Then press the TEMP button to set the cook temperature to 350°F. Press START/STOP to start preheating. Arrange the chips in the Air Fry Basket. 4. When bottom oven is preheated, immediately slide the Basket in LEVEL 2 position. Close door to start cooking. 5. When cooking is up, serve as a snack.

Per Serving: Calories 46; Fat 3.35g; Sodium 422mg; Carbs 0.8g; Fiber 0.2g; Sugar 0.23g; Protein 3.22g

Yummy Mozzarella Snack

Prep Time: 5 minutes | Cook Time: 5 minutes | Serves: 8

2 cups mozzarella, shredded	husk powder
¾ cup almond flour	¼ teaspoon sweet paprika
2 teaspoons psyllium	

1. Put the mozzarella in a bowl and melt it in the microwave for 2 minutes, add all the other ingredients quickly and stir really until a dough forms. 2. Divide the dough into 2 balls, roll them on 2 baking sheets and cut into triangles. 3. Arrange the tortillas in the sheet pan. Press TOP and turn the dial until BAKE is illuminated. Press TEMP/SHADE and set the temperature to 370°F, then press TIME/SLICES and set the time to 5 minutes. Press START/STOP to start preheating. 4. When the unit has preheated, immediately put the sheet pan on the wire rack in the Bottom Oven Level 1. Close oven door. 5. When cooking is up, transfer to bowls and serve as a snack.

Per Serving: Calories 41; Fat 0.07g; Sodium 210mg; Carbs 1.06g; Fiber 0.5g; Sugar 0.43g; Protein 8.99g

Easy Cheese Rounds

Prep Time: 10 minutes | Cook Time: 6 minutes | Serves: 4

1 cup Cheddar cheese,	shredded

1. Press BOTTOM and turn the dial until AIR FRY illuminates. Press the TIME/SLICES buttons to set the cook time to 6 minutes. Then press the TEMP button to set the cook temperature to 400°F. Press START/STOP to start preheating. 2. Line the Air Fry Basket with baking paper. Sprinkle the cheese on the baking paper in the shape of small rounds. 3. When bottom oven is preheated, immediately slide the Basket in LEVEL 2 position. Close door to start cooking. Cook until the cheese is melted and becomes crispy. 4. When cooking is up, serve.

Per Serving: Calories 134; Fat 11.16g; Sodium 213mg; Carbs 0.44g; Fiber 0g; Sugar 0.09g; Protein 7.93g

Healthy Bacon Avocado Wraps

Prep Time: 5 minutes | Cook Time: 15 minutes | Serves: 4

2 avocados, peeled, pitted and cut into 12 wedges	12 bacon strips 1 tablespoon ghee, melted

1. Wrap each avocado wedge in a bacon strip and brush them with the ghee. 2. Press BOTTOM and turn the dial until AIR FRY illuminates. Press the TIME/SLICES buttons to set the cook time to 15 minutes. Then press the TEMP button to set the cook temperature to 360°F. Press START/STOP to start preheating. 3. Place the avocado wedge on the Air Fry Basket. When bottom oven is preheated, immediately, place the wire rack in LEVEL 1 position of the bottom oven and place the sheet pan on top. Slide the Basket in LEVEL 2 position of bottom oven. Close door to begin cooking. 4. When cooking is up, serve as an appetizer.

Per Serving: Calories 237; Fat 22.56g; Sodium 227mg; Carbs 9.52g; Fiber 7.1g; Sugar 0.66g; Protein 3.61g

Cream Cheese Breadsticks

Prep Time: 5 minutes | Cook Time: 15 minutes | Serves: 6

½ cup almond meal Sea salt and ground black pepper, to taste ¼ teaspoon smoked paprika ½ teaspoon celery seeds	6 ounces mature Cheddar, cold, freshly grated 2 tablespoons cream cheese 2 tablespoons cold butter

1. Press TOP and turn the dial until BAKE is illuminated. Press TEMP/SHADE and set the temperature to 330°F, then press TIME/SLICES and set the time to 15 minutes. Press START/STOP to start preheating. Line the sheet pan with parchment paper. 2. In a mixing bowl, thoroughly combine the almond meal, black pepper, salt, paprika, and celery seeds. 3. Then combine the cheese and butter in the bowl of a stand mixer. Slowly stir in the almond meal mixture and mix to combine well. 4. Then pack the batter into a cookie press fitted with a star disk. Pipe the long ribbons of dough across the parchment paper. Then cut into six-inch lengths. 5. When the unit has

preheated, immediately put the sheet pan on the wire rack in the Bottom Oven Level 1. Close oven door. 6. Repeat with the remaining dough. When cooking is up, let the cheese straws cool on a rack. The cheese straws can be stored between sheets of parchment in an airtight container. Bon appétit

Per Serving: Calories 166; Fat 14.97g; Sodium 623mg; Carbs 0.94g; Fiber 0.2g; Sugar 0.28g; Protein 7.32g

Chili Shrimp Toasts

Prep Time: 10 minutes | Cook Time: 8 minutes | Serves: 4-6

½ pound raw shrimp, peeled and de-veined 1 egg (or 2 egg whites) 2 scallions, plus more for garnish 2 teaspoons grated fresh ginger 1 teaspoon soy sauce ½ teaspoon toasted	sesame oil 2 tablespoons chopped fresh cilantro or parsley 1 to 2 teaspoons sriracha sauce 6 slices thinly-sliced white sandwich bread ½ cup sesame seeds Thai chili sauce

1. Combine the shrimp, egg, fresh ginger, sesame oil, scallions, soy sauce, cilantro (or parsley) and sriracha sauce in a food processor and process into a chunky paste, scraping down the sides of the food processor bowl as necessary. 2. Cut the crusts off the sandwich bread and generously spread the shrimp paste onto each slice of bread. Place the sesame seeds on a plate and invert each shrimp toast into the sesame seeds to coat, pressing down gently. Slice each slice of bread into 4 triangles. 3. Press TOP and turn the dial until BAKE is illuminated. Press TEMP/ SHADE and set the temperature to 400°F, then press TIME/ SLICES and set the time to 8 minutes. Press START/STOP to start preheating. 4. Transfer one layer of shrimp toast triangles to the sheet pan. When the unit has preheated, immediately put the sheet pan on the wire rack in the Bottom Oven Level 1. Close oven door. Cook until the sesame seeds are toasted on top. 5. When cooking is up, serve warm with a little Thai chili sauce and some sliced scallions as garnish.

Per Serving: Calories 321; Fat 25.46g; Sodium 424mg; Carbs 2.67g; Fiber 1.7g; Sugar 0.61g; Protein 21.25g

Spicy Scallops and Bacon Kabobs

Prep Time: 5 minutes | Cook Time: 6 minutes | Serves: 6

1 pound sea scallops	½ pound bacon, diced
½ cup coconut milk	1 shallot, diced
1 tablespoon vermouth	1 teaspoon garlic powder
Sea salt and ground black pepper, to taste	1 teaspoon paprika

1. In a ceramic bowl, place the sea scallops, vermouth, salt, coconut milk, and black pepper and let it marinate for 30 minutes. 2. Assemble the skewers alternating the scallops, bacon, and shallots. Sprinkle the garlic powder and paprika all over the skewers. 3. Press TOP and turn the dial until BAKE is illuminated. Press TEMP/SHADE and set the temperature to 400°F, then press TIME/SLICES and set the time to 6 minutes. Press START/STOP to start preheating. 4. Place the skewers on the sheet pan. When the unit has preheated, immediately put the sheet pan on the wire rack in the Bottom Oven Level 1. Close oven door. 5. When cooking is up, serve warm and enjoy!

Per Serving: Calories 276; Fat 19.77g; Sodium 1012mg; Carbs 4.94g; Fiber 1.8g; Sugar 1.05g; Protein 22.03g

Spicy Garlic Chicken Wings

Prep Time: 10 minutes | Cook Time: 36 minutes | Serves: 4

2 cloves garlic, smashed	black pepper, to taste
3 tablespoons melted butter	8 chicken wings
Sea salt and ground	A few dashes of hot sauce

1. Steam chicken wings for 8 minutes. Then pat them dry and refrigerate for about 55 minutes. 2. Transfer the chicken wings to the Air Fry Basket. 3. Press BOTTOM and turn the dial until AIR FRY is illuminated. Press TEMP and set to 335°F, then press TIME and set to 28 minutes. Press START/STOP to begin preheating. 4. When preheating is complete, insert the Air Fry Basket in LEVEL 2 position of the bottom oven. Close the door to begin cooking. Flip halfway through the cooking time. 5. Meanwhile, prepare the sauce by mixing the remaining ingredients. 6. To serve, toss air fried chicken wings with the

sauce and serve immediately.

Per Serving: Calories 153; Fat 10.73g; Sodium 131mg; Carbs 0.71g; Fiber 0.1g; Sugar 0.03g; Protein 12.99g

Lime Parmesan Chicken Meatballs

Prep Time: 15 minutes | Cook Time: 11 minutes | Serves: 4

½ cup almond flour	1 teaspoon dried basil
2 eggs	½ teaspoon Hungarian paprika
1½ tablespoons melted butter	⅓ cup Parmesan cheese, preferably freshly grated
⅓ teaspoon mustard seeds	½ lime, zested
1-pound ground chicken	1 teaspoon fine sea salt
2 garlic cloves, finely minced	⅓ teaspoon ground black pepper, or more to taste

1. In a nonstick skillet over medium heat, add the ground chicken and garlic; cook until the chicken is no longer pink and the garlic starts to brown, about 3 minutes. 2. Then transfer the chicken to a large bowl. Add in the remaining ingredients and toss until well combined. Shape the mixture into golf-sized balls. 3. Lightly grease the Air Fry Basket and place the chicken balls inside. 4. Press BOTTOM and turn the dial until AIR FRY is illuminated. Press TEMP and set to 385°F, then press TIME and set to 8 minutes. Press START/STOP to begin preheating. 5. When preheating is complete, insert the Air Fry Basket in LEVEL 2 position of the bottom oven. Close the door to begin cooking. When cooking is complete, serve immediately.

Per Serving: Calories 406; Fat 26.29g; Sodium 876mg; Carbs 13.71g; Fiber 1.9g; Sugar 0.5g; Protein 28.55g

Thai-Style Turkey Bites

Prep Time: 15 minutes | Cook Time: 18 minutes | Serves: 6

1½ pounds turkey wings, cut into pieces	lemongrass
1 teaspoon ginger-garlic paste	1 teaspoon cayenne pepper
1½ tablespoons rice wine	Sea salt flakes and ground black pepper, to savor
1½ tablespoons coconut oil, melted	⅓ cup Thai chili sauce
½ palmful minced	

1. Place the turkey wings in a bowl and toss with the remaining ingredients except the Thai sweet chili sauce and lemon wedges. Then arrange them in the Air Fry Basket. 2. Press BOTTOM and turn the dial until AIR FRY is illuminated. Press TEMP and set to 355°F, then press TIME and set to 18 minutes. Press START/STOP to begin preheating. 3. When preheating is complete, insert the Air Fry Basket in LEVEL 2 position of the bottom oven. Close the door to begin cooking. 4. When cooking is complete, serve with Thai sweet chili sauce and lemon wedges. Bon appétit!

Per Serving: Calories 276; Fat 17.86g; Sodium 457mg; Carbs 4.22g; Fiber 1.4g; Sugar 1.64g; Protein 23.6g

Bacon & Onion Cheese Bombs

Prep Time: 15 minutes | Cook Time: 5 minutes | Serves: 6

2 onions, sliced	8 ounces soft cheese
1 cup bacon, finely chopped	2 ½ tablespoons canola oil
½ cup Colby cheese, shredded	2 eggs

1. In a bowl, mix together all the ingredients and form the mixture into bite-sized balls. Place the balls in the Air Fry Basket. 2. Press BOTTOM and turn the dial until AIR FRY is illuminated. Press TEMP and set to 390°F, then press TIME and set to 5 minutes. Press START/STOP to begin preheating. 3. When preheating is complete, insert the Air Fry Basket in LEVEL 2 position of the bottom oven. Close the door to begin cooking. When cooking is complete, serve warm.

Per Serving: Calories 386; Fat 32.12g; Sodium 707mg; Carbs 2.66g; Fiber 0.7g; Sugar 0.48g; Protein 22.38g

Mushroom Meatballs with Tzatziki Dip

Prep Time: 15 minutes | Cook Time: 10 minutes | Serves: 6

Greek Keftedes:

½ pound mushrooms, chopped	1 teaspoon dried rosemary
½ pound pork sausage, chopped	1 teaspoon dried basil
1 teaspoon shallot powder	1 teaspoon dried oregano
1 teaspoon granulated garlic	2 eggs
	2 tablespoons golden flaxseed meal

Tzatziki Dip:

½ Lebanese cucumbers, grated, juice squeezed out	juice
	1 garlic clove, minced
1 cup full-fat Greek yogurt	1 tablespoon extra-virgin olive oil
1 tablespoon fresh lemon	½ teaspoon salt

1. Mix together all ingredients for the Greek keftedes in a bowl. 2. Form the meat mixture into bite-sized balls and arrange them in the Air Fry Basket. 3. Press BOTTOM and turn the dial until AIR FRY is illuminated. Press TEMP and set to 380°F, then press TIME and set to 10 minutes. Press START/STOP to begin preheating. 4. When preheating is complete, insert the Air Fry Basket in LEVEL 2 position of the bottom oven. Close the door to begin cooking. Shake the basket halfway through the cooking time. 5. Meanwhile, prepare the tzatziki dip by mixing all ingredients. Serve the keftedes with cocktail sticks and tzatziki dip on the side. Enjoy!

Per Serving: Calories 301; Fat 13.51g; Sodium 600mg; Carbs 34.95g; Fiber 5.7g; Sugar 4.32g; Protein 14.87g

Coconut Zucchini and Bacon Cakes Ole

Prep Time: 15 minutes | Cook Time: 13 minutes | Serves: 4

⅓ cup Swiss cheese, grated	grated
⅓ teaspoon fine sea salt	½ teaspoon freshly cracked black pepper
⅓ teaspoon baking powder	1 teaspoon Mexican oregano
⅓ cup scallions, finely chopped	1 cup bacon, chopped
½ tablespoon fresh basil, finely chopped	¼ cup almond meal
1 zucchini, trimmed and	¼ cup coconut flour
	2 small eggs, lightly beaten

1. In a large bowl, combine all ingredients and stir to mix well. 2. Form the mixture into small balls and gently flatten each ball. Spray them with nonstick cooking oil and place in the sheet pan in a single layer. 3. Press TOP and turn the dial until BAKE is illuminated. Press TEMP/SHADE and set to 305°F, then press TIME/SLICES and set to 13 minutes. Press START/STOP to begin preheating. When preheating is complete, place the sheet pan on the rack. Close the door to begin cooking. Serve warm with tomato ketchup and mayonnaise if desired.
Per Serving: Calories 190; Fat 15.58g; Sodium 774mg; Carbs 5.17g; Fiber 1.6g; Sugar 1.1g; Protein 9.66g

Cheese Tomato Chips

Prep Time: 5 minutes | Cook Time: 10 minutes | Serves: 4

4 Roma tomatoes, sliced	1 teaspoon Italian seasoning mix
2 tablespoons olive oil	
Sea salt and white pepper, to taste	½ cup Parmesan cheese, grated

1. Spray the Air Fry basket with nonstick cooking oil. 2. Toss the sliced tomatoes with the remaining ingredients and arrange them in the Air Fry basket in one layer. 3. Press BOTTOM and turn the dial until AIR FRY is illuminated. Press TEMP and set to 350°F, then press TIME and set to 5 minutes. Press START/STOP to begin preheating. 4. When preheating is complete, insert the Air Fry Basket in LEVEL 2 position of the bottom oven. Close the door to begin cooking. When cooking time

is up, shake the basket and cook for 5 minutes more. 5. Serve with Mediterranean aioli for dipping, if desired. Enjoy!
Per Serving: Calories 122; Fat 10.28g; Sodium 279mg; Carbs 3.81g; Fiber 0.4g; Sugar 1.06g; Protein 3.94g

Beef Steak and Onion Sliders

Prep Time: 15 minutes | Cook Time: 10 minutes | Serves: 8

1-pound top sirloin steaks, about ¾-inch thick	Horseradish Mayonnaise:
	1 cup light mayonnaise
Salt and pepper	4 teaspoons prepared horseradish
2 large onions, thinly sliced	2 teaspoons Worcestershire sauce
1 tablespoon extra-light olive oil	1 teaspoon coarse brown mustard
8 slider buns	

1. Place steak in the Air Fry Basket. 2. Toss the onion slices with the oil and place in the sheet pan. 3. Press BOTTOM and turn the dial until AIR FRY is illuminated. Press TEMP and set to 390°F, then press TIME and set to 10 minutes. 4. Press TOP and turn the dial until BAKE is illuminated. Press TEMP/SHADE and set to 390°F, then press TIME/SLICES and set to 6 minutes. Press SMART FINISH, then press START/STOP to begin preheating. 5. When preheating is complete, place the sheet pan on the top oven rack. Then insert wire rack in LEVEL 1 position of the bottom oven, place the air fry basket on the rack. Close the door to begin cooking. Flip the steak halfway through the cooking time. 6. Meanwhile, prepare the Horseradish Mayonnaise by whisking all ingredients together. 7. When steak is cooked, remove from the oven and season with salt and pepper to taste, set aside to cool. then cut the steak into thin slices. 8. Spread slider buns with the horseradish mayo and pile on the meat and onions. Serve with remaining horseradish dressing for dipping.
Per Serving: Calories 530; Fat 34.91g; Sodium 639mg; Carbs 36.61g; Fiber 1.9g; Sugar 18.9g; Protein 16.87g

Parmesan-Crusted Bell Pepper Chips

Prep Time: 10 minutes | Cook Time: 7 minutes | Serves: 4

1 egg, beaten	¾ pound bell peppers,
½ cup parmesan, grated	deveined and cut to
1 teaspoon sea salt	¼-inch strips
½ teaspoon red pepper	2 tablespoons grapeseed
flakes, crushed	oil

1. In a bowl, mix together the egg, salt, parmesan, and red pepper flakes. 2. Dip bell peppers into the egg mixture and transfer them to the Air Fry basket. Brush them with the grapeseed oil. 3. Press BOTTOM and turn the dial until AIR FRY is illuminated. Press TEMP and set to 390°F, then press TIME and set to 4 minutes. Press START/STOP to begin preheating. 4. When preheating is complete, insert the Air Fry Basket in LEVEL 2 position of the bottom oven. Close the door to begin cooking. When cooking time is up, shake the basket and cook for 3 minutes more. 5. Season to taste with the seasonings and serve.

Per Serving: Calories 166; Fat 9.89g; Sodium 728mg; Carbs 12.83g; Fiber 1.4g; Sugar 4.94g; Protein 8.06g

Spinach Chips with Chili Yogurt Dip

Prep Time: 15 minutes | Cook Time: 10 minutes | Serves: 3

3 cups fresh spinach	1 teaspoon garlic powder
leaves	Chili Yogurt Dip:
1 tablespoon extra-virgin	¼ cup yogurt
olive oil	2 tablespoons
1 teaspoon sea salt	mayonnaise
½ teaspoon cayenne	½ teaspoon chili powder
pepper	

1. Place the spinach leaves in a bowl and toss with the olive oil and seasonings. Then transfer the spinach to the Air Fry Basket. 2. Press BOTTOM and turn the dial until AIR FRY is illuminated. Press TEMP and set to 350°F, then press TIME and set to 10 minutes. Press START/STOP to begin preheating. 3. When preheating is complete, insert the Air Fry Basket in LEVEL 2 position of the bottom oven. Close the door to begin cooking. Shake the cooking basket occasionally during the cooking time. 4. Meanwhile, prepare the chili yogurt dip by mixing all ingredients in a bowl. Serve the spinach with the sauce. Enjoy!

Per Serving: Calories 75; Fat 6.09g; Sodium 940mg; Carbs 3.5g; Fiber 1.1g; Sugar 1.25g; Protein 2.45g

Buffalo Chees Stuffed Chicken Bites

Prep Time: 15 minutes | Cook Time: 13 minutes | Serves: 4

1-pound ground chicken	cheese, cut into 16 cubes
8 tablespoons buffalo	1 tablespoon maple
wing sauce	syrup
2 ounces Gruyère	

1. Place the ground chicken in a bowl and toss with 4 tablespoons buffalo wing sauce. 2. Shape chicken into a log with your hands and divide into 16 equal portions. 3. Place a cube of cheese in the center of each chicken portion and shape into a firm ball. 4. Arrange the balls in one layer in the Air Fry Basket. 5. Press BOTTOM and turn the dial until AIR FRY is illuminated. Press TEMP and set to 390°F, then press TIME and set to 5 minutes. Press START/STOP to begin preheating. 6. When preheating is complete, insert the Air Fry Basket in LEVEL 2 position of the bottom oven. Close the door to begin cooking. 7. Then shake the basket and lower the temperature to 360°F. Cook for an additional 5 to 6 minutes. 8. Meanwhile, mix together the remaining 4 tablespoons of buffalo wing sauce and maple syrup in a medium bowl. Add the cooked meatballs and toss to coat well. 9. Place the meatballs back into air fry basket and air fry at 390°F for 2 to 3 minutes to set the glaze. Skewer each with a toothpick and serve.

Per Serving: Calories 472; Fat 32.9g; Sodium 695mg; Carbs 9.89g; Fiber 0.4g; Sugar 4.2g; Protein 33.17g

Garlic Cheese Zucchini Fries

Prep Time: 15 minutes | Cook Time: 12 minutes | Serves: 2

1 zucchini, slice into strips	Sea salt and black pepper, to your liking
2 tablespoons mayonnaise	1 tablespoon garlic powder
¼ cup almond meal	½ teaspoon red pepper flakes
½ cup Romano cheese, shredded	

1. Place the zucchini in a bowl and toss with mayonnaise until well coated. 2. In a shallow bowl, mix together the Romano cheese, almond meal, and spices. 3. Roll the zucchini sticks in the cheese mixture and place in the Air Fry Basket. 4. Press BOTTOM and turn the dial until AIR FRY is illuminated. Press TEMP and set to 400°F, then press TIME and set to 12 minutes. Press START/STOP to begin preheating. 5. When preheating is complete, insert the Air Fry Basket in LEVEL 2 position of the bottom oven. Close the door to begin cooking. Shake the basket halfway through the cooking time. When cooking is complete, serve immediately.

Per Serving: Calories 299; Fat 20.24g; Sodium 934mg; Carbs 9.42g; Fiber 1.2g; Sugar 2.51g; Protein 20.49g

Crunchy Cheese Wafers

Prep Time: 15 minutes | Cook Time: 6 minutes | Serves: 6

4 ounces sharp Cheddar cheese, grated	¼ teaspoon salt
¼ cup butter	½ cup crisp rice cereal
½ cup flour	Oil for misting or cooking spray

1. Cream the butter and grated cheese with a stand mixer. 2. Sift the flour and salt together and add it to the cheese mixture. Stir to mix until well blended. Stir in the cereal. 3. Place dough on waxed paper and pinch into long rolls about 1 inch in diameter. Wrap in waxed paper and refrigerate at least 4 hours. 4. Then cut the cheese roll into ¼-inch slices. 5. Spray the air fry basket with cooking oil and place the slices in a single layer inside, close but not touching. 6. Press BOTTOM and turn the dial until AIR FRY is illuminated. Press TEMP and set

to 360°F, then press TIME and set to 6 minutes. Press START/STOP to begin preheating. 7. When preheating is complete, insert the Air Fry Basket in LEVEL 2 position of the bottom oven. Close the door to begin cooking. 8. When cooking is complete, place them on paper towels to cool.

Per Serving: Calories 148; Fat 9.53g; Sodium 378mg; Carbs 11.89g; Fiber 0.3g; Sugar 1.63g; Protein 3.84g

Delicious Corn Dog Muffins

Prep Time: 15 minutes | Cook Time: 10 minutes | Serves: 8

1¼ cups sliced kosher hotdogs (3 or 4, depending on size)	1 egg
	2 tablespoons canola oil
½ cup flour	8 foil muffin cups, paper liners removed
½ cup yellow cornmeal	Cooking spray
2 teaspoons baking powder	Mustard or your favorite dipping sauce
½ cup skim milk	

1. Cut each hotdog in half lengthwise, then cut into ¼-inch half-moon slices and set aside. 2. Mix together the flour, cornmeal, and baking powder in a large bowl. 3. Whisk the egg, milk, and oil in a small bowl until just blended. 4. Pour egg mixture into the dry ingredients and stir to mix well. Stir in the sliced hot dogs. 5. Lightly spray the muffin cups cooking spray. 6. Divide mixture evenly into the muffin cups. 7. Place the muffin cups in the air fry basket. 8. Press BOTTOM and turn the dial until AIR FRY is illuminated. Press TEMP and set to 360°F, then press TIME and set to 5 minutes. Press START/STOP to begin preheating. 9. When preheating is complete, insert the Air Fry Basket in LEVEL 2 position of the bottom oven. Close the door to begin cooking. 10. When cooking time is up, lower the temperature to 360°F and air fry for 3 to 5 minutes or until toothpick inserted in center of muffin comes out clean. You may cook the muffins in batches.
Serve with mustard or other sauces for dipping.

Per Serving: Calories 274; Fat 10.15g; Sodium 548mg; Carbs 41.83g; Fiber 1.6g; Sugar 11.98g; Protein 5.1g

Savory Cabbage Steaks

Prep Time: 15 minutes | Cook Time: 25 minutes | Serves: 4

1-pound white cabbage, cut into steaks	1 teaspoon apple cider vinegar
1 tablespoon avocado oil	½ teaspoon mustard
1 teaspoon salt	

1. Place the white cabbage steaks in a bowl and toss with the avocado oil, apple cider vinegar, salt, and mustard. 2. Then place them in the air fry basket in a single layer. 3. Press BOTTOM and turn the dial until AIR FRY is illuminated. Press TEMP and set to 375°F, then press TIME and set to 15 minutes. Press START/STOP to begin preheating. 4. When preheating is complete, insert the Air Fry Basket in LEVEL 2 position of the bottom oven. Close the door to begin cooking. 5. When cooking time is up, flip and cook for 10 more minutes.

Per Serving: Calories 67; Fat 3.7g; Sodium 619mg; Carbs 8.41g; Fiber 2.4g; Sugar 4.35g; Protein 1.64g

Sweet Cinnamon Pita Chips

Prep Time: 5 minutes | Cook Time: 4 minutes | Serves: 4

2 tablespoons sugar	whole grain or white
2 teaspoons cinnamon	Oil for misting or
2 whole 6-inch pitas,	cooking spray

1. In a small bowl, mix up the sugar and cinnamon. 2. Cut each pita in half and each half into 4 wedges. Break apart each wedge at the fold. 3. Spray one side of pita wedge with oil and sprinkle with half of the cinnamon sugar. 4. Turn the pita over, oil the other side and sprinkle with the remaining cinnamon sugar. 5. Place the pita wedges in air fry basket. 6. Press BOTTOM and turn the dial until AIR FRY is illuminated. Press TEMP and set to 330°F, then press TIME and set to 4 minutes. Press START/STOP to begin preheating. 7. When preheating is complete, insert the Air Fry Basket in LEVEL 2 position of the bottom oven. Close the door to begin cooking. Shake the basket halfway through the cooking time. 8. When cooking is complete, serve immediately.

Per Serving: Calories 104; Fat 0.91g; Sodium 142mg; Carbs 22.65g; Fiber 3.1g; Sugar 4.2g; Protein 3.19g

Garlic Rutabaga Fries

Prep Time: 5 minutes | Cook Time: 20 minutes | Serves: 4

15 ounces rutabaga, cut into fries	oil
4 tablespoons avocado	1 teaspoon garlic powder

1. Place the rutabaga in a bowl and toss with garlic powder and avocado oil. Then arrange them in the Air Fry Basket. 2. Press BOTTOM and turn the dial until AIR FRY is illuminated. Press TEMP and set to 360°F, then press TIME and set to 20 minutes. Press START/STOP to begin preheating. 3. When preheating is complete, insert the Air Fry Basket in LEVEL 2 position of the bottom oven. Close the door to begin cooking. 4. Shake the basket twice during the cooking time to prevent burning. When cooking is complete, serve immediately.

Per Serving: Calories 166; Fat 14.18g; Sodium 13mg; Carbs 9.73g; Fiber 2.5g; Sugar 4.76g; Protein 1.28g

Keto Cauliflower Mac & Cheese

Prep Time: 10 minutes | Cook Time: 10 minutes | Serves: 4

2 cups cauliflower, chopped	½ cup Monterey Jack, shredded
1 teaspoon avocado oil	½ cup of heavy cream
1 teaspoon salt	½ teaspoon coconut oil
1 teaspoon dried oregano	

1. Place the cauliflower in the air fry basket and toss with avocado oil, salt, heavy cream, dried oregano, and coconut oil. Top with Monterey Jack cheese. 2. Press BOTTOM and turn the dial until AIR FRY is illuminated. Press TEMP and set to 400°F, then press TIME and set to 10 minutes. Press START/STOP to begin preheating. 3. When preheating is complete, insert the Air Fry Basket in LEVEL 2 position of the bottom oven. Close the door to begin cooking. When cooking is complete, serve immediately.

Per Serving: Calories 133; Fat 11.69g; Sodium 688mg; Carbs 3.35g; Fiber 1.2g; Sugar 1.52g; Protein 4.82g

Cheese BLT

Prep Time: 15 minutes | Cook Time: 4 minutes | Serves: 4

2 tomatillos

¼ cup almond flour

2 eggs, beaten

¼ teaspoon ground black pepper

¼ teaspoon chili powder

1 oz. Monterey Jack cheese, shredded

4 lettuce leaves

1. Cut the tomatillos into 4 slices and sprinkle with black pepper and chili powder. 2. Whisk the eggs in a small shallow bowl. Place the almond flour in another shallow bowl. 3. Dip the tomatillos in the eggs and then roll in the almond flour. Repeat this step one more time. 4. Place the tomatillos in the air fry basket. 5. Press BOTTOM and turn the dial until AIR FRY is illuminated. Press TEMP and set to 400°F, then press TIME and set to 4 minutes. Press START/STOP to begin preheating. 6. When preheating is complete, insert the Air Fry Basket in LEVEL 2 position of the bottom oven. Close the door to begin cooking. Flip halfway through the cooking time. 7. When cooking is complete, place the cooked tomatillos on the lettuce leaves. Top with Monterey Jack cheese and serve.

Per Serving: Calories 101; Fat 7.24g; Sodium 100mg; Carbs 2.25g; Fiber 0.6g; Sugar 1.33g; Protein 6.68g

Cheesy Eggplant Mash

Prep Time: 8 minutes | Cook Time: 15 minutes | Serves: 4

½ cup Mozzarella, shredded

2 eggplants, trimmed

and chopped

1 tablespoon avocado oil

½ teaspoon dried cilantro

1. Place the eggplants in the Air Fry Basket and sprinkle with avocado oil. 2. Press BOTTOM and turn the dial until AIR FRY is illuminated. Press TEMP and set to 360°F, then press TIME and set to 15 minutes. Press START/STOP to begin preheating. 3. When preheating is complete, insert the Air Fry Basket in LEVEL 2 position of the bottom oven. Close the door to begin cooking. 4. When cooking is complete, transfer them to a blender. Add cilantro and cheese. 5. Blend the mixture until smooth.

Per Serving: Calories 119; Fat 3.99g; Sodium 110mg; Carbs 16.61g; Fiber 8.5g; Sugar 9.88g; Protein 7.16g

Chapter 7 Dessert Recipes

Coconut Cupcakes with Peanuts

Prep Time: 15 minutes | Cook Time: 10 minutes | Serves: 8

4 egg whites	tartar
2 whole egg	½ stick butter, softened
½ teaspoon pure vanilla extract	⅓ teaspoon almond extract
½ cup swerve	1 cup almond flour
½ cup confectioners' swerve	½ cup coconut flour
⅓ teaspoon cream of	2 tablespoons unsalted peanuts, ground

1. Beat the softened butter and swerve until fluffy. 2. Whisk in the egg and mix again; carefully add in the flour, ground peanuts, vanilla extract and almond extract. 3. Line 8 muffin cups with muffin papers and divide the batter among the muffin cups. 4. Press BOTTOM and turn the dial until AIR FRY is illuminated. Press TEMP and set to 325°F, then press TIME and set to 10 minutes. Press START/STOP to begin preheating. 5. When preheating is complete, insert wire rack in LEVEL 1 position of the bottom oven, place the muffin cups on the rack. Close the door to begin cooking. 6. In the meantime, prepare the topping. Whip the egg and cream of tartar until it has an airy texture. 7. Gradually add the confectioners' swerve; continue mixing until stiff glossy peaks form. Decorate the cupcakes and serve them on a nice serving platter.

Per Serving: Calories 217; Fat 7.76g; Sodium 62mg; Carbs 30.78g; Fiber 2.6g; Sugar 13.97g; Protein 7.33g

Coconut Sesame Seeds Cookies

Prep Time: 15 minutes | Cook Time: 10 minutes | Serves: 8

1 cup almond flour	¼ cup Splenda
2 tablespoons coconut shred	3 tablespoons sesame seeds
2 eggs, beaten	1 tablespoon coconut oil, softened
1 teaspoon baking powder	

1. Combine all the ingredients in a mixing bowl and knead into dough. 2. Form the dough into small balls and press them gently in the shape of the cookies. 3. Arrange the cookies in the air fry basket in one layer. 4. Press BOTTOM and turn the dial until AIR FRY is illuminated. Press TEMP and set to 360°F, then press TIME and set to 10 minutes. Press START/STOP to begin preheating. 5. When preheating is complete, insert the Air Fry Basket in LEVEL 2 position of the bottom oven. Close the door to begin cooking. When cooking is complete, allow the cookies to cool and serve.

Per Serving: Calories 80; Fat 6.03g; Sodium 32mg; Carbs 4.19g; Fiber 0.4g; Sugar 3.34g; Protein 2.91g

Easy Chocolate Cake

Prep Time: 10 minutes | Cook Time: 9 minutes | Serves: 2

1 egg	1 tablespoon vegetable oil
2 tablespoons unsweetened cocoa powder	½ teaspoon baking powder
2 tablespoons water	⅛ teaspoon vanilla extract
2 tablespoons Swerve sugar replacement	Pinch of salt
1 tablespoon flaxseed meal	Sugar-free whipped topping (optional)

1. Press TOP and turn the dial until BAKE is illuminated. Press TEMP/SHADE and set the temperature to 350°F, then press TIME/SLICES and set the time to 9 minutes. Press START/STOP to start preheating. Coat the cake pan with vegetable oil and set aside. 2. In a small bowl, combine the baking powder, egg, water, Swerve, cocoa powder, flaxseed meal, vegetable oil, and vanilla. Stir until thoroughly combined. Transfer the mixture to the prepared cake pan. Sprinkle the top with a pinch of salt. When the unit has preheated, immediately put the sheet pan on the wire rack in the Bottom Oven Level 1. Close oven door. Cook for 8 to 9 minutes until the edges begin to firm.

3. When cooking is up, let the cake cool for a few minutes before taking it out of the oven Serve warm, with whipped topping (if desired).

Per Serving: Calories 199; Fat 14.5g; Sodium 638mg; Carbs 14.13g; Fiber 3.1g; Sugar 8.48g; Protein 6.47g

Blackberry Cocoa Cake

Prep Time: 15 minutes | Cook Time: 22 minutes | Serves: 8

⅓ cup fresh blackberries	½ cup cocoa powder, melted
½ cup butter, room temperature	1 teaspoon baking soda
⅓ teaspoon baking powder	4 whole eggs
2 ounces swerve	1 cup almond flour
	1 teaspoon orange zest

1. Add the butter, swerve and orange zest to a bowl and beat with an electric mixer. Carefully whisk in the eggs, one at a time; beat well after each addition. 2. Stir in the almond flour, cocoa powder, baking powder, baking soda, and orange juice. 3. Pour the prepared batter into the sheet pan. Spread the fresh blackberries on top. 4. Press TOP and turn the dial until BAKE is illuminated. Press TEMP/SHADE and set to 335°F, then press TIME/SLICES and set to 22 minutes. Press START/STOP to begin preheating. When preheating is complete, place the sheet pan on the rack. Close the door to begin cooking. 5. Check for doneness and let it cool on a wire rack. Serve.

Per Serving: Calories 184; Fat 14.4g; Sodium 125mg; Carbs 13.31g; Fiber 2g; Sugar 9.26g; Protein 4.03g

Lemon Coconut Cheese Tart

Prep Time: 15 minutes | Cook Time: 15 minutes | Serves: 8

2 eggs plus 6 egg yolks	¾ cup shredded coconut
¼ cup lemon juice	1¼ cups cream cheese, room temperature
4 tablespoons unsalted butter	1 teaspoon apple pie spice blend
½ cup powdered swerve	1 teaspoon pure vanilla extract
4 tablespoons heavy cream	⅛ teaspoon salt
Crust:	½ teaspoon ground anise star
1 cup blanched almond meal	

1. Whisk the eggs in a mixing bowl. Stir in the butter, lemon juice, zest, powdered swerve. Place in a stainless-steel bowl over boiling water. 2. Continue stirring until temperature reaches 170°F. Remove from heat and add heavy cream. 3.

Cover with plastic wrap and cool in the refrigerator. 4. Mix together all of the crust ingredients in the sheet pan. 5. Press TOP and turn the dial until BAKE is illuminated. Press TEMP/SHADE and set to 350°F, then press TIME/SLICES and set to 5 minutes. Press START/STOP to begin preheating. When preheating is complete, place the sheet pan on the rack. Close the door to begin cooking. 6. Once done, spread the prepared cream over the crust. Keep them refrigerated until serving. Enjoy!

Per Serving: Calories 274; Fat 25.23g; Sodium 235mg; Carbs 9.01g; Fiber 3.4g; Sugar 3.02g; Protein 7.43g

Chocolate Fudge Brownies

Prep Time: 15 minutes | Cook Time: 25 minutes | Serves: 8

1 cup granulated swerve	2 eggs, room temperature
2 tablespoons unsweetened cocoa powder, sifted	1 teaspoon vanilla
	2 tablespoons Baileys
½ cup almond flour	2 ounces unsweetened chocolate chips
½ cup coconut flour	½ cup sour cream
¼ teaspoon salt	⅓ cup powdered erythritol
¼ teaspoon baking powder	3 ounces Ricotta cheese, room temperature
½ cup butter, melted then cooled	

1. In a bowl, mix together the flour, granulated swerve, cocoa powder, salt, and baking powder. 2. Whisk in the eggs, butter, and vanilla. 3. Lightly grease the sheet pan and add in the batter. 4. Press BOTTOM and turn the dial until AIR FRY is illuminated. Press TEMP and set to 355°F, then press TIME and set to 25 minutes. Press START/STOP to begin preheating. 5. When preheating is complete, insert the Air Fry Basket in LEVEL 2 position of the bottom oven. Close the door to begin cooking. 6. When cooking is complete, place the sheet pan on a cooling rack and set aside. 7. Microwave the chocolate chips until all are melted; cool the mixture to room temperature. 8. Then, add the ricotta cheese, Baileys, sour cream, and powdered erythritol and stir until all is well combined. 9. Spread the mixture over the top of the brownies. Refrigerate and serve.

Per Serving: Calories 372; Fat 21.59g; Sodium 297mg; Carbs 35.78g; Fiber 1.8g; Sugar 30.08g; Protein 10.72g

Coconut Orange Galettes

Prep Time: 15 minutes | Cook Time: 15 minutes | Serves: 6

1 cup almond meal	nutmeg, preferably
½ cup coconut flour	freshly ground
3 eggs	1½ teaspoons baking
⅓ cup milk	powder
2 tablespoons monk fruit	3 tablespoons orange
2 teaspoons grated	juice
lemon peel	A pinch of turmeric
⅓ teaspoon ground	

1. Mix together the dry ingredients in a bowl. 2. In a separate bowl, mix together all the wet ingredients. Add the wet mixture to the dry and stir until smooth. Then add the batter to the sheet pan. 3. Press TOP and turn the dial until BAKE is illuminated. Press TEMP/SHADE and set to 345°F, then press TIME/SLICES and set to 15 minutes. Press START/STOP to begin preheating. 4. When preheating is complete, place the sheet pan on the rack. Close the door to begin cooking. Dust with confectioners' swerve if desired. Enjoy!
Per Serving: Calories 197; Fat 12.2g; Sodium 201mg; Carbs 5.05g; Fiber 0.5g; Sugar 3.27g; Protein 15.98g

Orange Custard

Prep Time: 15 minutes | Cook Time: 38 minutes | Serves: 6

6 eggs	½ teaspoon orange rind,
7 ounces cream cheese,	grated
at room temperature	1½ cardamom pods,
2 ½ cans condensed	bruised
milk, sweetened	2 teaspoons vanilla paste
½ cup swerve	¼ cup fresh orange juice

1. Melt the swerve in a saucepan over low heat, about 10 to 12 minutes. Immediately pour the melted sugar into six ramekins, tilting the ramekins so coat the bottoms and leave them to cool slightly. 2. Beat the cheese until smooth in a bowl and whisk in the eggs, one at a time, and beat until pale and creamy. 3. Stir in the orange rind, vanilla, orange juice, cardamom, and the milk. Pour the mixture over the caramelized sugar. Then arrange the ramekins on the Air Fry Basket. 4. Press BOTTOM

and turn the dial until AIR FRY is illuminated. Press TEMP and set to 325°F, then press TIME and set to 28 minutes. Press START/STOP to begin preheating. 5. When preheating is complete, insert the Air Fry Basket in LEVEL 2 position of the bottom oven. Close the door to begin cooking. When cooking is complete, garnish with berries or other fruits and serve.
Per Serving: Calories 307; Fat 21.13g; Sodium 273mg; Carbs 15.06g; Fiber 0.1g; Sugar 14.12g; Protein 13.35g

Mini Chocolate Cheesecakes

Prep Time: 15 minutes | Cook Time: 18 minutes | Serves: 8

For the Crust:

⅓ teaspoon grated	8 tablespoons melted
nutmeg	butter
1½ tablespoons	1 teaspoon ground
erythritol	cinnamon
1½ cups almond meal	A pinch of kosher salt

For the Cheesecake:

2 eggs	4 ounces soft cheese
½ cups unsweetened	½ cup swerve
chocolate chips	½ teaspoon vanilla
1½ tablespoons sour	essence
cream	

1. Line 8 mini muffin cups with paper liners. 2. To make the crust, mix together the almond meal, cinnamon, nutmeg, erythritol, and kosher salt. 3. Stir in the melted butter to moisten the crumb mixture. 4. Divide the crust mixture among the muffin cups. Press gently to make even layers. 5. In a separate bowl, whip together the sour cream, soft cheese, and swerve until smooth. Whisk in the eggs and the vanilla essence. 6. Divide chocolate chips among the prepared muffin cups. Spread the cheese mix on top of each muffin cup. 7. Press TOP and turn the dial until BAKE is illuminated. Press TEMP/SHADE and set to 345°F, then press TIME/SLICES and set to 18 minutes. Press START/STOP to begin preheating. When preheating is complete, place the muffin cups on the rack. Close the door to begin cooking. You can cook in batches. 8. Once done, transfer the mini cheesecakes to a cooling rack; store in the fridge.
Per Serving: Calories 262; Fat 19.51g; Sodium 361mg; Carbs 17.74g; Fiber 0.2g; Sugar 7.69g; Protein 4.92g

Coconut Pound Cake

Prep Time: 15 minutes | Cook Time: 30 minutes | Serves: 8

1 stick butter, at room temperature	¼ teaspoon salt
1 cup swerve	A pinch of freshly grated nutmeg
4 eggs	A pinch of ground star anise
1½ cups coconut flour	
½ teaspoon baking powder	½ cup buttermilk
½ teaspoon baking soda	1 teaspoon vanilla essence

1. Coat the bottom and sides of the sheet pan with cooking spray. 2. Using a hand mixer, beat the butter and swerve until creamy. Then, whisk in the eggs, one at a time, and mix well until fluffy. 3. Fold in the flour and the remaining ingredients. Stir to mix well. Pour the batter into the prepared sheet pan. 4. Press TOP and turn the dial until BAKE is illuminated. Press TEMP/SHADE and set to 320°F, then press TIME/SLICES and set to 15 minutes. Press START/STOP to begin preheating. When preheating is complete, place the sheet pan on the rack. Close the door to begin cooking. 5. When cooking time is up, rotate the pan and bake for 15 minutes longer.

Per Serving: Calories 276; Fat 13.99g; Sodium 304mg; Carbs 31.61g; Fiber 0.7g; Sugar 13.18g; Protein 5.84g

Chocolate Rum Cake

Prep Time: 15 minutes | Cook Time: 10 minutes | Serves: 4

2½ ounces butter, at room temperature	swerve
3 ounces chocolate, unsweetened	½ cup almond flour
	1 teaspoon rum extract
2 eggs, beaten	1 teaspoon vanilla extract
½ cup confectioners'	

1. Grease the sides and bottom of the sheet pan with cooking spray. 2. Melt the chocolate and butter in a microwave-safe bowl. Whisk the eggs and confectioners' swerve in a bowl and mix until frothy. 3. Pour the chocolate mixture into the egg mixture. Add in the almond flour, vanilla extract and rum extract; stir to mix well. 4. Pour the batter into the prepared sheet pan. 5. Press TOP and turn the dial until BAKE is illuminated.

Press TEMP/SHADE and set to 370°F, then press TIME/SLICES and set to 10 minutes. Press START/STOP to begin preheating. When preheating is complete, place the sheet pan on the rack. Close the door to begin cooking. 6. Once done, let rest for 2 to 3 minutes. Invert on a plate and serve warm

Per Serving: Calories 427; Fat 21.15g; Sodium 238mg; Carbs 41.2g; Fiber 1g; Sugar 26g; Protein 15.92g

Coconut Swiss Rolls

Prep Time: 20 minutes | Cook Time: 12 minutes | Serves: 6

½ cup milk	temperature
¼ cup swerve	¼ teaspoon salt
1 tablespoon yeast	1 cup almond flour
½ stick butter, at room temperature	1 cup coconut flour
	2 tablespoons fresh orange juice
1 egg, at room	
Filling:	
2 tablespoons butter	cinnamon
4 tablespoons swerve	1 teaspoon vanilla paste
1 teaspoon ground star anise	½ cup confectioners' swerve
¼ teaspoon ground	

1. Warm the milk in a microwave-safe bowl, then pour the hot milk into the bowl of a stand electric mixer. Add ¼ cup swerve and yeast; mix well. Cover and let stand until the yeast is foamy. 2. Then mix in the butter on low speed. Add the eggs and mix well again. Add salt and flour. Add the orange juice and mix on medium speed until a soft dough forms. 3. Knead the dough on a lightly floured surface. Cover the dough loosely and let it rest in a warm place for about 1 hour, until it has doubled in size. 4. Roll out the dough into a rectangle. 5. Spread 2 tablespoons butter on dough. 6. In a bowl, mix up 4 tablespoons of swerve, cinnamon, ground star anise, and vanilla; sprinkle evenly over the dough. 7. Roll up the dough to form a log and cut into 6 equal rolls. 8. Line the sheet pan with parchment and place the rolls inside. Spray them with cooking oil. 9. Press TOP and turn the dial until BAKE is illuminated. Press TEMP/SHADE and set to 350°F, then press TIME/SLICES and set to 12 minutes. Press START/STOP to begin preheating. When preheating is complete, place the sheet pan on the rack. Close the door to begin cooking. Flip halfway through the cooking time. 10. Dust with confectioners' swerve and serve warm!

Per Serving: Calories 310; Fat 14.47g; Sodium 277mg; Carbs 36.26g; Fiber 2.5g; Sugar 20.64g; Protein 9.66g

Orange Coconut Cake

Prep Time: 15 minutes | Cook Time: 17 minutes | Serves: 6

¾ cup coconut flour	1 ¼ cups almond flour
⅓ cup coconut milk	½ teaspoon baking
2 tablespoons orange	powder
jam, unsweetened	⅓ teaspoon grated
1 stick butter	nutmeg
¾ cup granulated swerve	¼ teaspoon salt
2 eggs	

1. Grease the inside of a cake pan that fits the oven with cooking spray. 2. In a bowl, beat the butter and swerve until fluffy. 3. Whisk in the eggs until smooth. Then stir in the coconut flour, nutmeg and salt; slowly pour in the coconut milk, almond flour, orange jam and baking powder. Continue stirring to create the cake batter. 4. Press the batter into the prepared cake pan. 5. Press TOP and turn the dial until BAKE is illuminated. Press TEMP/SHADE and set to 355°F, then press TIME/SLICES and set to 17 minutes. Press START/STOP to begin preheating. When preheating is complete, place the cake pan on the rack. Close the door to begin cooking. 6. When cooking is complete, remove the cake pan from the oven and allow to cool on a rack. Frost the cake and serve chilled.

Per Serving: Calories 438; Fat 20.28g; Sodium 242mg; Carbs 58.5g; Fiber 1.5g; Sugar 26g; Protein 6.65g

Coconut Walnuts Rum Cookies

Prep Time: 15 minutes | Cook Time: 15 minutes | Serves: 8

½ cup walnuts, ground	2 tablespoons rum
½ cup coconut flour	½ teaspoon pure vanilla
1 cup almond flour	extract
¾ cup swerve	½ teaspoon pure almond
1 stick butter, room	extract
temperature	

1. Add the butter, vanilla, swerve, and almond extract to a bowl and beat until light and fluffy. Stir in the flour, ground walnuts and rum. 2. Form the mixture into a soft dough. 3. Cover and refrigerate for 20 minutes. Then roll the dough into small cookies and place them on the Air Fry Basket. Gently press

each cookie with a spoon. 4. Press BOTTOM and turn the dial until AIR FRY is illuminated. Press TEMP and set to 330°F, then press TIME and set to 15 minutes. Press START/STOP to begin preheating. 5. When preheating is complete, insert the Air Fry Basket in LEVEL 2 position of the bottom oven. Close the door to begin cooking. When cooking is complete, serve warm.

Per Serving: Calories 183; Fat 14.86g; Sodium 107mg; Carbs 10.69g; Fiber 0.5g; Sugar 9.74g; Protein 1.04g

Chocolate Blueberry Muffins

Prep Time: 15 minutes | Cook Time: 15 minutes | Serves: 6

3 teaspoons cocoa	1 teaspoon pure rum
powder, unsweetened	extract
½ cup blueberries	½ teaspoon baking soda
1¼ cups almond flour	1 teaspoon baking
½ cup milk	powder
1 stick butter, room	¼ teaspoon grated
temperature	nutmeg
3 eggs	½ teaspoon ground
¾ cup granulated	cinnamon
erythritol	⅛ teaspoon salt

1. In a bowl, mix together the almond flour, erythritol, baking soda, salt, baking powder, cinnamon, nutmeg and cocoa powder. 2. In a second bowl, whisk the egg, butter, rum extract, and milk together. Add the wet mixture to the dry mixture. Stir in the blueberries. 3. Lightly grease a 6-cup muffin tin and divide the prepared batter mixture among them. 4. Press TOP and turn the dial until BAKE is illuminated. Press TEMP/SHADE and set to 345°F, then press TIME/SLICES and set to 15 minutes. Press START/STOP to begin preheating. When preheating is complete, place the muffin tins on the rack. Close the door to begin cooking. 5. Use a toothpick to check if the cupcakes are baked. Enjoy!

Per Serving: Calories 335; Fat 21.12g; Sodium 339mg; Carbs 32.47g; Fiber 0.8g; Sugar 30.8g; Protein 5.65g

White Chocolate Cookies

Prep Time: 15 minutes | Cook Time: 11 minutes | Serves: 10

¾ cup butter	⅓ teaspoon ground allspice
1⅔ cups almond flour	
½ cup coconut flour	⅓ teaspoon grated nutmeg
2 tablespoons coconut oil	
	¼ teaspoon fine sea salt
¾ cup granulated swerve	8 ounces white
⅓ teaspoon ground anise star	chocolate, unsweetened
	2 eggs, well beaten

1. In a bowl, mix together all of the ingredients except 1 egg. Knead the mixture into a soft dough with your hand. Refrigerate for 20 minutes. 2. Then roll the chilled dough into small balls and flatten the balls in the sheet pan. 3. Whisk the remaining egg in a small bowl and brush the top of the cookies. 4. Press TOP and turn the dial until BAKE is illuminated. Press TEMP/SHADE and set to 350°F, then press TIME/SLICES and set to 11 minutes. Press START/STOP to begin preheating. When preheating is complete, place the sheet pan on the rack. Close the door to begin cooking. Serve.
Per Serving: Calories 359; Fat 17.9g; Sodium 102mg; Carbs 46.33g; Fiber 1.3g; Sugar 26.65g; Protein 3.99g

Monk Fruit Pecan Cookies

Prep Time: 15 minutes | Cook Time: 25 minutes | Serves: 10

¾ cup coconut oil, room temperature	grated nutmeg
	⅓ teaspoon ground cloves
1½ cups coconut flour	
1 cup pecan nuts, unsalted and roughly chopped	½ teaspoon baking powder
	⅓ teaspoon baking soda
3 eggs plus an egg yolk, whisked	½ teaspoon pure vanilla extract
1½ cups extra-fine almond flour	½ teaspoon pure coconut extract
¾ cup monk fruit	⅛ teaspoon fine sea salt
¼ teaspoon freshly	

1. In a bowl, mix together the flour, baking powder and baking

soda. 2. In another bowl, whisk the eggs with coconut oil. Add the egg mixture to the flour mixture and stir until well combined. 3. Stir in the remaining ingredients, mixing well. Shape the mixture into cookies and arrange on the sheet pan in one layer. 4. Press TOP and turn the dial until BAKE is illuminated. Press TEMP/SHADE and set to 370°F, then press TIME/SLICES and set to 25 minutes. Press START/STOP to begin preheating. When preheating is complete, place the sheet pan on the rack. Close the door to begin cooking. Serve.
Per Serving: Calories 249; Fat 25.04g; Sodium 114mg; Carbs 6.68g; Fiber 1.6g; Sugar 4.74g; Protein 2.1g

Almond Monk Fruit Cookies

Prep Time: 15 minutes | Cook Time: 25 minutes | Serves: 8

½ cup slivered almonds	⅓ teaspoon ground cloves
1 stick butter, room temperature	
	1 tablespoon ginger powder
4 ounces monk fruit	
⅔ cup blanched almond flour	¾ teaspoon pure vanilla extract
⅓ cup coconut flour	

1. Combine the monk fruit, butter, vanilla extract, ground cloves, and ginger in a mixing bowl and beat until light and fluffy. Then fold in the almond flour, coconut flour, and slivered almonds. 2. Mix until a soft dough forms. Cover and chill for 35 minutes. 3. Then roll the dough into small cookies and place them on the sheet pan; gently press each cookie using the back of a spoon. 4. Press TOP and turn the dial until BAKE is illuminated. Press TEMP/SHADE and set to 315°F, then press TIME/SLICES and set to 13 minutes. Press START/STOP to begin preheating. When preheating is complete, place the sheet pan on the rack. Close the door to begin cooking. Serve.
Per Serving: Calories 121; Fat 7.89g; Sodium 74mg; Carbs 11.3g; Fiber 0.6g; Sugar 2.9g; Protein 1.32g

Chocolate Raspberry Cake

Prep Time: 15 minutes | Cook Time: 20 minutes | Serves: 4

⅓ cup monk fruit

¼ cup unsalted butter, room temperature

1 egg plus 1 egg white, lightly whisked

3 ounces almond flour

2 tablespoons Dutch-process cocoa powder

½ teaspoon ground cinnamon

1 tablespoon candied ginger

⅛ teaspoon table salt

For the Filling:

2 ounces fresh raspberries

⅓ cup monk fruit

1 teaspoon fresh lime juice

1. Grease the inside of two cake pans that fits the oven with cooking spray. 2. Combine the monk fruit and butter in a bowl and beat until creamy and uniform. Whisk in the eggs. Then, stir in the almond flour, cinnamon, cocoa powder, ginger and salt. 3. Press batter into two cake pans and smooth the surface with a wide spatula. 4. Press TOP and turn the dial until BAKE is illuminated. Press TEMP/SHADE and set to 315°F, then press TIME/SLICES and set to 20 minutes. Press START/STOP to begin preheating. When preheating is complete, place the cake pans on the rack. Close the door to begin cooking. 5. When cooking time is up, insert a wooden stick to the center of the cake and it should be completely dry when it comes out. 6. Meanwhile, in a medium saucepan over high heat, mix together all of the ingredients for the filling. Stir constantly and mash with the back of a spoon. Bring to a boil, then reduce the heat and continue to cook, stirring until the mixture thickens, for another 7 minutes. Allow the filling to cool to room temperature. 7. Spread half of the raspberry filling over the first crust. Put another crust on top. Then top with the remaining filling. Spread frosting over top and sides of your cake. Enjoy!
Per Serving: Calories 197; Fat 8.43g; Sodium 100mg; Carbs 27.93g; Fiber 2.9g; Sugar 8.17g; Protein 4.42g

Cranberry Cake with Ricotta Frosting

Prep Time: 15 minutes | Cook Time: 20 minutes | Serves: 8

1 cup almond flour

⅓ teaspoon baking soda

⅓ teaspoon baking powder

¾ cup erythritol

½ teaspoon ground cloves

⅓ teaspoon ground cinnamon

½ teaspoon cardamom

1 stick butter

½ teaspoon vanilla paste

2 eggs plus 1 egg yolk, beaten

½ cup cranberries, fresh or thawed

1 tablespoon browned butter

For Ricotta Frosting:

½ stick butter

½ cup firm Ricotta cheese

1 cup powdered

erythritol

¼ teaspoon salt

Zest of ½ lemon

1. In a bowl, mix together the flour, baking powder, baking soda, erythritol, cinnamon, ground cloves, and cardamom. 2. In another bowl, whisk 1 stick butter, vanilla paste and eggs until light and fluffy. Add the dry mixture to the wet mixture. Fold in the cranberries and browned butter. 3. Pour the mixture into a greased cake pan. 4. Press TOP and turn the dial until BAKE is illuminated. Press TEMP/SHADE and set to 355°F, then press TIME/SLICES and set to 20 minutes. Press START/STOP to begin preheating. When preheating is complete, place the sheet pan on the rack. Close the door to begin cooking. 5. In the meantime, in a food processor, whip ½ stick butter and Ricotta cheese until there are no lumps. 6. Slowly add the powdered erythritol and salt until a thick-consistency mixture is achieved. Add lemon zest, stir to combine, and cool completely. 7. Frost the cake and enjoy!
Per Serving: Calories 273; Fat 23.1g; Sodium 334mg; Carbs 18.79g; Fiber 3.4g; Sugar 11.57g; Protein 4.26g

Raspberry Muffins

Prep Time: 15 minutes | Cook Time: 15 minutes | Serves: 6

½ cup raspberries	⅓ teaspoon ground
¾ cup swerve	allspice
½ cup coconut oil	⅓ teaspoon ground anise
1 cup sour cream	star
1¼ teaspoons baking	½ teaspoon grated lemon
powder	zest
2 cups almond flour	¼ teaspoon salt
2 eggs	

1. Mix together the almond flour, salt, baking powder, swerve, anise, allspice and lemon zest in a bowl. 2. In a separate bowl, whisk the sour cream, coconut oil, and eggs together. Then, add the wet mixture to the dry mixture. Fold in the raspberries. 3. Lightly grease a muffin tin and press the batter mixture inside. 4. Press TOP and turn the dial until BAKE is illuminated. Press TEMP/SHADE and set to 345°F, then press TIME/SLICES and set to 15 minutes. Press START/STOP to begin preheating. When preheating is complete, place the sheet pan on the rack. Close the door to begin cooking. 5. Use a toothpick to check if the muffins are baked. Enjoy!

Per Serving: Calories 302; Fat 23.88g; Sodium 151mg; Carbs 21.02g; Fiber 0.8g; Sugar 16.67g; Protein 3.47g

Delicious Chocolate-Maple Bacon

Prep Time: 10 minutes | Cook Time: 15 minutes | Serves: 4

8 slices sugar-free bacon	free chocolate chips
1 tbsp. granular erythritol	1 tsp. coconut oil
⅓ cup low-carb sugar-	½ tsp. maple extract

1. Press BOTTOM and turn the dial until AIR FRY illuminates. Press the TIME/SLICES buttons to set the cook time to 6 minutes. Then press the TEMP button to set the cook temperature to 350°F. Press START/STOP to start preheating. 2. Place the bacon in Air Fry Basket and add the erythritol on top. When bottom oven is preheated, immediately, place the wire rack in LEVEL 1 position of the bottom oven and place the sheet pan on top. Slide the Basket in LEVEL 2 position of bottom oven. Close door to begin cooking. 3. Turn the bacon over. Leave to cook another six minutes until the bacon is sufficiently crispy. 4. When cooking is up, take the bacon out of and leave it to cool. 5. Microwave the coconut oil and chocolate chips together for half a minute. 6. Remove from the microwave and mix together before stirring in the maple extract. 7. Set the bacon flat on a piece of parchment paper and pour the mixture over. Allow to harden in the refrigerator for roughly five minutes before serving.

Per Serving: Calories 247; Fat 22.98g; Sodium 315mg; Carbs 2.85g; Fiber 0.1g; Sugar 0.96g; Protein 7.65g

Honeyed Balsamic Roasted Strawberry Tart

Prep Time: 15 minutes | Cook Time: 30 minutes | Serves: 2

1 pound (455 g)	1 sprig basil
strawberries, hulled and	1 sheet frozen puff
thinly sliced	pastry, thawed according
1 tablespoon (15 ml)	to package instructions
balsamic vinegar	1 egg beaten with 1
1 tablespoon (20 g)	tablespoon (15 ml) water
honey	

1. Press TOP and turn the dial until BAKE is illuminated. Press TEMP/SHADE and set the temperature to 325°F (170°C), then press TIME/SLICES and set the time to 30 minutes. Press START/STOP to start preheating. Place the strawberries in the sheet pan and mound them slightly in the center. Whisk together the honey and balsamic vinegar in a small bowl. Drizzle the mixture over the strawberries. Slice the leaves from the sprig of basil into ribbons and sprinkle them over the strawberries. 2. Cut out an 8-inch (20 cm) square from the sheet of puff pastry. Drape the pastry over the strawberries in the pan. Poke holes in the puff pastry with the tines of a fork. Brush the top of the pastry with the egg wash. When the unit has preheated, immediately put the sheet pan on the wire rack in the Bottom Oven Level 1. Close oven door. 3. Bake for 25 to 30 minutes until the top of the pastry is golden brown and glossy and the underside of the pastry is cooked. 4. When cooking is up, remove the pan. If desired, cut the pastry in half and divide the dessert among 2 plates. Alternatively, for less mess, two people can enjoy this tart right out of the pan.

Per Serving: Calories 306; Fat 14.46g; Sodium 114mg; Carbs 38.57g; Fiber 4.9g; Sugar 21.41g; Protein 7.83g

Lime Caramelized Peach Shortcakes

Prep Time: 15 minutes | Cook Time: 28 minutes | Serves: 4

1 cup (125 g) self-rising flour	unsalted butter, melted
½ cup (120 ml) plus 1 tablespoon (15 ml) heavy cream	2 teaspoons brown sugar
	1 teaspoon cinnamon
	Whipped Cream
Vegetable oil for spraying	1 cup (240 ml) cold heavy cream
Caramelized Peaches	1 tablespoon (13 g) granulated sugar
2 peaches, preferably freestone	½ teaspoon vanilla extract
1 tablespoon (14 g)	Zest of 1 lime

1. To make the shortcakes, place the flour in a medium bowl and whisk for removing any lumps. Make a well in the center of the flour. While stirring with a fork, pour in ½ cup (120 ml) plus 1 tablespoon (15 ml) of the heavy cream slowly. Continue to stir until the dough has mostly come together. With the hands, gather the dough, incorporating any dry flour, and form into a ball. 2. Place the dough on a lightly floured board and pat into a rectangle that is ½ to ¾ inch (1.3 to 2 cm) thick. Fold in half. Turn and repeat. Pat the dough into a ¾-inch-thick (2 cm) square. Cut dough into 4 equally sized square biscuits. 3. Press BOTTOM and turn the dial until AIR FRY illuminates. Press the TIME/SLICES buttons to set the cook time to 18 minutes. Then press the TEMP button to set the cook temperature to 325°F(170°C). Press START/STOP to start preheating. Spray the Air Fry basket with oil to prevent sticking. Place the biscuits in the Basket. When bottom oven is preheated, immediately slide the Basket in LEVEL 2 position. Close door to start cooking. Cook until the tops are browned and the insides fully cooked. (May be done ahead.) When cooking is up, set aside. 4. To make the peaches, cut the peaches in half and remove the pit. Brush the peach with the melted butter and sprinkle ½ teaspoon of the brown sugar and ¼ teaspoon of the cinnamon on each peach half. Arrange the peaches in a single layer in the Basket. Cook at 375°F (190°C) for 8 to 10 minutes until the peaches are soft and the tops caramelized. 5. While the peaches are cooking, whip the cream. Pour the cold heavy cream, sugar, and vanilla if using, into the bowl of a stand mixer or a metal mixing bowl. Beat with the whisk attachment for the stand mixer or a handheld electric mixer on high speed for about 1 minute until stiff peaks form. 6. To assemble the shortcakes, cut each biscuit in half horizontally. Place a peach on the bottom half of each biscuit and place the top half on top of the peach. Top each shortcake with whipped cream and a sprinkle of lime zest. Serve immediately.

Per Serving: Calories 393; Fat 20.62g; Sodium 397mg; Carbs 49.56g; Fiber 3.2g; Sugar 23.41g; Protein 5.28g

Butter Caramelized Pineapple

Prep Time: 15 minutes | Cook Time: 28 minutes | Serves: 4

1 pineapple	2 tablespoons (12 g) fresh mint, cut into ribbons
4 tablespoons (55 g) unsalted butter, melted	
	1 lime
2 tablespoons (30 g) plus 2 teaspoons brown sugar	

1. Cut off the top and bottom of the pineapple and stand it on a cut end. Slice off the outer skin, cutting deeply enough to remove the eyes of the pineapple. Cut off any pointy edges to make the pineapple nice and round. Cut the peeled pineapple into 8 circles, approximately ½ to ¾ inch (1.3 to 2 cm) thick. Remove the core of each slice using a small, circular cookie or biscuit cutter, or simply cut out the core with a paring knife. Place the pineapple rings on a plate. 2. Press BOTTOM and turn the dial until AIR FRY illuminates. Press the TIME/SLICES buttons to set the cook time to 10 minutes. Then press the TEMP button to set the cook temperature to 400°F (200°C). Press START/STOP to start preheating. Brush the pineapple rings with the melted butter on both sides. Working in 2 batches, arrange 4 slices in a single layer in the Air Fry Basket. Sprinkle ½ teaspoon brown sugar on the top of each ring. When bottom oven is preheated, immediately, place the wire rack in LEVEL 1 position of the bottom oven and place the sheet pan on top. Slide the Basket in LEVEL 2 position of bottom oven. Close door to begin cooking. Cook until the top side is browned and caramelized. With the tongs, carefully flip each ring and sprinkle brown sugar on the second side. Cook for an additional 5 minutes until the second side is browned and caramelized. Remove the cooked pineapple and repeat with the remaining pineapple rings. 3. When cooking is up, arrange all the cooked pineapple rings on a serving plate or platter. Sprinkle with mint and spritz with the juice of the lime. Serve warm.

Per Serving: Calories 194; Fat 7.99g; Sodium 8mg; Carbs 32.87g; Fiber 3.2g; Sugar 24.7g; Protein 1.73g

Sweet Cream Cheese Cinnamon Cupcake

Prep Time: 10 minutes | Cook Time: 25 minutes | Serves: 6

½ cup plus 2 tablespoons almond flour	2 tablespoons heavy cream
2 tablespoons low-carb vanilla protein powder	Cream Cheese Frosting:
⅛ teaspoon salt	4 ounces cream cheese, softened
1 teaspoon baking powder	2 tablespoons unsalted butter, softened
¼ teaspoon ground cinnamon	½ teaspoon vanilla extract
¼ cup unsalted butter	2 tablespoons powdered Swerve sugar replacement
¼ cup Swerve sugar replacement	
2 eggs	1–2 tablespoons heavy cream
½ teaspoon vanilla extract	

1. Press BOTTOM and turn the dial until AIR FRY illuminates. Press the TIME/SLICES buttons to set the cook time to 25 minutes. Then press the TEMP button to set the cook temperature to 320°F. Press START/STOP to start preheating. Lightly coat 6 silicone muffin cups with vegetable oil and set aside. 2. In a medium bowl, combine the almond flour, salt, protein powder, baking powder, and cinnamon, and then set aside. 3. In a stand mixer fitted with a paddle attachment, beat the butter and Swerve until creamy. Add the vanilla, heavy cream, and eggs, and beat again until thoroughly combined. Add half the flour mixture at a time to the butter mixture, mixing after each addition, until a smooth, creamy batter forms. 4. Divide the batter evenly among the muffin cups, filling each one about three-fourths full. Arrange the muffin cups in the Air Fry Basket. When bottom oven is preheated, immediately slide the Basket in LEVEL 2 position. Close door to start cooking. Cook for 20 to 25 minutes until a toothpick inserted into the center of a cupcake comes out clean. 5. When cooking is up, transfer the cupcakes to a rack and let cool completely. 6. To make the cream cheese frosting: Beat the cream cheese, butter, and vanilla in a stand mixer fitted with a paddle attachment until fluffy. Add the Swerve and mix again until thoroughly combined. With the mixer running, pour in the heavy cream a tablespoon at a time until the frosting is smooth and creamy. Frost the cupcakes as desired.
Per Serving: Calories 226; Fat 19.39g; Sodium 192mg; Carbs 7.83g; Fiber 0.3g; Sugar 6.46g; Protein 5.39g

Lemony Apple Turnovers with Raisins

Prep Time: 20 minutes | Cook Time: 30 minutes | Serves: 4

3½ ounces (100 g) dried apples (about 2½ cups)	½ teaspoon cinnamon
¼ cup (35 g) golden raisins	1 pound (455 g) frozen puff pastry, defrosted according to package instructions
1 tablespoon (13 g) granulated sugar	1 egg beaten with 1 tablespoon (15 ml) water
1 tablespoon (15 ml) freshly squeezed lemon juice	Turbinado or demerara sugar for sprinkling

1. Place the dried apples in a medium saucepan and cover with about 2 cups (480 ml) of water. Bring the mixture to a boil over medium-high heat and reduce the heat to low. Cover and simmer for about 20 minutes until the apples have absorbed most of the liquid. Remove the apples from the heat and let cool. Add the lemon juice, raisins, sugar, and cinnamon to the rehydrated apples and set aside. 2. On a well-floured board, roll the puff pastry out to a 12-inch (30 cm) square. Cut the square into 4 equal quarters. Divide the filling equally among the 4 squares, mounding it in the middle of each square. Brush the edges of each square with water and add the pastry diagonally over the apple mixture, creating a triangle. Press them with the tines of a fork to seal the edges. Transfer the turnovers to a sheet pan lined with parchment paper. 3. Press TOP and turn the dial until BAKE is illuminated. Press TEMP/SHADE and set the temperature to 325°F (170°C), then press TIME/SLICES and set the time to 3 minutes. Press START/STOP to start preheating. Brush the top of 2 turnovers with egg wash and sprinkle with turbinado sugar. Make 2 small slits in the top of the turnovers for venting. When the unit has preheated, immediately put the sheet pan on the wire rack in the Bottom Oven Level 1. Close oven door. Bake for 25 to 30 minutes until the top is browned and puffed and the pastry is cooked through. 4. When cooking is up, remove the cooked turnovers to a cooling rack and cook the remaining 2 turnovers in the same manner. Serve warm or at room temperature.
Per Serving: Calories 758; Fat 45.76g; Sodium 331mg; Carbs 78.47g; Fiber 4.5g; Sugar 23.36g; Protein 11.13g

Vanilla Cream Cheese Cookies

Prep Time: 20 minutes | Cook Time: 15 minutes | Serves: 12

½ cup unsalted butter, softened	2 eggs
4 ounces plain cream cheese, softened	1 tablespoon vanilla extract
1 cup Swerve sugar replacement	1 teaspoon salt
	6 cups almond flour

1. Line the Air Fry Basket with parchment paper. Press BOTTOM and turn the dial until AIR FRY illuminates. Press the TIME/SLICES buttons to set the cook time to 15 minutes. Then press the TEMP button to set the cook temperature to 350°F. Press START/STOP to start preheating. 2. In a stand mixer fitted with a paddle attachment, beat the butter, Swerve, and cream cheese, until fluffy. Beat in the eggs, vanilla extract, and salt. Set the mixer to the lowest speed and add the almond flour, ½ cup at a time slowly until thoroughly combined. 3. Working in batches, roll a spoonful of dough into a ball, flatten it between the palms, and arrange in the Basket, leaving enough space between the cookies so they don't touch. 4. When bottom oven is preheated, immediately, place the wire rack in LEVEL 1 position of the bottom oven and place the sheet pan on top. Slide the Basket in LEVEL 2 position of bottom oven. Close door to begin cooking. Cook 12 to 15 minutes until the edges become lightly golden. 5. When cooking is up, cool completely before removing from the oven, and the cookies will harden as they cool.

Per Serving: Calories 135; Fat 9.75g; Sodium 256mg; Carbs 9.08g; Fiber 0.1g; Sugar 8.75g; Protein 2.6g

Crispy Peanut Butter Cookies

Prep Time: 20 minutes | Cook Time: 15 minutes | Serves: 6

½ cup peanut butter	replacement
½ cup Swerve sugar	1 egg

1. Line the Air Fry Basket with parchment paper. Press BOTTOM and turn the dial until AIR FRY illuminates. Press the TIME/SLICES buttons to set the cook time to 15 minutes. Then press the TEMP button to set the cook temperature to 350°F. Press START/STOP to start preheating. 2. In a stand mixer fitted with a paddle attachment, beat the peanut butter and Swerve until fluffy. Beat in the egg. 3. Working in batches, roll a spoonful of dough into a ball, arrange in the Basket, and use the back of a fork to flatten the cookies and make the traditional crisscross pattern, leaving enough space between the cookies. 4. When bottom oven is preheated, immediately slide the Basket in LEVEL 2 position. Close door to start cooking. Cook for 12 to 15 minutes until the edges are lightly golden. 5. When cooking is up, cool completely before removing and the cookies will harden as they cool.

Per Serving: Calories 116; Fat 5.45g; Sodium 338mg; Carbs 13.77g; Fiber 0.4g; Sugar 12.36g; Protein 3.01g

Vanilla Chocolate Brownies

Prep Time: 10 minutes | Cook Time: 20 minutes | Serves: 8

1 cup almond flour	½ cup unsalted butter, melted and cooled
½ cup unsweetened cocoa powder	3 eggs
½ teaspoon baking powder	1 teaspoon vanilla extract
⅓ cup Swerve sugar replacement	2 tablespoons mini semisweet chocolate chips
¼ teaspoon salt	

1. Press TOP and turn the dial until BAKE is illuminated. Press TEMP/SHADE and set the temperature to 350°F, then press TIME/SLICES and set the time to 20 minutes. Press START/STOP to start preheating. Line the cake pan with parchment paper and brush with vegetable oil. 2. In a large bowl, combine the baking powder, Swerve, almond flour, cocoa powder, and salt. Add the butter, eggs, and vanilla. Stir until thoroughly combined. The batter will be thick. Transfer the batter to the prepared pan and scatter the chocolate chips on top. 3. When the unit has preheated, immediately put the sheet pan on the wire rack in the Bottom Oven Level 1. Close oven door. Cook for 15 to 20 minutes until the edges are set. 4. When cooking is up, let cool completely before slicing. To store, cover and refrigerate the brownies for up to 3 days.

Per Serving: Calories 200; Fat 13.02g; Sodium 118mg; Carbs 18.54g; Fiber 1.9g; Sugar 14.5g; Protein 4.99g

Conclusion

In conclusion, the Ninja Foodi Double Oven Cookbook opens the doors to a culinary journey that is both innovative and inspiring. As you delve into its pages, you embark on a voyage of taste and creativity, empowered by the remarkable features of the Ninja Foodi Double Oven. With its FlexDoor™ technology, FlavorSeal innovation, and Smart Cook System, this cookbook becomes your guide to crafting two meals, two ways, all in one space. From delectable desserts to savory roasts, from quick snacks to elaborate feasts, the possibilities are as limitless as your imagination.

Through these recipes, you'll not only discover the art of simultaneous cooking but also the art of precision and convenience. The Smart Finish™ technology ensures synchronization, while the leave-in thermometer brings an element of accuracy to your culinary endeavors. The diverse cooking functions cater to your every craving, whether it's the crispiness of air-fried delights or the warmth of freshly baked bread.

As you navigate through these recipes, remember that the Ninja Foodi Double Oven Cookbook is not just a collection of instructions; it's a gateway to culinary mastery. Embrace its offerings with an open mind, and let your creativity flourish within the realms of its pages. Whether you're a seasoned chef or a kitchen enthusiast, this cookbook invites you to create, innovate, and elevate your cooking game to new heights.

With every sizzle, every aroma, and every perfected dish, the Ninja Foodi Double Oven Cookbook will be your companion on a gastronomic expedition, redefining the way you approach cooking. So, set your tables, gather your ingredients, and let this cookbook be the catalyst for a symphony of flavors, an exploration of techniques, and a celebration of the artistry that is cooking with the Ninja Foodi Double Oven.

Appendix 1 Measurement Conversion Chart

WEIGHT EQUIVALENTS

US STANDARD	METRIC (APPROXINATE)
1 ounce	28 g
2 ounces	57 g
5 ounces	142 g
10 ounces	284 g
15 ounces	425 g
16 ounces (1 pound)	455 g
1.5pounds	680 g
2pounds	907 g

VOLUME EQUIVALENTS (DRY)

US STANDARD	METRIC (APPROXIMATE)
⅛ teaspoon	0.5 mL
¼ teaspoon	1 mL
½ teaspoon	2 mL
¾ teaspoon	4 mL
1 teaspoon	5 mL
1 tablespoon	15 mL
¼ cup	59 mL
½ cup	118 mL
¾ cup	177 mL
1 cup	235 mL
2 cups	475 mL
3 cups	700 mL
4 cups	1 L

TEMPERATURES EQUIVALENTS

FAHRENHEIT(F)	CELSIUS（C） (APPROXIMATE)
225 °F	107 °C
250 °F	120 °C
275 °F	135 °C
300 °F	150 °C
325 °F	160 °C
350 °F	180 °C
375 °F	190 °C
400 °F	205 °C
425 °F	220 °C
450 °F	235 °C
475 °F	245 °C
500 °F	260 °C

VOLUME EQUIVALENTS (LIQUID)

US STANDARD	US STANDARD (OUNCES)	METRIC (APPROXIMATE)
2 tablespoons	1 fl.oz	30 mL
¼ cup	2 fl.oz	60 mL
½ cup	4 fl.oz	120 mL
1 cup	8 fl.oz	240 mL
1½ cup	12 fl.oz	355 mL
2 cups or 1 pint	16 fl.oz	475 mL
4 cups or 1 quart	32 fl.oz	1 L
1 gallon	128 fl.oz	4 L

Appendix 2 Recipes Index

Made in the USA
Columbia, SC
30 November 2024

47462546R00067